JOHN C. CALHOUN

Also by John L. Thomas

The Liberator: William Lloyd Garrison

Slavery Attacked

John C. Calhoun

A PROFILE

EDITED BY

JOHN L. THOMAS

AMERICAN PROFILES

General Editor: Aïda DiPace Donald

HILL AND WANG : NEW YORK

Contents

v

Introduction

In 1843 as Americans prepared for a Presidential election there appeared an anonymous campaign biography, the *Life of John C. Calhoun, presenting a condensed history of political events from 1811 to 1843*. Calhoun's hand may not have actually drawn the sketch, but there is no doubt that he supplied the materials for the profile of the "perfect statesman" against which voters were invited to measure his own Presidential stature. Calhoun and his followers rested his case for political preferment on his "matchless constancy," his "turn of mind naturally philosophical," and his "faculty of considering circumstances in their combinations, and of determining their relative power in propelling events." True statesmanship, Calhoun insisted, depended upon the reasoned application of principles derived from an objective political science. "My politics, I think I may say with perfect truth," he once wrote in explaining his beliefs, "has been a system founded on certain fixed principles; and to carry them into effect has been my highest ambition."

Calhoun's "fixed principles," outlined in the *South Carolina Exposition* (1828) and the Fort Hill Letter (1832) and fully established in his two great political treatises, the *Disquisition on Government* and the *Discourse on the Constitution and Government of the United States* (1851), uphold two fundamental propositions: the theory of the concurrent majority and the doctrine of nullification. All good governments, Calhoun believed, must supply both power to the community and liberty to its members. Yet governments, because they are run by men motivated in large part by self-interest, naturally tend to exceed the limits of authority set by their founders and to encroach upon the liberties of their citizens. By 1830 Calhoun was convinced that the American people were being victimized by an oppressive federal government and that it was his task to recall to them the first principles of the Founding Fathers whose clear understanding of the nature of political power had been lost. He defined his problem as the constitutional one of re-establishing an equilibrium of powers through an "organization" which would "furnish the means by which resistance may be systematically and peaceably made on the part of the ruled, to oppression and abuse of power on the part of the rulers." For such protection of minority interests within the American community the mere separation of powers in the government and simple majority rule based on universal suffrage were obviously not enough: majorities through the mechanism of the political party could and would gain control of all three branches of the government and proceed to violate the rights of minorities. What was needed, Calhoun argued, was a principle "of the character calculated to prevent any one interest or combination of interests from using the powers of government to aggrandize itself at the expense of the others." That principle he defined as the rule of the concurrent majority.

Unlike the rule of the numerical majority, which takes the sense of the community as a whole by counting heads, the concurrent or "constitutional" majority "regards interests as well as numbers." The numerical majority provides the government with the power and will to act; the concurrent majority functions as a "mutual negative," a cease-and-desist order held by aggrieved minorities in constant readiness against the encroachments of the central government. "It is this negative power," Calhoun concluded, "the power of preventing or arresting the action of the government— be it called by what terms it may: veto, interposition, nullification, check, or balance of power—which, in fact, forms the constitution."

How does this "mutual negative" work? What is the device for registering the concurrent majority? Calhoun found the solution to the problem of governmental invasion of minority rights in the doctrine of nullification based on elaborate historical arguments for state sovereignty. From his reading of the records of the Founding Fathers, the Constitution emerged as an agreement made by sovereign states. As parties to the constitutional compact, the states retain the right, unrestricted in all areas not surrendered to the federal government, to judge the extent of their obligations imposed by the compact or constitution. Specifically, this reserved right means the right to judge and, if necessary, to nullify federal laws.

Nullification, according to Calhoun, is simple and effective: should the federal government overstep the limits to its authority, the legislature of any state may call a special convention which then declares the offensive law unconstitutional and hence null and void. By this exercise of its veto power the state forces the federal government to submit the question for adjudication to the several states through the amendment process. If its assumption of power is clearly unwarranted, the amendment will fail of the necessary three-fourths majority and the verdict of the aggrieved state will be vindicated. In the unlikely event of passage, the state retains the right to secede from the Union. To those of his contemporaries inclined to doubt the workability of nullification Calhoun expounded its merits as chiefly psychological. The very process of nullification—its constant availability as a remedy—would provide the necessary atmosphere for compromise.

By giving to each interest or portion the power of self-protection, all strife and struggle between them for ascendency is prevented; and, thereby, not only every feeling calculated to weaken the attachment to the whole is suppressed, but the individual and the social feelings are made to unite in one common devotion to country. Each sees and feels that it can best promote its own prosperity by conciliating the goodwill and promoting the prosperity of the others. And hence there will be diffused throughout the whole community kind feelings between its different portions; and instead of antipathy, a rivalry amongst them to promote the interests of each other, as far as this can be done consistently with the interests of all. Under the combined influence of these causes, the interests of each would be merged in the common interests of the whole; and thus the community would become a unit, by becoming the common centre of attachment of all its parts. And hence, instead of faction, strife, and struggle for party ascendency, there would be patriotism, nationality, harmony, and a struggle only for supremacy in promoting the common good of the whole.

Despite the implied universality of his political principles, Calhoun's doctrine of the concurrent majority and nullification is clearly a product of the sectional discord in pre-Civil War America and, in particular, the crisis over slavery. When after 1830 Calhoun spoke of "interests," he meant sectional interests. When he referred to an "oppressive majority," he meant an industrial North. When he invoked the rights of an "oppressed minority," he meant an agrarian South. First among the "liberties" which he saw threatened by the federal government was the Southern planter's right to hold slaves. The theory of the concurrent majority rested on the assumed beneficence of slavery, and nullification was designed to preserve the institution. Of the essential rightness of slavery Calhoun was fully convinced: it was a "positive good," the only conceivable social arrangement which would benefit both whites and blacks. "To destroy the existing relation between the free and servile races at the South," he warned, "would lead to consequences unparalleled in history. They cannot be separated, and cannot live together in peace and harmony or to their mutual advantage except in their present relation." Whatever new meanings Calhoun's political theory may have acquired in our own day, it was originally offered and for three decades served as a formidable defense of the institution of slavery.

The fact that Calhoun's transcendent cause—the preservation of the Union with slavery—ended in ruin has tended to obscure his record as a brilliant parliamentarian, skilled legislative draftsman, painstaking diplomatist, and bureaucratic innovator of considerable talent. His career falls into two parts, split by the nullification crisis into an early nationalist phase and a later period of opposition to the federal government. As a young House chairman of the Committee on Foreign Relations he prepared the bill declaring war against England and throughout the War of 1812 lent invaluable nationalist support to Madison's hard-pressed administration. During the Era of Good Feelings he continued to guide Congress along the course set by his nationalist vision, drafting the bill for the second Bank of the United States in 1816, offering a sensible plan for internal improvements, and supporting the tariff. Appointed Secretary of War by Monroe in 1817, he proved a model public official, holding the impetuous General Andrew Jackson in check during the Florida campaign and fighting valiantly to save his own system of national defense from the dismantling operations of his political enemies. As Vice-President, first under the National Republican John Quincy Adams and then under the Democrat Jackson, he managed the Senate with an efficiency unknown to his predecessors. Then in 1828 came the Tariff of Abominations, South Carolina's heated response, and the beginning of Calhoun's protracted war against the centralizing tendencies of Jacksonian Democracy. After breaking with Jackson over nullification, he took his regular seat in the Senate which, along with Henry Clay and Daniel Webster, he dominated until his death in 1850. For nearly a decade a man without a party, suspected by Northern Whigs and regular Democrats alike, he served the South as an unyielding opponent of national consolidation, a tireless defender of slavery and sectional interests, and the scourge of both parties. He served briefly but effectively as Tyler's Secretary of State in 1844, and during the long Southern vigil which began with the Mexican War managed to complete the *Disquisition* and the *Discourse* on which his followers relied so heavily in their defense of slavery after his death. By any standards his was an impressive career.

Historians, however, have been quick to note that it was also a career marked by paradox. The "matchless constancy" of Calhoun the political theorist celebrated by his admirers does not characterize Calhoun the politician. Entering political life as an eager nationalist intent on strengthening the powers of the federal government, he spent the last twenty years trying to reverse the very trend he had set in motion. As a broad constructionist he first deplored the kind of hair-splitting constitutional analysis upon which he later came to rely so heavily. "I am no advocate for refined arguments on the Constitution," the young nationalist announced in championing the use of federal power. "The instrument was not intended as a thesis for the logician to exercise his ingenuity on. . . ." Once convinced of the threat to Southern institutions posed by Northern humanitarians, however, he put his own considerable ingenuity to work in erecting just such an intricate constitutional defense of slavery. He possessed a genuine if qualified love for the Union, yet no man of his time provided his followers with better arguments for breaking it up. Dedicated as he was to an objective science of politics, he remained, as he once admitted, "a good deal attached" to his own prejudices and a partisan reading of events. He was a defender of minorities but also a guardian of the "peculiar institution," and protection of minorities in his system did not extend to those who doubted the value of slavery to a democracy. Although his analysis of divergent economic and social forces in ante-bellum America penetrated to the core of the sectional conflict, he misjudged both the timing and the real meaning of that struggle and threw his influence on the side of reaction. A theorist with a strong sense of history who began by repudiating the overly mechanical contractualism of Locke, he ended by devising one of the most complex constitutional mechanisms ever contrived for the management of a republican society. And despite his self-styled realism, his political thought is tinged with a pronounced utopian shade highlighting predicted consequences which his premises made unlikely.

Of all the qualities of statesmanship Calhoun put most emphasis on the genius for systematic analysis characterizing the truly disinterested leader, the ability to see "circumstances in combination" and the wisdom to recognize their power in "propelling events." "The prosperity of our country," he wrote, "never has, perhaps, depended much on the conduct of any single individual. . . . Provided our country be powerful and moderate in her councils, I care not whether I have principal sway or not." Yet the crowning irony of a life filled with ideological and political contradictions was that Calhoun spent most of it in constant pursuit of the "principal sway" never accorded him. No other contender for the office of President in the Age of Jackson desired it more fervently than Calhoun. From his first announcement of Presidential ambitions in 1821 until he was passed over a final time in 1848 he never ceased to think of himself as a major candidate and possible favorite. His repeated attempts and perennial failure raise important questions as to the survival value of a theory of democratic politics based on principles rather than personality and a knowledge of the machinery of politics. It was Calhoun's neglect of the political machinery —his distaste for compromise, his contempt for spoilsmen and party hacks, and his morbid fear of faction and intrigue—which helped defeat his hopes at every turn and eventually isolated him from the sources of national power. More than once his fierce longing for the Presidency distorted his vision of the Jacksonian political terrain and indicated circuitous routes across it. Ill-founded expectations of succeeding Jackson delayed his public acknowledgment of nullification, and even after the break with the administration—the turning point in his political fortunes—he could console himself with the illusion that Old Hickory's fall from power was "almost certain" and Van Buren's prospects "hopeless." In the years that followed, systematic defense of principle was frequently attended by political miscalculation. Neither during the nullification crisis nor during his subsequent twenty-year search for a party to carry his doctrinal banner did he succeed in winning widespread support for his ideas or his leadership.

The generation which came to maturity after 1830 knew Calhoun chiefly as an abstractionist, impassioned, forceful and brilliant, but also cold, inflexible and distant, a theoretician seemingly obsessed with constitutional subtleties only tenuously attached to the body of American politics. This was the figure mercilessly lampooned by Henry Clay as an anguished dialectician—"tall, careworn, with furrowed brow, haggard and intensely gazing, looking as if he were dissecting the last abstraction which sprung from the metaphysician's brain, and muttering to himself in half-uttered tones, 'This is indeed a real crisis.'" Here was Harriet Martineau's cast-iron man looking as though he had never been born and could never be extinguished. "His mind," she noted with obvious relish for an imagined symbol of Southern isolation, "has long lost all power of communicating with any other. I know no man who lives in such intellectual solitude." Even Calhoun's lieutenants, otherwise faithful, found his intensity disconcerting and his claims on their loyalty excessive. His friend and disciple, Richard K. Crallé, confessed that Calhoun was "too intelligent, too industrious, too intent on the struggle of politics to suit me except as an occasional companion," and Judge Prioleau admitted privately to hating a man who made him think so much. Nor could these adherents always fathom his intricate schemes and strategies. "He marches and countermarches all who follow him," complained James H. Hammond, "until after having broken from the bulk of his followers he breaks from his friends one by one and expends them in breaking down his late associates—so all ends in ruin."

The dramatic reversal of Calhoun's political stance, the relentless logic of his reasoning, his failure to win and hold support for his ideas, all reflected the frustrations and contradictions involved in the general Southern defense of slavery. Seen in the light of the conflagration of the Civil War, his career appears to follow a course from initial indifference to the slavery question to a virtual obsession with it. His early nationalism, like that of South Carolina, was a conditional mood dependent upon internal stability and high cotton prices. Nevertheless, as late as 1820, the height of the Missouri debates, he failed to respond to Jefferson's fire-bell in the night and stressed the need for sectional concessions:

We to the South [he explained to a friend] ought not to assent easily to the belief that there is a conspiracy either against our property, or just weight in the Union. A belief of the former might, and probably would, lead more directly to disunion with all of its horrors. That of the latter would cooperate, as it appears to me, directly with the scheme of the few designing men to the north, who think they see their interest in exciting a struggle between the two portions of our country. If we, from such a belief, systematically oppose the north, they must of necessity resort to similar opposition to us. Our true system is to look to the country; and to support such measures and men without a regard to sections as are best calculated to advance the general interest.

Ten years later on the eve of nullification, the few designing men had assumed the more menacing aspect of an abolitionist vanguard in a crusade against slavery, a threat which Calhoun saw lurking behind the tariff issue.

I consider the Tariff, but the occasion, rather than the real cause of the present unhappy state of things. The truth can no longer be disguised, that the peculiar domestick institutions of the Southern States, and the consequent direction which that and her soil and climate have given her industry, has placed them in regard to taxation and appropriation in opposite relation to the majority of the Union; against the danger of which, if there be no protective power in the reserved rights of the states, they must in the end be forced to rebel, or submit to have . . . their domestick institutions exhausted by Colonization and other schemes. Thus situated, the denial of the right of the state to interfere constitutionally in the last resort, more alarms the thinking than all other causes.

After 1830 it became clear that South Carolina's cause was that of the entire South which required at once a spokesman in Washington and a theorist capable of justifying and protecting its interest. This dual role Calhoun willingly assumed, expounding slavery as a "positive good," surrounding it with constitutional hedges in the states and proclaiming the Southern right to carry it into the territories. It proved a Sisyphean labor: by 1849, a year before his death, Calhoun's warnings of imminent emancipation had culminated in a despairing prophecy.

If it [emancipation] should be effected, it would be through the agency of the Federal Government, controlled by the dominant power of the Northern States of the Confederacy, against the resistance and struggle of the Southern. It can then only be effected by the prostration of the white race; and that would engender the bitterest feelings of hostility between them and the North. . . . The blacks and the profligate whites that might unite with them would become the principal recipients of federal offices and patronage and would, in consequence, be raised above the whites of the South in the political and social scale. We would, in a word, change conditions with them—a degradation greater than has ever yet fallen to the lot of a free and enlightened people, and one from which we could not escape, should emancipation take place (which it certainly will if not prevented), but by fleeing our homes of ourselves and ancestors and by abandoning our country to our former slaves, to become the permanent abode of disorder, anarchy, poverty, misery and wretchedness.

Thus framed by these three quotations, Calhoun's thought appears to have the simple congruity of an apology for slavery, but it has continued to raise perplexing questions for the historian and the political scientist. Was he the far-sighted statesman his partisans thought him, the unheeded prophet who tried to turn the country from its self-destructive path? Or was he, for all his erudition, a short-sighted special pleader willing to save the Union with slavery

xvi   JOHN L. THOMAS

if he could, but determined at all costs to save slavery? Was his a compelling philosophy of minority rights or a narrow defense of minority privilege? Most important of all, is his political science best understood as the reckless strategy for a hard-pressed nineteenth-century planter class or does it have a modern significance for a twentieth-century pluralistic society?

Ex-Confederates dealt with the question of slavery in Calhoun's thought by dismissing it. Although Jefferson Davis did not publish his essay until 1886, he had forgotten nothing and forgiven little, and he was particularly concerned with clearing Calhoun's name along with his own of charges of disunionism and disloyalty. He accepts, therefore, Calhoun's definition of terms, distinguishing between nullification and disunion and, like his mentor, rejecting as a "vicious heresy" the principle of simple majority rule. For Davis the real issue at stake in the Civil War was not the moral question of slavery but the constitutional one of the nature of the Union, and he credits Calhoun with the lofty motives of a great leader who "sacrificed personal ambition and party ties to lead the few against the many, in defense of truth, justice, and liberty the Union was formed to secure and perpetuate." His essay is the account of an interested party restating Calhoun's premises with unqualified approval.

If Jefferson Davis and Alexander Stephens called Calhoun as a witness for the defense, representatives of the New South, writing in the twilight of the old agrarianism, frequently served the prosecution. Davis acquits Calhoun of charges of treason to the Union; William Peterfield Trent accuses him of a more subtle betrayal. Trent, who was born during the Civil War and received his training in the new historical criticism at Johns Hopkins, dismisses Calhoun's constitutional theory as a form of "fetish worship" and his arguments for the divisibility of sovereignty as "ludicrous." He concentrates, instead, on Calhoun's failure of moral imagination which he equates with a failure of statesmanship. The ante-bellum planters, Trent argues, needed enlightenment above all else but were blandly reassured by Calhoun that slavery was economically and socially a blessing. "If anyone can cry 'treachery and treason,' it is the Southern planter himself, when he realizes, as he does not often do, how the political leaders he trusted lured him onward like so many will-o'-the-wisps into pitfall after pitfall." In Trent's analysis Calhoun's tragic limitation was his moral callousness: in attempting to reconcile slavery and democracy he failed—"and so will any man who does not distinguish between right and wrong."

Both the spokesmen of the New South and the Whig-Republican school of historians have placed Calhoun outside the arena of nineteenth-century nationalism, a judgment which has not been widely challenged. In "A Footnote on John C. Calhoun," however, the intellectual historian Ralph Gabriel questions the assumed identification of the South Carolinian with sectionalism and calls attention to certain orthodox features of his nationalist outlook. Going behind what he calls Calhoun's "political devices" to the ideas themselves, Gabriel discovers several generally held mid-nineteenth-century postulates: belief in fundamental law, a doctrine of progress, the celebration of the free individual, and, perhaps most important, faith in a transcendent American destiny. "Calhoun's words were those of the scholar and theorist," Gabriel concludes, "but his thought was that of the run-of-the-mill American democrat."

Charles M. Wiltse, who has written the best if not the most impartial biography of Calhoun, describes him as the critic rather than the champion of democratic nationalism, a close student of the American and French Revolutions whose continuing purpose it was to check democratic excess and in particular what he conceived to be King Andrew's "one unbroken march toward despotism." According to Wiltse, the great enemies of Calhoun were partisan majorities, unchecked universal suffrage, a strong executive, and national consolidation—all achievements of Andrew Jackson. In Wiltse's view it was the operation of these larger forces which gave the slavery question its urgency: in opposing the abolitionists and the Whig proponents of federal power Calhoun was defending the eighteenth-century principle of balanced republican government against the onslaught of a new centralized nationalist democracy.

If Wiltse emphasizes Calhoun's diagnosis of the political ills of ante-bellum America and the remedies he proposed, Gerald M. Capers, another recent biographer of Calhoun, is less interested in the principles than in the political maneuvering involved in the attempt to effect them. Capers seeks to replace the antipodal myths of the disinterested statesman and the evil genius of the slavocracy with a more sophisticated analysis. "To explain his career in terms of enlightened self-interest and to describe his defense of himself and his actions as rationalization can be regarded as condemnation only to those who persist in identifying the fleshless symbol with the man." In his biography Capers presents a profile of an ambitious politician given to rationalizing his drive for power while pursuing it in a highly opportunistic fashion. In the essay reprinted here he concentrates on Calhoun's delayed conversion to states' rights which he interprets as a result of his strategy for retaining the allegiance of his home state while placating the nationalist followers of Jackson, a hazardous scheme which was wrecked by the more hot-headed of the Nullificationists. Forced to choose between states' rights and Jacksonian nationalism, Calhoun elected to go with South Carolina, "but by the same action he doomed himself to a position of isolation in the nation from which he never completely emerged."

The nullification crisis may have been the turning point in Calhoun's political fortunes, but the fact remains that his isolation deepened with the slavery conflict that followed it. In a chapter from her prize-winning biography Margaret Coit offers a sympathetic but critical analysis of Calhoun's position on slavery. He saw the Southern predicament clearly: "Slavery could no longer be termed a necessary evil because the very admission of evil was a concession of justice in the Northern point of view. But to defend slavery unitedly, without giving hope for its ultimate extinction, of course involved a revolution in Southern thinking." Calhoun's willingness to undertake such a revolution Mrs. Coit attributes to an "emotional error" which on the racial issue turned a keen-eyed analyst into a bigot.

Although Calhoun has continued to attract biographers for over a century, serious interest in his political thought is of fairly recent origin. In large part this revival accompanied the New Deal with its shift of emphasis to pluralism, interest groups and economic blocs. By 1940 political scientists and historians were beginning to examine Calhoun's theory—especially the idea of the concurrent majority—with a view to establishing its continued relevance to twentieth-century politics. One of these so-called neo-Calhounites is the political scientist Peter Drucker who finds the key to American politics in Calhoun's pluralism. The long neglect of Calhoun's works Drucker interprets as simply the partisan vote of Reconstruction which in no way invalidated his basic premises. In fact, Calhoun in his time clearly recognized the distinctive feature of the American political system: government by compromise of major interests, pressure groups and sections. The twentieth century, Drucker maintains, has merely substituted for Calhoun's veto power vested in the states "the much more powerful and much more elastic but extraconstitutional and extralegal veto power of sections, interests, pressure groups in Congress and within the parties." In this sense Calhoun's rule of the concurrent majority has become "the organizing principle of American politics" at work in the operation of the Congressional committee system, in the unofficial veto power over major pieces of legislation held by large interest groups, and in the structure and functioning of the party system.

The central problem in the neo-Calhounite interpretation lies in the use of modern examples. Is the "functional representation" in twentieth-century American politics a natural extension of Calhoun's rule of the concurrent majority or something altogether different? Would Calhoun have approved this extension of his idea to unlocalized economic interest blocs or was he exclusively concerned with the nineteenth-century state as a geographical unit? A sharp critic of both the original theory and the neo-Calhounite position is the historian Richard N. Current who defines Calhoun's legacy much more narrowly. "Wherever contemporary Bourbons take counsel together somewhere in their midst hovers the ghost of the Great Nullifier." The real key to Calhoun's theory, Current maintains, is his analysis of the conflict between social classes. On the question of class conflict he was strictly a reactionary although he anticipated in a crude way many of Marx's postulates. Calhoun was attempting to put this philosophy of reaction into effect when in the 1840's he sought to create a coalition of planters and Northern capitalists to forestall the social revolution of which abolition was the harbinger. Thus his legacy, according to Current, properly belongs, not to twentieth-century liberals who try to accommodate divergent interests, but to the reactionaries who supposedly are confronting the same problems of social control which their benefactor faced over a century ago.

A second negative verdict on Calhoun's thought is registered by Louis Hartz in his *The Liberal Tradition in America*. Hartz locates Calhoun far outside the American liberal consensus as a representative of the Reactionary Enlightenment, "a profoundly disintegrated political theorist" and a captive of his contradictory objectives. Hartz identifies as the most striking of these contradictions Calhoun's utopian insistence that state sovereignty would preserve rather than destroy national union, a fallacy which he traces to his confused attempt to combine an organic naturalism with the mechanical rule of the concurrent majority. Calhoun, he concludes, was "caught in the classic agony of the brink-of-war philosopher."

William H. Freehling also finds Calhoun's philosophy "hopelessly inconsistent," but for different reasons. The origins of Calhoun's confusion Freehling sees in his departure from a strict economic theory of politics. Freehling's Calhoun is a split personality, part philosopher and part eighteenth-century patrician with a consuming fear of parties and patronage. "The key to Calhoun's thought is not just his concern with class or any other kind of economic interests, not just his concern with moral fanatics, not just his concern with demagogic spoilsmen. Rather, the secret of his political philosophy—the reason why it is inevitably inconsistent—is that Calhoun distrusted democracy for so many exaggerated and contradictory reasons."

The final selection, a careful study of the ideas in the *Disquisition* by Ralph Lerner, proceeds from the assumption that "Calhoun was one of the first to construct a science of politics on partially articulated principles that we can fairly identify as belonging to today's behavioral science." Calhoun's self-imposed task was the establishment of a true constitution which the Founding Fathers somehow had failed to secure, and it was an assignment which to a greater degree than is generally realized he was able to detach from the political struggles over slavery. If there is a weakness in the completed theory, Lerner argues convincingly, it does not lie in a failure of detachment but in a system in which the "process" of realizing the concurrent majority, in default of a larger community of interests, itself becomes the common good. Despite this limitation Calhoun realized, if only occasionally, the way democratic politics really works. "Not Madison, but Calhoun, had the clearer and fuller understanding of the multifarious and shifting alliances that constitute the political behavior of groups."

Whether or not Calhoun will appear to have met the requirements of the philosopher-statesman prescribed in his campaign biography will depend finally on the reader's estimate of the qualities essential to great political leadership. But these essays make one fact undeniably clear: Calhoun approached the problems of his day with a theoretical intensity and a practical involvement unmatched by any of his contemporaries. No one who seeks to understand American politics before the Civil War or, on a deeper level, to assess the qualities of statesmanship, can afford to ignore his record.

JOHN L. THOMAS

Brown University
June 1967

John Caldwell Calhoun, 1782–1850

John Caldwell Calhoun was born near Abbeville in Ninety-Six District, South Carolina, on March 18, 1782. In 1802 he entered Yale as a junior and graduated two years later. After studying law at Judge Tapping Reeve's Litchfield school he returned to Abbeville and was admitted to the South Carolina bar. In 1807 he was elected to the South Carolina General Assembly where he served for two years. He was elected to the House of Representatives in 1810 and took his seat for the first of three successive terms a year later. In 1811 he married a distant cousin, Floride Bonneau Calhoun, by whom he had seven children.

In the Twelfth Congress Calhoun served as one of the leaders of the War Hawks and, as temporary chairman of the House Committee on Foreign Relations, introduced the bill declaring war on England. Subsequently, during the Era of Good Feelings he played a major nationalist role in Congress, supporting the tariff, presenting a bill for internal improvements and introducing the bill chartering the Second Bank of the United States. In 1817, before the end of his third Congressional term, he was appointed Secretary of War, an office which he held for eight years. He first declared for the Presidency in 1821 but later withdrew and was elected Vice-President in 1824. By 1827 his nationalist views were changing, and a year later in the *South Carolina Exposition* he first outlined his theory of nullification. Elected Vice-President again under Jackson in 1828, he broke with the administration within two years. After openly acknowledging nullification, he resigned his office in 1832 and was triumphantly returned to the Senate. In 1833 he further developed the principle of states' rights in his famous speech on the Force Bill; in 1836 he launched his counter-attack against the abolitionists and attempted to exclude their publications from the mails; and by 1837 he was defending slavery as a "positive good." He again declared for the Presidency in 1843 but withdrew once more to accept appointment as Secretary of State. During his brief tenure he negotiated the Texas annexation treaty, which however failed of Senate acceptance. At this time he also began work on the *Disquisition on Government* and the *Discourse on the Constitution and Government of the United States,* which were not published until after his death. Returning to the Senate in 1845, he vigorously opposed first the Mexican War and then the Wilmot Proviso which would have prohibited slavery from all territories acquired from Mexico. After the war he continued to insist on the right of slave owners to take their slaves into the new territories, called on the South to unite in resisting Northern demands for free soil, and in his last great speech on March 4, 1850, denounced the Compromise of 1850, the final attempt of his generation of statesmen to solve the slavery question. On March 31, 1850, he died of tuberculosis.

J.L.T.

JOHN C. CALHOUN

✪

Life of John C. Calhoun

For ourselves, we can truly say, that our estimate of his public services has increased with our opportunities for studying them, and that our admiration of his character has grown as his private and political history became more familiar to us. Indeed, it would almost seem to us, at times, that it belonged to the destiny of the American people to have reared up such a man, and that one of its necessities required him to pursue that long and stormy career, through which he has watched and helped to steer the ship of state with an eye that never winked and an energy that never tired. It required his indomitable will, and a nature thus rarely constituted, to have maintained this eager and incessant labor for the happiness of the American people, and to have led, for so long a period, the triumphal march of our glorious institutions. With a turn of mind naturally philosophical, his great power of analysis and his faculty of attentive observation early enabled him to form a system for the conduct of life, both in his private and public relations, and to determine within his own mind upon the true ends of human action; ends which he has pursued with a matchless constancy, while a knowledge of his ultimate destination and of the high objects of his journey has cheered him along through the

Reprinted from the *Life of John C. Calhoun, presenting a condensed history of political events from 1811 to 1843* (New York, 1843), pp. 69–74. The question of the authorship of this campaign biography has not been settled. For conflicting views on Calhoun's involvement, see works by Charles M. Wiltse and Gerald M. Capers listed in the Bibliographical Essay.

thorny paths of public life. Of all the men whom we have ever
seen, he seems to us to have surveyed most completely the whole
ground of human action. To these advantages he adds another,
which constitutes, perhaps, his highest quality as a statesman. It is
the faculty of considering circumstances in their combinations, and
of determining their relative power in propelling events. To analyze this combination, or "juncture" (as he sometimes calls it),
and to determine the resultant of all these forces, is, in his opinion, the highest and rarest faculty of a statesman. If he values
this power more than most others, it is because he has derived
more benefit from its use, and well may he estimate highly that
quality which, by affording him an insight into futurity far beyond
the usual range of human vision, has given him such control over
events. These were the gifts in whose strength he presented himself on the stage of the world in the very commencement of his
public life, as one fully grown and armed for the trials which
belonged to the time and the place. True to those noble instincts
which spring more from a Divine source than from human reason,
he ever leaned to liberty as against power, and early learned to
resist those temptations which so often lead man to increase the
power of the mass, which he is content to share as a member, at
the expense of those separate and individual rights of which nature
constituted him the peculiar guardian, and which were only given
as the means of self-culture, and as indispensable to the moral
elevation of his being.

His public life may be divided into two grand epochs: the first,
in which he put forth his whole energies to enable his countrymen
to maintain their independence against foreign aggression; and
the second, in which he undertook the more difficult task of free-
ing their domestic legislation from those devices by which one
was enabled to prey upon another. In each of these periods he has
been emphatically "the man of his time," and he has ever regarded
the tenets of the Republican party as indicating the best means of
attaining these ends under our form of government. Of all men
now living, he, perhaps, has contributed most to illustrate and
establish that political creed. We are aware that we expose ourselves here to the sneers of some of those literal expositors of the
law, who believe that man was made for the Sabbath and not the

Sabbath for man. But we repeat the assertion, that in all the public exigencies in which he was called to act, he made the nearest practical approach to the great ends of the Republican party which human wisdom or foresight could then devise. In all the great measures of our government since he first entered Congress, his influence has been felt either in their origination or modification, and to this influence more than any other the Republican party is indebted for its present proud position before the world.

Morally considered, the great objects of the Republican party are simple and few. Its first is to preserve, as far as possible, the independence of individual action and pursuit; and it rejects all limitations upon this independence which are not essential to the great ends of social organization. It regards all of those powers which man wields in his aggregate or corporate capacity as so many limitations upon his individual rights, and it yields those which are indispensable to the institution of society as so many concessions which necessity has extorted from liberty. These are the terms upon which they would grant government its powers; and they would administer the power thus limited with an equal regard for all who are entitled to share the benefits of the trust. Tried by these tests, Mr. Calhoun has nothing to fear, when the circumstances are considered under which he was called to act.

In the first epoch of his public life, we were forced to defend ourselves in a war with the most formidable nation of the globe, and with the only power whose arm was long enough to reach us in our distant position, and within the defenses of so many natural barriers. In its commencement it was a war of independence, and it might become a contest for existence. In this state of things, it was in our aggregate power alone that we were to find the strength to resist foreign assaults, and every American patriot sought the means of increasing it as far as the limitations of the Constitution would permit. The war was a measure of the Republican party, and the unpatriotic course of the opposition devolved upon them alone the duty of devising the means to prosecute it. Under these circumstances, the Republican party deflected from the natural line of their direction, and sought to concentrate as much power in the government as they then believed indispensable for the successful conduct of the war. How far they were right or wrong, it is not our province here to determine; but certain it is, that there was much in the overruling power of circumstances to justify their course and excuse their errors, if errors they may be called. With how much more justice may the same apology be made for Mr. Calhoun himself. The leading advocate of hostilities and the chairman of the committee which reported the declaration of war, with a deep responsibility to the country for the success of that contest, which he was accused of precipitating; young, ardent, and indignant at the course of foreign and domestic enemies, it is surprising that he was not less scrupulous of the Constitution in calling forth the means of defending it, and our people against foreign expositions of law and justice, which ultimately might have overturned all, unless arrested by our successful resistance. And yet, upon how many great occasions did he restrain the Republican party from aberrations from their principles.

It was he who opposed the restrictive system against the majority of the party. It was he, too, who took a prominent part in resisting the system of forced loans in the case of the merchants' bonds, and who defeated Mr. Dallas's vast scheme of a national bank to issue irredeemable paper, which was recommended by a Republican President and supported by the party. Session after session did he combat it, until he succeeded in restoring to the country a specie-paying paper, and something like uniformity in the medium in which its taxes were collected. And although the opinions of that day, growing out of the exigencies of the war, exaggerated the necessity for roads and canals as military defenses, and called for the general use of a power which was given by the Constitution within the narrowest limits, it is remarkable that he has nowhere expressly affirmed the existence of such a power in the federal government.

His views of the proper use to be made of this power, if it existed, or could be obtained, when given in obedience to a call of the House of Representatives, were perhaps the ablest ever taken of the relation of this subject to our military defenses, yet he cautiously abstained from deciding the constitutional question. This was before the Republican party had paused in that career in which they were concentrating power within to defend themselves against attacks from without. In a review of this period of his life, it may with truth be said, that all those acts for which he has been reproached as departures from the states'-rights creed, were substitutes for much worse measures, which, but for him, his party would have adopted; and, although some of them were neither the wisest nor best, according to the present standard of information, they were each the nearest approach to the true Republican line of action which was permitted by the state of public knowledge and feeling at the time. But, whatever may have been the errors of the early part of his *public* life, he nobly redeemed them in the second period, which commenced from his election to the Vice-Presidency. It was during the interval then allowed for reflection that he first examined thoroughly the working of the machinery of the government in its internal as well as its external relations. He was among the first of the Republican party to pause in that career by which power had been consolidated in the federal government, without due reflection upon its consequences to the states and the people. He saw that the distribution of the political powers of our system, as contemplated by the Constitution, had been deranged, and that vast affiliated stock interests had been permitted to grow up almost unconsciously, which threatened to absorb the whole power and influence of the Confederacy, and to substitute a government of the few for that of the many; and, worse than all, he saw many of the Republican party so deeply entangled in the consequences of past action, and so little aware of the mischiefs which threatened them, that it was impossible to receive their cooperation in the efforts which were necessary to save the government from deep organic derangement, and the party itself from utter annihilation. His position gave him a deep interest in the unity of the party, if he had looked to himself alone; the road to office was open and easy; but the higher and more alluring path to fame lay along a steeper route and over rugged and difficult precipices. Between these alternatives he did not hesitate, but determined at once to strike the blows he believed to be necessary to save the country and restore the party to its pristine purity of faith and practice. We have given the history of the memorable contest in which, with unexampled odds against him, he maintained his foothold and accomplished his grand design.

We have seen the series of skillful movements and masterly combinations by which, with comparatively few forces, he occupied and manfully contested every inch of disputed territory, until he finally struck down the protective system with blows from which it never can entirely recover in the face of the formidable array against him, wielding the battle-axe of Richard or the cimeter of Saladin, as strength or skill might best serve his turn. Ever ready, cheerful, and confident, he sometimes obtained concessions from mere respect to his gallantry and prowess, which no force at his disposal could then have extorted. Experience now proved that he had not been a moment too soon in striking at the protective system. The Republican party had been gradually wasting under the assaults of their open enemies, and the moral influences of the stock interests. The banks, deprived for the time of their natural ally the tariff, were forced to take the field alone, and the difficulty which the Republicans experienced in coping with this single interest, proved how impossible it would have been for them to have resisted the whole affiliated system if its strength had been unimpaired, and its united forces directed against them. They now saw that Mr. Calhoun had been warring all along, not against them, but a common enemy, which, but for him, might have overwhelmed all together. Mr. Calhoun, who had left his ancient friends in their strength to reform, but not to destroy, now returned to them in their weakness to cheer, to animate, to rally, and defend them, and was prouder of their alliance upon principle in their period of adversity than he would have been of all the honors which they could have heaped upon him in their prosperity. It was not in his nature to regard the execrations which these stock interests poured out upon him. They had too often tried the temper of his steel not to know the force of the arm which wielded it, and it was perhaps with as much of despair as rage that privilege saw its ancient and well-trained adversary take the field with additional strength against it. Mr. Calhoun did not now direct his attention so much to mere affairs of outposts as to placing the party upon that solid platform of principle, in which he well knew that the whole battering train of the federal hosts could never effect a breach. With a true military eye, he readily seized all the advantages of position, and under his advice mainly, they have, at every sacrifice, directed column after column upon this elevated post, where they now command the field, and from which, if not abandoned or lost by want of vigilance, they must ultimately recover the country.

He is now about to retire from the theater of public life, neither wearied nor worn, but because his work is done, so far, at least, as senatorial life can afford him any useful part to play. If there be any new field of action worthy of his powers, and as yet untrodden by him, it is in that highest executive sphere, for which the character of his mind and the experience of his life have so eminently fitted him. It is, perhaps, only upon this theater that his countrymen would not now exclaim, "Superfluous lags the veteran on the stage," and it is there that they will probably require him to consummate, as perhaps he alone can do, those great Republican reforms so cherished by the party, as destined to commend it to the grateful regards of posterity. We cannot better close this sketch than by extracting a portrait of Mr. Calhoun as a man and an orator, which was drawn by a friendly hand, it is true, but which we recognize as being so just and well executed that we gladly adopt it as our own.

In his person Mr. Calhoun is slender and tall. His countenance, at rest, is strikingly marked with decision and firmness. In conversation it is highly animated, expressive, and indicative of genius. His eyes are large, dark, brilliant, and penetrating, and leave no doubt, at first view, of a high order of intellect. His manners are easy, natural, and unassuming, and as frank as they are cordial and kind. In all his domestic relations his life is without a blemish. He has none of the cautious reserve and mystery of common politicians; for he has nothing to conceal or disguise. He is accessible to all, agreeable, animated, instructive, and eloquent in conversation, and communicates his opinions with the utmost freedom. Some politicians seek popularity by carefully avoiding responsibility. Whatever popularity Mr. Calhoun possesses has, on the contrary, been acquired by bold and fearless assumption of responsibility on all critical and trying occasions. His judgment is so clear and discriminating, that he seems to possess a sort of prophetic vision of future events, and on occasions when most men doubt and hesitate, he decides with confidence, follows up his decision with undoubting firmness, and has never failed in the end to be justified by time, the arbiter of all things.

Few men have been called upon to pass through scenes of higher political excitement, and to encounter more vigorous and unrelenting opposition than Mr. Calhoun; yet, amid all the prejudices which party feeling engenders, and all the jealousy of political rivals, and all the animosity of political opponents, no one has yet ventured to hazard his own reputation for judgment or sincerity so far as to doubt one moment his great and commanding talents.

As an orator, Mr. Calhoun stands in the foremost rank of parliamentary speakers. On first rising in debate, he always felt the anxiety of diffidence, arising from a sensibility which is almost always the companion of true genius. His manner of speaking is energetic, ardent, rapid, and marked by a solemn earnestness, which leaves no doubt of his sincerity and deep conviction. His style is pure, forcible, logical, and condensed; often figurative for illustration, never for ornament. His mind is well stored with the fruits of learning, but still better with those of observation and reflection. Hence depth, originality, and force characterize all his speeches. He lays his premises on a foundation too broad, solid, and deep to be shaken; his deductions are clear and irresistible; "the strong power of genius," to adopt the language of the eloquent Pinkney, in referring to Mr. Calhoun's splendid speech on the treaty-making power, "from a higher region than that of argument, throws on his subjects all the light with which it is the prerogative of genius to invest and illustrate everything." And his speeches, full of the most elevated and patriotic sentiments, after conquering the understanding, take the heart entirely captive, and carry along his hearers, often unconsciously, and sometimes against their will, to the point he desires.

Mr. Calhoun had attained so high a reputation as a member of Congress, that it was thought by many that he was leaving his appropriate field when he accepted the appointment of Secretary of War. On the contrary, his new situation only presented another theater for the exercise of his great and diversified talents. The distinguishing feature of his mind, the power of analysis, was now to be exercised in the practical business of government, and at once, as by enchantment, order, efficiency, and perfect accountability sprang from the chaos in which he found the department, and demonstrated that his energy in execution was equal to his wisdom in organizing, and left it doubtful whether his legislative talents were not surpassed by his practical ability in administration. As a statesman, in the most enlarged and elevated sense of the term, Mr. Calhoun has no superior. A philosophical observer of men and of their affairs, he analyzes and reduces all things to their original elements, and draws thence those general principles, which, with inconceivable rapidity and unerring certainty, he applies on all occasions, and banishes the perplexity and doubt by which ordinary minds are overwhelmed and confounded. By this wonderful faculty, he is enabled to decide at once, not only what measures are at present necessary for a government novel in its principles, and placed in circumstances of which there is no precedent in the history of mankind, but, by discerning results through their causes, to look into futurity, and to devise means for carrying on our beloved country in a direct path to the high and glorious destiny which, under the guidance of wisdom and virtue, awaits her.

To the highest powers of mind Mr. Calhoun unites those elevated moral qualities, which are equally essential with ability to complete the character of a perfect statesman: inflexible integrity, honor without a stain, disinterestedness, temperance, and industry; a firmness of purpose which disdains to calculate the consequences of doing his duty; prudence and energy in action, devotion to his country, and inextinguishable love of liberty and justice. To these great qualities, perhaps, we ought to add a lofty ambition; but it is an ambition that prefers glory to office and power, which looks upon the latter only as a means for acquiring the former, and which, by the performance of great and virtuous actions for the accomplishment of noble ends, aims at the establishment of a widely extended and ever-during fame. This ingredient, which enters into the composition of all great and powerful minds, seems intended by Providence to stimulate them to the highest pitch of exertion in the service of mankind; and if it be a defect, it is one which Mr. Calhoun shares, as well as all their high qualities, with the most perfect models of Greek and Roman excellence.

To those who have not been attentive observers of the life, character, and conduct of Mr. Calhoun, or who may have been

alienated by political conflicts, the above portraiture may seem to
derive some of its coloring from the partial pencil of friendship.
If an intimate connection of that kind for more than a quarter of
a century may be supposed to tincture the writer's mind with
partiality, it will be allowed, at the same time, that it affords the
best possible opportunity of forming an accurate estimate of the
moral and political character of the subject of this memoir. His
statements of fact and opinion he knows to be entirely authentic;
and after a deliberate review of every sentence and word he has
written, he finds nothing which a reverence for justice and truth
will allow him to alter.

✪

Life and Character of the
Hon. John Caldwell Calhoun

Grateful appreciation of the services and veneration for the character of a distinguished statesman has overcome the reluctance belonging to a consciousness of inability to do adequate justice to the theme. A long personal acquaintance would enable me to say much learned in friendly intercourse, but I shall rely upon those official records which are within the reach of all who choose to consult them.

No public man has been more misunderstood and misrepresented than Mr. Calhoun. Not unfrequently he has been described as a "hair-splitting abstractionist," a "sectionist" and a "disunionist." That he was eminently wise and practical, that his heart and his mind embraced the whole country, that he was ardently devoted to the Union of the Constitution as our fathers made and construed it, his official acts and published speeches clearly demonstrate.

The subject of this sketch was of Scotch-Irish descent, a stock characterized by sturdy integrity, intrepidity, and intellectual vigor. They have been represented in our history by Presidents Monroe and Jackson, and many distinguished in the civil and military service.

Mr. Calhoun was born in 1782, the last year of the Revolution-

Reprinted from the *North American Review*, Vol. CXLV (September 1887), pp. 246–260.

ary War, and while negotiations were pending which terminated in the treaty of peace, recognizing the declared sovereignty and independence of the several states, late colonies of Great Britain.

At the time of his birth the state of his nativity, South Carolina, was a member of the confederacy styled the "United States of America," being bound by articles of confederation and perpetual union between the states enumerated. Rocked in the cradle of the Revolution, his earliest years amid the shouts of a people triumphant in their liberation from foreign rule, and the enjoyment of community independence, may he not fairly be regarded as having imbibed with his first sensations the belief in states' rights, maintained with such ardent devotion in defiance of all the clamor which pursued him to the end of his life, and stops not even at his grave?

Reared in a rural district of South Carolina, with such preparation as the country schools of that day could give, he entered Yale College and was graduated with distinction, evincing at that early period the exact and analytic character of his mind by a special proficiency in mathematics. He read law as a profession, but practiced little, and at an early age became the representative of his district in the House of Representatives of the legislature of his state, and subsequently a Representative in the Congress of the United States. He entered the House of Representatives in 1811, a period of intense excitement, of depredations upon our commerce, and upon the rights of seamen, citizens of the United States, which had aroused a just spirit of resistance. The policy of nonintercourse no longer satisfied the prouder spirits among our people; but, timidity and selfishness magnifying the danger of conflict with Great Britain, contended both in and out of Congress for further toleration of the ills we had, sooner than brave "those we knew not of." It was such a time as this that naturally brought forward men who loved their country, their *whole* country, and who would as soon fight for the commerce and sailors of New England as if they had belonged to their own state or section; and thus it was that, foremost of those who advocated defiance to Great Britain, and war with all its consequences, stood Calhoun of South Carolina and Clay of Kentucky. So ardent and effective were Calhoun's invocations as to cause a jeer to be thrown at those advocating the protection of our sailors, as "backwoodsmen who never saw a ship till convened here." Mr. Calhoun claimed that such sympathy was commendable, and said: "It constitutes our real Union, the rest is form; the wonder is, in fact, on the other side. Since it cannot be denied that American citizens are held in foreign bondage, how strange that those who boast of being neighbors and relations should be dead to all sympathy." In his speech December 12, 1811, he put to his opponents the searching question: "Which shall we do, abandon or defend our commercial and maritime rights and the personal liberties of our citizens employed in exercising them?" Again he answered to the excuse of those who opposed preparation for war by representing the defenseless state of the country for which the majority, not the minority, was to be held responsible, and said: "It is no less the duty of the minority than a majority to endeavor to defend the country. For that purpose we are sent here and not for that of opposition." In the same spirit of broad patriotism he rebuked those who were pleading against the necessary expense which would attend armed opposition. "But it may be, and I believe was said, that the people will not pay taxes, because the rights violated are not worth defending; for that the defense will cost more than the gain. Sir, I enter my solemn protest. There is, sir, one principle necessary to make us a great people—to produce not the form, but the real spirit of union—and that is to protect every citizen in the lawful pursuit of his business."

After the war of 1812 had been successfully ended, to which success Calhoun, in civil life, and his compatriot, Jackson, in the army, had been recognized as mainly contributing, we see him laboring with the same zeal, though under different form, for the general welfare and common defense.

On January 31, 1816, referring to the condition and future prospects of the country, he thus spoke: "We are now called upon to determine what amount of revenue is necessary for this country in time of peace. This involves the additional question, What are the measures which the true interests of the country demand?" Treating of the defense of the country on land, he advocated a regular draft from the body of the people in preference to recruiting an army by individual enlistment, and of the latter said: "Uncertain, slow in its operation, and expensive, it draws from society only its worst materials, introducing into our army, of necessity, all the severities which are exercised in that of the most despotic governments. Thus composed, our armies, in a great degree, lose that enthusiasm with which citizen soldiers, conscious of liberty and fighting in defense of their country, have ever been animated." Then, with the same deep concern for every interest of the broad Union to which he was proud to belong, he proceeded to discuss material questions as follows: "I shall now proceed to a point of less, but still of great importance—I mean the establishing of roads and the opening of canals through various parts of the country." Referring to the widely dispersed condition of our population, and the difficulty in the then condition of the country of collecting the military means at a menaced point, he said: "The people are brave, great, and spirited, but they must be brought together in sufficient numbers, and with a certain promptitude, to enable them to act with effect. . . . Let us make great permanent roads; not like the Romans, with views of subjecting and ruling provinces, but for the more honorable purpose of defense and of connecting more closely the interests of various sections of this great country." This he enforced by reference to the embarrassments felt for the want of facilities in transportation during the preceding war, and then proceeded to consider what encouragement could properly be given to the industry of the country. He said: "In regard to the question, How far manufactures ought to be fostered, it is the duty of this country, as a means of defense, to encourage its domestic industry, more especially that part of it which provides the necessary materials for clothing and defense. . . . Laying the claims of manufacturers entirely out of view, on general principles, without regard to their interests, a certain encouragement should be extended at least to our woollen and cotton manufactures." After the war of the Revolution, it will be remembered that President Washington recommended special encouragement for the manufacture of materials requisite in time of war, and indicated the payment of bounties for the same. A like experience of the sufferings of the defenders of the country during the suspension of foreign trade suggested to both the propriety of guarding against such want in the future. Mr. Calhoun, in the same speech, called attention to the preparation which should be made for the defense of our coast and navigable rivers, and answered the argument which was opposed to the taxation which would be required, that it would impair the moral power of the country, and in that connection said: "Let us examine the question, whether a tax laid for the defense, security, and lasting prosperity of a country is calculated to destroy its moral power, and more especially of this country. If such be the fact, indispensable as I believe these taxes to be, I would relinquish them; for of all the powers of the Government, the power of a moral kind is most to be cherished. We had better give up all our physical power than part with this. But what is moral power? The zeal of the country and the confidence it reposes in the administration of its government."

After stating the obligation of the representatives as agents of the people, and their duty to influence their constituents to agree to whatever sacrifices were necessary for the security and prosperity of the country, he said: "I know of no situation so responsible, if properly considered, as ours. We are charged by Providence, not only with the happiness of this great and rising people, but, in a considerable degree, with that of the human race. We have a government of a new order, perfectly distinct from all others which have preceded it—a government founded on the rights of man; resting, not on authority, not on prejudice, not on superstition, but reason. If it shall succeed, as fondly hoped by its founders, it will be the commencement of a new era in human affairs." To men of the present day, the full significance of the argument of Mr. Calhoun for the encouragement of the manufactures which had grown up under the necessities of the war may not be appreciated in their antisectional character; it may, therefore, be not inappropriate to say that it was before the invention of steamships and steam locomotives, and that the manufactures were almost exclusively in the Northern states, and it would have required prophetic vision to foresee their introduction into the land of Calhoun. Commerce was then conducted on the sea and in sailing vessels. A wide plain lay between the mountains of South Carolina and the sea. If the water power at the base of the mountains had been utilized for purposes of manufacture, the transportation across the plain would have been too slow and expensive for a profitable commerce. Therefore, the agricultural products, chiefly in the country near to the sea, were transported in ships to places where the water power was near to a harbor, and thus it will be seen that to advocate encouragement to the manufacturers was to benefit, not the people of his own section, but those far away from it, and that in this, as well as in his zealous efforts for the vindication of the rights of sailors, he rose above any considerations of sectional interest or feeling, and stood forward as the champion of his countrymen, to whatever state they might belong. I now submit it to any candid and intelligent reader whether I have not disproved the charge of sectionalism as made against Calhoun.

The services rendered by him in the House of Representatives during the war of 1812 and immediately thereafter, not merely by the ability he exhibited, but by the purity and patriotism which characterized his course, gave to him a high reputation in every portion of the country. He was invited by Mr. Monroe and accepted a seat in his Cabinet as Secretary of War, but many of Mr. Calhoun's best friends objected to his accepting the appointment, believing that the Parliamentary field was one for the labors of which he was peculiarly fitted. They underrated the universality of his genius. His administrative ability was soon exhibited in so marked a degree as to induce the belief that he was then in his most appropriate sphere. Many eminent men had occupied that post, and, without detracting from their merit, the fact must be noted that there was a want in the system of accountability and the general conduct of our military affairs, which was marked by a very large amount of unsettled accounts and more or less of confusion in all the operations of the department, which at that time included the conduct of our relations with the Indian tribes. Rapidly a system of accountability was established, so perfect as to require very little modification by his successors, at least for the next quarter of a century. Under that system default by disbursing officers of the War Department became a very rare exception, though new posts were being established on the remote frontier, requiring heavy expenditures beyond the limits of commercial facilities, and that the only foreign war in which our country has been engaged was also embraced within the period I have named. The exclusion of party considerations in appointments and preferments may not have originated, but was certainly perpetuated by him, so that the War Department and the officers of the old army were so far removed from political influence, and politics were so rarely discussed in army circles, that if an officer had been asked to what party one of his most intimate friends belonged, he probably would have answered that he could not tell.

It was during Mr. Calhoun's occupancy of the War Office that the system of seacoast defenses received its great impulse, and army discipline and instruction were nurtured by schools of practice. In this, as in every other public office he held, a broad and comprehensive view of the general interests of the country, together with a strict observance of the powers and limitation conferred by the Constitution on the government of the United States, was the polar star by which his course was directed. At the close of his service in the War Office the popular verdict was that he had done well in all his stewardship, and should go up still higher. Thus, by a rare unanimity, in 1824, he was elected Vice-President, at a time when many candidates for the Presidency divided the people into earnestly contending parties.

Thus the breath of life was breathed into the Union. It was created by the states, its purposes and powers expressly enumerated and restricted by the compact. The Constitution was the soul, the form of government the body of the Union. Whoso adhered to the Constitution, and maintained its validity, defending its principles and upholding its purposes, was a friend of the Union, and he who perverted it from its declared purposes, thus breaking the only bond which held the states together, was logically and criminally a disunionist. To claim, because he still adhered to the form of the government, that he was, therefore, a friend of the union of the states is as if the man who should take the life of his neighbor could, by embalming his body, prove himself to have been his friend.

In the beginning of Mr. Calhoun's career we find him the champion of the honor and independence of the United States, and subsequently advocating a policy of a tariff and internal improvements as a means of providing for the common defense. His patriotism and generosity caused him to overlook the danger which lurked beneath measures which, distorted from their real purpose, could be made to serve the aggrandizement of one sec-

tion, the impoverishment of another, and taxation, not for common defense, but for the benefit of individuals and corporations.
In this, as in other instances of his public career, we find evidence of the extent to which his broad patriotism, generosity,
and purity engendered a confidence which never proved misplaced.
When abuses, progressing in geometrical ratio, warned him of the
evils which threatened the perpetuity of the Union, he labored
assiduously, even unto the end of his life, to point out the danger
and invoke the application of appropriate remedies. It is but justice
to him to say that his ardent devotion to the Union of the Constitution was the source of whatever his friends will admit were
the errors of his political life, and it is a tribute to his elevated
nature that he did not anticipate all that sordid avarice and narrow
selfishness would build on the small foundation which patriotic
credulity had laid.

Imposts designed to provide revenue, like the costs of transportation from foreign countries, were of advantage, and served
to encourage home manufactures, and insofar as the benefit thus
resulted to individuals in any of the states, Mr. Calhoun did not
object; but when duties were made, not to provide the means necessary for the support of government, but were discriminations
intended solely for the profit of particular classes—*this* was not
the scheme to which he had ever given favor; and then he invoked
the Constitution as the shield of the minority to protect it against
oppression. In pointing out the landmarks of the fathers, and
showing how they were being obliterated, and the tendency of
such crime to produce disunion, he was not expressing a thought
which originated in desire, but warning those who, he hoped,
would, like himself, recoil from the approach of so great a disaster,
that they might, in time, retrace their steps, and, before it was too
late, avert the threatened calamity. He was too wise to ignore how
many and grievous would be the consequences of disrupting the
bonds which held the states together; not only the compact,
but the traditions, memories, and historical glories which cemented
them as a family together. To those who knew him well, and
remember how regardless he was of his personal safety, when,
with a disease that was rapidly carrying him to the grave, he
rejected all solicitation to remain quietly at home, and came, at an

eventful period, to renew his labors in defense of the Constitution and the preservation of the Union, it must seem absurdly strange that currency could have been obtained for a report that he desired to destroy a confederation to which his life had been devoted, and in the annals of which all his glories were recorded. This may, perhaps, be due to the fact that the unreflecting have confounded nullification with disunion, when, in point of fact, the idea of nullification, so far as South Carolina is concerned, was adopted as a remedy *within* the Union. The hope was, by state interposition, to induce the call of a convention of states, to which would be submitted the constitutional question of laying duties; otherwise, imposing taxes upon the whole people for the benefit of a particular class. The question to be presented was, What was the proper limit of the powers delegated by the states to the general government? All else was expressly reserved to the states or the people. The phrase "the people" necessarily meant the people of the several states, as there were no other people known to the Constitution. The language must have been intended to convey the state governments and the people of the states so far as they possessed rights and powers with which their governments had not been invested. The whole proceeding of South Carolina was on the ground that the Constitution did not authorize the general government to impose and collect duties on imports for the benefit of manufacturers, *i.e.*, a protective, not a revenue tariff. In this connection Mr. Calhoun referred to the constitutional provision for amendment, and it was in the nature of his profound intellect to believe that, if the states were assembled in convention, any imperfection which experience had proved to exist would be remedied, and additional safeguards provided to protect the people from the usurpations of government. It would be needless to inquire, in the light shed by the experience of 1860 and 1861, especially of the peace congress, whether that hope would have been realized. I am now treating of the question as it was presented to his mind and that of his associates. Thus it is evident that their remedy looked, not to a dissolution of the Union, but to the purification of its general government, the happiness and contentment of the people, and the perpetuity of their fraternal relations. No more dangerous and vicious heresy has grown up than the supposition that ours is a government made and controlled by a majority of the people of the United States *en masse*.

Let us now examine the odious and unfounded accusation that he was a disunionist.

To the clear understanding of the charge it is necessary, in the first place, to define the true meaning of the word "union." The history of its formation irrefutably proves that it was a confederation of sovereign states, each acting separately and for itself alone. The states so agreeing to unite entered into a compact styled "The Constitution of the United States of America." This constitution was declared to be binding between the states ratifying the same, and that "The ratification of the conventions of nine States shall be sufficient for the establishment of the constitution between the States so ratifying the same."—Art. VII.

The men who founded our constitutional government were too profound as statesmen and philosophers, after having achieved their independence of Great Britain, to transfer the liberties they had acquired to the control of a majority of the people, *en masse*. The most careless reading of the Constitution, and the laws enacted to carry out its provisions, will show there is not a department or officer of the federal government who derives power and authority from a majority of the people of the United States. The power of amending the Constitution was given to the states, not to the people collectively. From the speech of Mr. Calhoun delivered in the Senate February 15 and 16, 1833, I make the following extract:

"To maintain the ascendency of the Constitution over the law-making majority is the great and essential point on which the success of the system must depend. Unless that ascendency can be preserved, the necessary consequence must be that the laws will supersede the Constitution; and finally, the will of the executive, by the influence of his patronage, will supersede the laws; indications of which are already perceptible. This ascendency can only be preserved through the action of the States as organized bodies, having their own separate governments, and possessed of the right, under the structure of our system, of judging of the extent of their separate powers, and of interposing their authority to arrest the unauthorized enactments of the general government within their respective limits." Additional evidence could be abundantly offered that nullification was intended to conserve, not to destroy the Union, and in the manner proposed to secure a remedy short of secession. It would be unfair to judge of the practicability of the plan by the state of the country at a subsequent date, and we must presume that it was more feasible in 1833 than it was in 1860.

In 1850, during the long and exciting debate over what was known as the compromise measures of that year, Mr. Calhoun was generally confined to his lodgings, being too ill and debilitated to occupy his seat in the Senate. In that condition he wrote the speech read for him to the Senate on March 4, 1850. It was the effort of a dying man whose affections clung so tenaciously to the Union he had long and faithfully served, that, though unable to deliver the speech, he submitted the MSS. to the Senate. To him earthly ambition was a thing of the past, but the love of truth and justice, devotion to the cause of liberty, and hopes for the people's welfare and happiness under the Constitution, all of which could not die, sustained his sinking frame for this last supreme effort in his country's cause. A few brief extracts from that speech are here inserted. Referring to the supposition of states held together by force, he said:

"It may indeed keep them connected; but the connection will partake much more of the character of subjugation, on the part of the weaker to the stronger, than the union of free, independent, and sovereign States in one confederation as they stood in the early stages of the government, and which only is worthy of the sacred name of Union." Then, referring to frequent eulogies on the Union, he said:

"It usually comes from our assailants. But we cannot believe them to be sincere; for, if they loved the Union, they would necessarily be devoted to the Constitution. It made the Union, and to destroy the Constitution would be to destroy the Union."

The day after the reading of the speech from which these extracts have been made, a Senator made a speech in review, Mr. Calhoun being absent; but, when his colleague, Mr. Butler, had commenced a reply Mr. Calhoun came in. After expressing his regret that a member of the body should have commented upon his speech during his absence and before the hour for the consideration of the question under discussion, he said: "I had not the advantage of hearing the remarks of the Senator of Mississippi. Did he accuse me of disunion? Did he mean to insinuate that?" To which Mr. Foote, the Senator referred to, replied that he "had not the slightest intention to impute to him designs hostile to the Union." . . . "I have always maintained that he is one of the most devoted friends of the Union in this body."

The evident purpose for which the question was put was to answer the charge or insinuation, if made, by the most emphatic denunciation. This was the last time Mr. Calhoun appeared in the United States Senate. Death had laid its icy hand upon him; he was aware of the near approach, and with the heroism of a martyr strove with his last breath to bear testimony to the faith in which he had lived and labored.

If a young man should ask me where he could, in a condensed form, get the best understanding of our institutions and the duties of an American patriot, I would answer, "In Calhoun's speech in the Senate on what is known as 'The Force Bill.' "

No one has so fully and clearly expounded the Constitution, no one has so steadily invoked a strict observance of it, as the means of securing the blessings of liberty to ourselves and our posterity, for which the more perfect union was formed. It required neither his dying assertion nor the testimony of others to exculpate him from the charge of desiring to destroy our Constitutional Union. His whole life speaks trumpet-tongued denial.

Another accusation was his inconsistency—to which it may be briefly answered, he was practical as well as logical, and was consistent to principle, to truth, to the Constitution, and to the duties of a patriot. Consistency as to measures when every day brings forth unforetold phases could honestly belong only to one having more than human foresight, or to one having less than human capacity to learn.

The questions agitating the country to such degree as to threaten convulsion were the subjects under discussion when Mr. Calhoun last addressed the Senate. They were the slavery and territorial questions. Long he had foreseen and given warning of the danger of the hostile and unconstitutional interference with the domestic institution of African servitude. The states having that institution had become a minority and claimed the protection which the compact of union had expressly promised to give.

In regard to the territories outside of the limits of any state, there were three divisions of opinion. The one, that they belonged to the United States, and consequently that the citizens of every state, with every species of property recognized by the United States, had equal right therein; another, that they belonged to the immigrants who should settle thereon; and another, that the United States government had proprietary right over them. This last form of opinion, which has grown with the political decadence of our time, was, in 1850, the least dangerous, because it was then, as it is now, the least defensible. The general government was formed to be the agent of the states for specific purposes and with enumerated powers; it was penniless, could only collect revenue as the agent of the states, and as the agent of the states only had the means or authority to acquire anything. The authority conferred upon Congress to dispose of and make all needful rules and regulations respecting the territory or other property belonging to the United States applied equally to the public lands within the new states as to the outlying territories, save and except such regulations as might be necessary in the outlying territories with a view to the exercise of the granted power. The arguments of Mr. Calhoun were directed to support the first-named opinion and to demonstrate the fallacy of the other two. His proposition was maintained with the conclusiveness of a mathematical demonstration, but we shall be verging on the millennium when reason shall prevail over passion and prejudice, and the lust of dominion shall yield to truth and justice: it was a contest of might and right.

The permitted limit of this article does not allow me to follow the career of this great statesman through that period when he sacrificed personal ambition and party ties to lead the few against the many, in defense of truth, justice, and the liberty the Union was formed to secure and perpetuate. Exposing himself as a target to serried ranks of foes, he stood like a sentinel on the watchtower warning the people he loved.

In my early manhood I enjoyed the personal acquaintance of Mr. Calhoun, and perhaps received especial consideration from the fact that, as Secretary of War, he had appointed me a cadet in the United States Military Academy. In 1845, as a member of the House of Representatives, I frequently visited Mr. Calhoun, who was then a Senator, at his residence. His conversation was always instructive and peculiarly attractive. The great question of the day was on giving notice to Great Britain of a termination of the joint occupation of Oregon. He and his colleague, the brilliant orator McDuffie, did not fully concur, as I had occasion to learn, being one of several in a private consultation. There was great excitement in the country, and there was believed to be imminent danger of a war with Great Britain. Under these circumstances, Mr. Calhoun, though in such feeble health as to require rest, responded to the call for his services in the Senate, and went to Washington to labor in the cause of peace. War was to him an evil which only defense of the honor and rights of his country would justify. That state of the case made him the advocate of the war of 1812, but, in 1845, he saw no such justification, and was, therefore, in favor of negotiation, by which he believed war could be averted without the surrender of the rights of our country.

As a Senator he was a model of courtesy. He politely listened to each one who spoke, neither reading nor writing when in his seat, and as long as his health permitted was punctual and constant in his attendance. His correspondence was conducted by rising at dawn and writing before breakfast. Issues growing out of the disposal of the public lands within the states occupied much of the time of Congress, and for this and more important reasons he proposed, on certain conditions, to surrender the public lands to the new states in which they lay. This was but another exhibition of his far-reaching patriotism and wisdom, as shown in his argument for the measure.

Always earnest, often intense in debate, he was never rhetorical, seldom sought the aid of illustration, simile, or quotation, but, concisely and in logical sequence, stated his views like one demonstrating a problem, the truth of which was so clear to his mind that he did not doubt its acceptance by all who listened to the proof. Perhaps he was too little of a party man to believe, as the English parliamentarian did, that opinions might be, but votes were never changed by a speech.

Wide as was his knowledge, great as was his foresight, reaching toward the domain of prophecy, his opinions were little derived from books or from conversation. Data he gathered on every hand, but the conclusions were the elaboration of his brain—as much his own as is honey not of the leaf, but of the bag of the bee. He paid little attention to style—probably undervalued it; words were to him merely the medium to convey his thoughts, and these flowed on unbroken and with the resistless power of a mighty river.

The death of Mr. Calhoun, though anticipated by those who saw him, with tottering steps, enter the Senate Chamber for the last time, and feebly struggle to repel misconstruction, created the deep impression which his high and reverend character commanded. His great political antagonist, Mr. Webster, had always been his personal friend; they were born in the same year, 1782. There was a custom in the old Senate that, at the beginning of each session, Senators should give one another a friendly salutation as evidence that past controversies were buried. On one occasion I remember that Mr. Webster approached Mr. Calhoun, and with cordial greeting said: "How do the men of '82 stand on their pins?" When the death was announced in the Senate, Mr. Webster said: "I think there is not one of us, when he last addressed us from his seat in the Senate, who did not feel that he might imagine that we saw before us a Senator of Rome, when Rome survived. He had the basis, the indispensable basis of all high character, and that was unspotted integrity—unimpeached honor and character. If he had aspirations, they were high, and honorable, and noble. There was nothing groveling, or low, or meanly selfish that came near the head or the heart of Calhoun. . . . We shall delight to speak of him to those who are rising up to fill our places. And when the time shall come that we ourselves shall go, one after another, in succession, to our graves, we shall carry with us a deep sense of his genius and character, his honor and integrity, his amiable deportment in private life, and the purity of his exalted patriotism."

[1] I have relied mainly on the lives by John S. Jenkins and Hermann von Holst, on the latter's *Constitutional History*, and on Calhoun's *Works* in six volumes. I have also studied the nullification movement in original sources, and have found much help from South Carolina newspapers.

Reprinted from *Southern Statesmen of the Old Regime* (Boston and New York: Thomas Y. Crowell & Company, 1897), pp. 153-193.

John Caldwell Calhoun[1]

If the two great statesmen, Washington and Jefferson . . . belong more to the nation than to the South, the man whose career I am now about to discuss belongs, at least during the more important part of his life, pre-eminently to that region. Of purely Southern, and, therefore, sectional politics, John C. Calhoun was the coryphæus,—his like was not before him, nor has been since.

Yet even Calhoun himself is not, in all respects, a typical Southerner: he has not that peculiar flexibility and mobility of character that marks the average inhabitant of his section; his Scotch-Irish inherited qualities giving him a sort of stiffness and rigidity of temperament which, while not uncommon in the South, has never been typical of it. Yet though not entirely of the dominant planter-aristocrat class, which Dr. Von Holst has somewhat misleadingly dubbed the slavocracy, he was with them and for them, and was, in fact, their leader.

The mention of Dr. Von Holst, however, reminds me that I may as well say at the outset of this attempt to estimate Calhoun and his work, that I shall be able to add little or nothing to the admirable account of the great statesman's career which the scholarly professor has contributed to the well-known "American States-

[1] I have relied mainly on the lives by John S. Jenkins and Hermann von Holst, on the latter's *Constitutional History,* and on Calhoun's *Works* in six volumes. I have also studied the nullification movement in original sources, and have found much help from South Carolina newspapers.

Reprinted from *Southern Statesmen of the Old Regime* (Boston and New York: Thomas Y. Crowell & Company, 1897), pp. 153–193.

men" series. While, however, my conclusions are bound to be in the main those of Dr. Von Holst, I may be able to throw a tiny ray of light here and there upon certain obscure topics.

Of Calhoun as a man, we know next to nothing; since his private life was simple and retiring, and his hitherto published correspondence practically deals with politics only. His contemporaries were far from knowing or understanding him, so that their comments are of little value in estimating his character; and it is doubtful if we ever shall know him as we do most of his notable contemporaries. The mystery of genius, however, does not, in my opinion, overhang him; and his personality is hardly sufficiently attractive to make us long for any information that does not throw light on his political career. That, I confess, is for me the only point of importance with regard to Calhoun; for I cannot help believing that if he had been a great man, *quà,* man, this fact would force itself upon us in a thousand ways, in personal anecdotes, and in little flashes of character in his published works.

I may, indeed, be utterly mistaken in this matter, but I think not. I am inclined to judge the greatness of men much as I judge the greatness of poetry,—both must appeal powerfully to my imagination in a noble and elevating way, nor will the possession of merely pathetic qualities suffice. Calhoun is a pathetic figure, but he is not inspiring, at least to me; and true genius, while it may be pathetic, is always inspiring. Calhoun lacked, I think, the power of creative and truthful imagination. His foresight was largely the result of deduction; and as his premises were always mixed with error, except in the matter of the antagonism between slavery and modern civilization, his foresight was of little practical service to himself or others. Where his foresight did not depend on deduction, it rested on apprehension. The foresight of the genuine seer, however, is creatively and truthfully imaginative; it enables him to visualize the future in the present, not as he would like to have it, but as it will and ought to be, and not merely for himself, but for others. Hence there can be no greater blessing to any people than to be possessed of a true political seer in any grave crisis; i.e., to have a statesman of genius.

It is the irony of fate that often the statesman of genius is a man of bad character, as, for example, Themistocles; while his

chief opponent possesses all the moral virtues, but lacks a creative
imagination, as, for example, Aristides. Calhoun is in many ways
the Aristides of our politics; a breath of genius would have made
him the Demosthenes. But the sturdy Scotch-Irish blood with
its puritan strain seems to give us talents rather than genius.
Indeed puritanism, wherever found, seems to run to talents rather
than to genius; and Cromwell, Milton, Hawthorne, are the exceptions that prove the rule. But I will not obtrude my speculations
upon you; let me rather give in outline the chief facts of Calhoun's
life, and then proceed to comment upon them.

John Caldwell Calhoun was born March 18, 1782, in Abbeville
district, South Carolina. His Scotch-Irish grandfather emigrated to
Pennsylvania in 1735, removing thence to Virginia, and afterward,
in 1756, to South Carolina. His father, Patrick Calhoun, was a
brave man and a great Indian fighter. He seems to have been a
born particularist in politics, for he opposed the adoption of the
federal Constitution on the ground that it would enable the other
states to tax South Carolina. The right of suffrage having been
denied him on one occasion, he is said to have shouldered his
rifle and obtained it.[2] He died in 1795, but not before he had
instilled some of his individualistic principles into his young son.

His father not believing much in education, that of Calhoun
was neglected at first; but later on he made up for it under the
direction of his brother-in-law, Dr. Waddell, a famous school-
master in his day. Entering Yale, he graduated in 1804, having
disputed on politics with President Dwight in so able a manner
that that worthy prognosticated his election to the Presidency of
the Union. Of more importance, as Dr. Von Holst remarks, was
the influence of New England thought upon his early political
opinions. He next studied law, first in Charleston, then in Abbeville,
thus becoming acquainted with low-country and up-country habits
and customs,—the two sections of the state being not a little
different in many important respects, as indeed they still are.

Accounts differ as to his success when he first began to practice
at Abbeville in 1807. Dr. Von Holst doubts whether he would
ever have been a great lawyer; because "he was not objective

---

[2] See John S. Jenkins, *John C. Calhoun* (Auburn and Buffalo, N. Y.,
1857).

enough to examine his premises with sufficient care;" but premises
in law are not like premises in politics, which very frequently do
not admit of examination. I am inclined to think that Calhoun,
in his absence of creative imagination, would have been in his
proper place at the bar; for I am forced to qualify Dr. Von Holst's
statement that he was a born leader of men, and therefore a born
politician. Calhoun led thought rather than men, and lacking
imagination, he led thought badly. In the sphere of law, however,
he would have been fenced in by precedents in such a way as to
keep him from grievously erratic thinking, and his wonderful
powers of analysis and of logical deduction would have found full
vent; but this, again, is speculation, for which I apologize.

Facts are what we want here; and facts seem to favor Dr. Von
Holst, for Calhoun was almost immediately sent to the legislature,
and in 1811 was elected to Congress. A little incident of his legislative service may be recorded for the light it throws on his
character. He opposed the candidacies of Madison and George
Clinton for the Presidency, and thought that South Carolina ought
to nominate, as a sort of reconciliation candidate, John Langdon
of New Hampshire. Here is the radical defect of Calhoun's character, and of that of his state, standing out in bold relief,—that
portentous lack of humor which never fails to lead men and nations
into trouble. Calhoun would have been saved many a blunder had
he been able to speak disrespectfully of the equator—or of South
Carolina.

While a legislator Calhoun had favored war with Great Britain;
it was natural, therefore, that he should throw in his lot with Clay
and the war party in Congress. It was equally natural that his
strong personality easily carried him to the front in spite of his
youth, for the compromising tactics of Jefferson and Madison had
so emasculated the people and their representatives that strength of
any kind was bound to count.

Calhoun would have made his mark in any Congress, but he
made it all the more speedily and conspicuously in the Twelfth.
His first set speech was against John Randolph; and his biographers are right in contending that the young representative, who
was virtually chairman of the Committee on Foreign Relations,
acquitted himself admirably. Indeed, most of Calhoun's qualities

as an orator are present in this speech; and I cannot see that he ever varied much from his solid, logical, unemotional, and slightly heavy method of presenting his ideas. Later on he grew more prolix and more subtle; but his style of presentation and exposition changed little—a fact which is characteristic of talents rather than of genius. A tendency to sophistry, which was to grow with his growth, is also to be detected in this maiden effort.

I need not dwell on this period of his career; because there is only one feature of it that is at all important to us, and that feature is well known. I refer to his pronounced Union proclivities and repudiation of the narrow strict constructionist views of the Virginia school. When, later, he became the Cato of the states'-rights party, he was, of course, twitted with his tergiversation, and had some little difficulty in defending himself. His honesty, however, cannot be called into question, nor is the cause of the change far to seek.

Slavery had been steadily looming up as a political issue, and slavery could be maintained in the Union only on principles of the strictest construction. Hence, to be consistent with himself in 1830, Calhoun had to be inconsistent with what he had been in 1815. He showed his unflinching courage by the calm way he changed front, and bore the taunts of his opponents. He did, indeed, sometimes try to make out that the change had not been as great as it really was, but this was only human nature. Certainly the Calhoun of 1811–1817 was as national in his proclivities as one could well have desired. He had no hesitation in using the word "nation," and in meaning it. He favored the protection of manufactures, though he afterward tried to show that he had been very slightly affected by the delusion. He was far from taking a Jeffersonian position on the subject of the national bank, and he was positively liberal in the matter of internal improvements.

Naturally his political notions are less metaphysical than they afterward became, but it is easy to trace the germs of the fetish-worship of the Constitution that was to be his bane. In his speech on the treaty-making power, he said of this instrument, "We ought scarcely to indulge a wish that its provisions should be different from what they are." A pious Mussulman could hardly say more about the Koran, but the Mussulman keeps his Koran in mind; while Calhoun must have forgotten this speech when he allowed John Tyler to play his joint-resolution game with regard to Texas. No one knew better than Calhoun the scope of the treaty-making power, and no one had ever marked out so strictly the limits of the legislative. But, after all, one feels like forgiving him his inconsistency, grievous and almost dishonest as it was, when one reads the noble words in which he took his stand against the pernicious folly that a legislator must implicitly obey the instructions of his constituents. "The Constitution is my letter of instruction," [3] he proudly said, and he meant it; only later he could not see that some evil spirit had slipped a distorting lens before his eyes.[4]

The young Calhoun, then, was a Union man and a patriotic one. He claimed that he never ceased to be, and in a certain sense his claim was true. But he gradually assumed the dreadful position of a mother who slowly poisons her child, thinking to save its life; now he was like a mother feeding her firstborn. His sincerity and

[3] See Richard K. Crallé, ed., *The Works of John C. Calhoun* (Charleston, S. C., New York, 1851–1856), II, 179.

[4] For Calhoun's Union sentiments see his speech on Repeal of Direct Tax, *ibid.*, p. 139. In the same speech he said, "We are the most growing nation on earth." For his views on protection, see his speeches of April 6, 1816, and February 4, 1817. He tried to justify these views in his speeches on the Force Bill, February 15 and 16, 1833. The following quotations should also be carefully noted.

A. From the speech of December 4, 1812:—

"Our Union cannot safely stand on the cold calculations of interest alone. It is too weak to withstand political convulsions. We cannot, without hazard, neglect that which makes men love to be members of an extensive community—the love of greatness, the consciousness of strength. So long as American is a proud name, we are safe; but the day we are ashamed of it, the Union is more than half destroyed."

B. From the speech of January 17, 1814 (which contains some ineffective rhetoric):—

"For my part, I think that a fair and moderate opposition ought at all times to be respected; but that our Constitution authorized that dangerous and vicious species which I have attempted to describe, I utterly deny. . . . If, then, our opponents have the right [to make that kind of factious opposition], it is because it is not expressly forbidden. In this sense there is no limitation to their constitutional rights."

honesty are no less apparent first than last; although it is, perhaps, admissible to think that a desire to oppose the dominant Virginian school may account in part for the rather lavish way in which the representative of a proud and rising, but still unimportant state gave his support to the national idea. Patriotism and love of the Union were, however, peculiarly characteristic of the up-country Carolinians down to the close of Calhoun's life.[5]

As Secretary of War in Monroe's administrations, Calhoun seems to have shown marked ability—not enough to save him from criticism, most of it captious, or enough to entitle him to claim the possession of executive powers of the first rank, but sufficient to add materially to his general reputation as a statesman. It is easy to praise his report on roads and canals, and, what is more to the point, to read it; it is also easy to agree with Dr. Von Holst, that his reports on Indian affairs are most creditable to his heart and to his head.

How far his Presidential aspirations, which now became great, tended to impair his efficiency as an officer of government or his character as a man it is hard to determine; but I do not think the questions important, in view of the turn affairs soon took. Calhoun may have developed some of the arts of the politician; but he soon dropped them, and depended for his influence upon his integrity and his brain—a fact which makes him almost a unique figure in our history. That he should have had the Presidential fever was natural, and honorable to him; but I do not believe that it affected his career seriously, except insofar as his subsequent perceptions of the hopelessness of his ambition tended to strengthen his independence, and to develop his power of leaving personal and transient considerations out of his reasoning upon affairs of state. That he deliberately set to work to split the Union that he might at least rule over one-half of it, is an old wives' tale.

The two terms as Vice-President that followed his cabinet service are important in Calhoun's political life as marking the turning point in his career. The split with Jackson, toward the end,

[5] This fact will be apparent to anyone who will make a study of such a newspaper as the *Edgefield Advertiser* between 1835 and 1845, noting especially the accounts given of the Fourth of July banquets.

left no hope that the main forces of the democracy could be as yet prevailed upon to accept Carolinian leadership, and the tariff of 1828 determined the fact that that leadership would be both fanatical and doctrinaire. Calhoun's leadership would probably have developed these qualities under any circumstances; but it is as well to remark that, if he had won the Presidency in 1824 or 1828, he might, like Jefferson, have found it hard to preserve his philosophical consistency, and that, if he had been in the House or Senate, he would have been using weapons instead of forging them. It was his position as Vice-President, half in and half out of the political arena, that furnished both opportunity and incentive for the development of his metaphysical views on the nature of constitutional government, and for that analysis of the problem presented by slavery which is now his chief claim to a sinister reputation. A strong Vice-President, like a full-blooded Prince of Wales, is likely to get into trouble; for another well-known potentate is famous for finding work of his own for idle hands to do.

Having now reached Calhoun's turning point, we shall be compelled to pause for a while to consider the political and social environment that produced so great a change in the man's life. Henceforward the man himself and his outward career will hardly concern us. He becomes the embodiment of an idea, which, long rejected, becomes at last the idea of a section, and leads to the greatest civil war of modern times.

Calhoun the Senator, the rival of Webster and Clay, is, of course, interesting as a figure, but as an unearthly figure, wielding in the combat arms as mixed and queer as those that Milton put into the hands of his angels. Calhoun as Secretary of State under Tyler is more a demon helmsman, somehow translated from the "Ancient Mariner" to the constitutional history of the United States, than the successor of Jefferson and Madison. The Calhoun who in 1850 tottered into the Senate chamber to hear his political testament read by a colleague is a prophetic Prometheus in a new and strange garb, yet still stretched upon the inevitable rack of pain, the protagonist, in short, of a drama embodying a phase of the old myth unknown to Aeschylus or to Shelley. With this shadowy Calhoun we shall henceforward have little to do, for our time will be fully taken up with endeavoring to thread the equally shadowy mazes of his constitutional theory.

The tariff of 1828, naturally pressing hard on an agricultural state like South Carolina, and no relief having been experienced from legislative resolutions and petitions, the politicians of the state would probably have been at a standstill had not Calhoun come to their assistance with his famous Exposition. This document did not so much create public sentiment as focus it. There had been for some years a strong party in South Carolina that had pushed the doctrine of strict construction to extremes under the leadership of Judge William Smith. This gentleman was now shoved aside to make room for Calhoun, such a recruit as the Vice-President being almost equivalent to a victory for the party. The result was the rapid formulation and pressing through of that strange instrument upon federal coercion known as nullification.

But the nullifiers did not triumph in the state without a hard struggle; for a party with the curious sobriquet of "Union and States'-Rights Party" fought every inch of the way with them, under the leadership of such men as Hugh S. Legaré, Joel R. Poinsett, T. S. Grimké, and J. L. Petigru.[6] The feeling was so intense in Charleston that families were divided among themselves, and blows and bloodshed were with difficulty prevented.

The various stages of the crisis are well known, and need not detain us. South Carolina would possibly have fought, and Jackson would certainly have crushed her; but neither side was averse to the compromise which reduced the tariff and passed an empty force bill. Calhoun was right, however, when he claimed the result as a practical victory for his state and for the political doctrine

[6] Professor D. F. Houston has shown clearly in his monograph on nullification in the new Harvard Series of Studies that South Carolina, in the person of some of her impetuous politicians, can be more truly said to have dragged Calhoun into nullification, than the great statesman can be said to have dragged his state into it. Even Calhoun's services as a formulator of the doctrine were not so great as is usually supposed; but the influence of his example was immense, and it is at least open to doubt whether, if he had held aloof, the minor politicians could have carried things with such a high hand. It should be remembered, furthermore, that while Calhoun's well-known papers on the subject were much indebted to local pamphlets like "The Crisis," long since forgotten, much of the reasoning of these latter can be traced back to the writings of the Virginian school, particularly to those of Jefferson and John Taylor of Carolina.

he had so subtly propounded in his address to the people of South Carolina and his letter to Governor Hamilton.[7]

These documents had certainly helped to make the mass of his constituents nullifiers as strenuous as himself and more hot-brained, while the same arguments in his celebrated speech on the Force Bill were to make themselves feared and half respected by nearly every thoughtful man in the Union. He posed willingly as their chief exponent, and was willing in addition to be regarded as their author, if Jefferson's friends repudiated the honor for their favorite.

Madison, who was still living, was positive in his assertion that the South Carolina doctrines were far more extreme than any that had been in his mind or Jefferson's in 1798; but Madison was old, and had been known to change his opinions in curious ways.

Calhoun was positive that he had discovered no new thing, in spite of John Randolph's declaration that nullification was nonsense, and although his own previous record forced him to admit that for a long time he himself had not understood the true nature of the Constitution. And Calhoun was in the main right. Nullification could be deduced from the Constitution if that instrument were regarded as a compact, and it was no trouble to show that the compact theory had been widely held in 1789. Nullification was the legitimate outcome of the Kentucky Resolutions, if the latter were subjected to the analysis of a searching mind, not afraid of its own conclusions, and, indeed, certain of those conclusions from the start. All Calhoun had to do was to press the commercial metaphor a bit, and his point was gained. If the states were partners to a compact, and were sovereign except insofar as they had delegated part of their powers to the general government, the latter might well be regarded as the agent of the states, whose actions might be subject to disavowal by any of the principals.[8]

Secession would be a dissolution of partnership; nullification would be the disavowal of the act of an agent. But the disavowal of an agent's acts need not at all mean that the principal must cease to employ the agent; on the contrary, the latter, having got his cue,

[7] This proposition is often denied; but when a doctrine like that of nullification is met only by an *assertion of force* the victory is with the doctrinaires, a fact which is clearly proved by South Carolina's subsequent actions.

[8] See the letter to Governor Hamilton.

would act accordingly, and be a better agent than he was before. Therefore nullification, far from being destructive of the Union, would be conservative of it; in fact, nullification was now the only peaceable way to insure the stability of the general government.[9]

Ludicrous as it may seem, this is Calhoun's doctrine of nullification stripped of its expository features. This is the doctrine of peaceable resistance to Northern encroachments upon Southern rights, which he preached from 1828 until his death. His opponents might laugh at it, his disciples might rush past it and clamor for secession out and out, the mass of simple-minded people might be perplexed by it; but he continued to expound it calmly and logically and consistently, just because he was not what admirers have always thought him—a political philosopher of the first order. A philosopher examines his premises as well as his deductions and conclusions. Calhoun unconsciously started with the conclusions he wanted, reasoned back to his premises, and would not, because he could not, examine them. In other words, he had come slowly to see that the preponderance of political power had shifted to the North and must stay there. This meant, he could not doubt, national consolidation, and national consolidation meant the overthrow of slavery. The retention of slavery in the Union, being what he desired, was the conclusion to be reached; this could be deduced only from something just the reverse of national consolidation.

The problem, therefore, was how to arrest this consolidation. An instrument for the latter purpose had been already forged for him—strict construction of the Constitution. Slavery was recognized by the Constitution—construe that instrument strictly, and you would find it impossible to legislate slavery out of the Union.

[9] It should be noted that Calhoun did not claim the right of a state to set aside a law of the general government, except in the manner described in the following extract from the letter to Governor Hamilton:—

"I do not claim for a State the right to abrogate an act of the general government. It is the Constitution that annuls an unconstitutional act. Such an act is of itself void and of no effect. What I claim is, the right of the State *as far as its citizens are concerned* to declare the *extent of the obligation*, and that *such declaration is binding on them*."

He asserts that "there is no immediate connection between the citizens of a State and the general government,"—one of the queerest perversions of fact for the sake of theory that is known to history.

But experience had shown that with a Supreme Court,[10] executive, and Congress grasping at power, and a people supine or conniving, loose construction of the Constitution and consequent national consolidation must be expected. Where, then, must resistance to this tendency be looked for? Plainly in the states affected by it, who, being partners in the Union, have the rights of partners— protest, and disavowal or withdrawal.

Where, now, is the weak spot in this reasoning? There is none in the reasoning itself; and in all Calhoun's voluminous speeches and writings you will find little to fault in the reasoning proper. You will occasionally smile at some proof of historical ignorance, or some instance of a portentous lack of humor; but with Calhoun as a dialectician one is tempted to marvel and admire, not to smile. Grant him but his premises, and he leads you willy-nilly to his conclusions. From these you start back with horror and amazement. What could the man have been thinking of? you exclaim; this is not government, it is anarchy; this would mean stagnation, the relapsing into barbarism. True enough for you in 1896, but not true for Calhoun or the average Southerner in 1836. They regarded slavery as a positive blessing, and wished to keep it. They did not want progress, and had no fear of anarchy within the borders of their own section.[11] They were not horrified, therefore, at their conclusions; their reasoning was sound, and they would have been more than human if they had strictly examined the premises which afforded such agreeable conclusions.

Besides, was it entirely their fault that their premises were unsound? Had they not with the rest of the country conspired to make a fetish out of the Constitution;[12] and was that instrument, as it came from the hands of the founders, a perfectly satisfactory piece of work? Had not the very ingenuity of its construction offered a premium to ingenious interpretation? Had not its framers flattered themselves with having given the world a new kind of government,

[10] John Taylor of Carolina had previously analyzed very subtly the part played and to be played by the court in the drama of consolidation.

[11] "It is not we, but the Union which is in danger," said Calhoun in his speech of March 9, 1836, with regard to abolitionist petitions.

[12] "That sacred instrument, the Constitution." Speech on the Power of Removal, February 1835.

in which that mysterious entity, sovereignty, had been nicely parceled out?

Finally, had not the Constitution been a compromise, and therefore, like all compromises, satisfactory to no one, and always provocative of tinkering? If Calhoun started out with the false premises involved in the idea that a government could be formed on the same principles as a partnership, he made no more serious blunder than the founders did when they introduced their fatal distinction between delegated and reserved powers. If Calhoun had no true conception of the indivisible nature of sovereignty, he was in no worse and no better predicament than many members of the Convention of 1787. If he was satisfied with the conclusions he reached,—nullification and the retention of slavery in the Union,—so were they with their conclusions,—a compromise Constitution and an embryo Union.

No, I for one find it impossible to blame Calhoun greatly for the fact that he did not examine his premises sufficiently; but that fact necessarily prevents me from considering him a thoroughly great and philosophic statesman. The founders of the Union were not as philosophic, either, as is sometimes imagined; but they, at least, made it possible that a union should be formed that would in time develop into a nation, and for this they deserve not merely the name of statesmen, but the affectionate and reverent regard of all who live under the government which they inaugurated.

But if we do not blame Calhoun for his premises, what are we to say of his conclusions, which really did much to determine those premises? As to the conclusion that nullification, or a separate state veto, was a practicable or constitutional expedient for doing away with undesirable federal laws, there can be no use at this late day of saying anything; the notion is worthy neither of refutation nor of scorn. Indeed, very few of the proslavery leaders after 1835 paid any attention to nullification *per se*. They admitted that it would be absurd to remain in the Union and not obey its laws, they would not remain in the Union if slavery were interfered with, therefore they abjured nullification and preached secession.

Calhoun could not restrain his own disciples; for they did not love the Union as he did, and while they regarded him as a fanatic on the subject of nullification, he was consistently holding to that palpable absurdity because it was the only means to preserve both the Union and slavery. If he saw no absurdity in his purpose, he was not likely to see absurdity in his means.

But why did he not see that his purpose to preserve the Union and slavery was absurd? He did probably see that, as matters stood and had been going, it was absurd; and yet he hoped against hope that matters might be changed. Even in his last speech it seemed a perfectly simple proposition to him that the North should change its ways of looking at things, go back to the good old views of the Constitution, and leave the South in the possession of her rights.

But how could a sensible man, a man who had been keen enough to see the irreconcilable antagonism between progressive democracy and slavery long before the mass of his fellow-citizens saw it, indulge even for a moment in the hope that the North would recede from her position, and leave the South to enjoy her peculiar institution unmolested? I doubt if, in his heart of hearts, he had any hope for the South when he made his pathetic last speech. If he had, it was a very slight one; but, like the old Roman that he was, he would keep the fight up, that it might be said of him, as of his prototype, Cato the Younger:—

Victrix causa deis placuit, sed victa Catoni.

It did seem a simple proposition that the North should respect Southern rights, but he knew or felt sure that his section would be continually worsted. He died asking what would become of the "poor South." And yet, marvelous as it seems, it did not occur to him that there could possibly be an error in his fundamental doctrine that slavery was necessary to the South and must be maintained at all costs; he never once faltered in his belief that slavery was a blessing; he never once doubted that the cause which was continually growing weaker and becoming more obnoxious to the rest of the world, was a cause worthy of the loyal devotion of men, and of the benevolent and protecting smile of God.

Strange irony of fate, that the subtlest dialectician this country has produced should have been utterly unable to analyze correctly a social and economic problem that had been probed by Washington and Jefferson half a century before. If Calhoun had said, "We do not know how to get rid of slavery, but we will manage our own problem ourselves," his position would have been more intelligible. But when he boldly cried out, "Slavery is a blessing which you of the North should never have abandoned, and of which the Territories must not be deprived," [13] he took a stand that seemed little short of madness.

And yet it was a position that is now perfectly intelligible to the calm student of our history. The South, owing largely to slavery, was the most conservative portion of the Union; it was also that portion in which feudal notions had been most deeply rooted, and had most thoroughly survived. On feudality and slavery had been erected an aristocracy which had naturally developed the chief traits of this form of government,—bravery, pride, and conservatism.

In the ferment of the Revolutionary period a few leaders—great statesmen like Washington and great philosophers like Jefferson— had been led to scrutinize the society on which they proposed to found their new governments, state and national, and had perceived that the slave basis of this society in the Southern group of states was rotten to the core. Neither Washington nor Jefferson saw clearly what could be done to remedy the evil, but both hoped that the master class might be brought to see the danger that confronted them.

Jefferson, moreover, had unbounded faith in his panacea, democracy. But before he died he foresaw that great perils were threatening his state and section; and he must have felt a doubt whether the new generation had come up to his expectation, and drunk in the principles of liberty as their mothers' milk. For the new generation was plainly inferior to that of which Madison was almost the last survivor. William Wirt noticed the change, and commented on it in some of his Addisonian essays; and in spite of the presence of Madison, Monroe and Marshall, the Virginia Convention of 1829–1830, which argued the question of emancipation, would have proved to a candid spectator that the glory was departing from Virginia.

At such a moment it was natural for new aspirants for power to step to the front; it was South Carolina's opportunity, and she seized it. But south of Virginia there had practically never been

[13] These are not Calhoun's actual words.

any antislavery sentiment; and when Virginia dropped the reins of power, there was no issue on which Southern leadership could be more securely based than on the slavery question. But how could slavery be made an issue if its defenders were to be always apologizing for it? Could politicians, who were fiery and arrogant by nature, be expected to endeavor to gain power by appealing to their opponents' sympathies? Besides, a party had arisen in the North—small, it is true, but making itself heard—that proclaimed slavery to be a cursed institution. Could fiery aristocrats stand that? Had not their fathers and their fathers' fathers owned slaves; how could it then be wrong? And now that the cotton gin had been invented, and the world was beginning to bow down to cotton as king, how could a system that furnished the only labor suited to Southern climatic conditions be shown to be unprofitable?

Yes, slavery was right and profitable; and on it had been built a civilization which for charm of manners, for social virtues, for masterful political energies, had had no superior in the world's history. It was true that abolitionists bandied terms of reproach like "slave driver," collected rare instances of inhuman treatment of slaves, and pointed to certain features of slave codes that seemed barbarous to outsiders.

But the Southern gentleman knew that he and his neighbors were not cruel tyrants, and he claimed that outsiders could not judge what laws were necessary to keep a servile race in proper subjection. Slavery was his own concern; it was a matter of municipal law; it was guaranteed by the Constitution; it stood on a thoroughly moral and legal basis. Should the democracy of the North be allowed to assail an institution so vital to the aristocracy of the South?

No—his conservative instincts, his ancestral pride, his masterful courage, forbade him to allow this for an instant. If Washington and Jefferson opposed slavery, it must have been because they really had not understood the institution.[14] If Northerners criticized it, was it not because they were jealous of the South's political and social prestige? If foreigners denounced it, was it not part and parcel of the newfangled and monstrous atheistical and revolution-

[14] A. H. Stephens proclaimed this later on, and it was a favorite idea with the essayists who wrote for *DeBow's Review*.

ary spirit of change that had been unloosed by the French Revolution?

So the old-time Southern planter argued, as he sat with his neighbors on his broad veranda, and smoked his after-dinner cigar. A disunionist and a traitor he never was—he could not have been; for all his instincts were loyal and conservative, and he was not given to great displays of energy. All he wanted was to be let alone; but if he were not let alone, he would peaceably withdraw from a partnership made for him by his ancestors when times were better than now; if anyone tried to stop him, he would fight.

Meanwhile, he hoped things would not come to this pass, especially as that able "up-countryman," John C. Calhoun, had taken up the constitutional cudgels, and trounced that Yankee Webster (who was, after all, a clever chap) in a way that would not be soon forgotten. So the old Southern planter argued, if we can apply such a term to his leisurely manner of arriving at conclusions. He let his politicians and editors argue for him, while he sat by and applauded.

And before the final struggle came the politicians and editors had persuaded him that slavery was more the occasion than the cause of all the trouble, that really it was nothing more nor less than a matter of constant violations of the Constitution on the part of the North; and that if a war should come, which was hardly likely, as shopkeepers would not fight, he would arm himself, and go to the field as the champion of local self-government and of vested and inalienable constitutional rights.

He went to the field, and fought heroically in this belief; and this belief he holds today, while recognizing that the old order has passed away forever. Slavery hardly enters his mind now; but when he does think of it he generally admits it to have been an evil, and is glad that it is over and done with. He is still, however, a strict constructionist.

Now, in all this nightmarish reasoning, what is there that is blameworthy or unnatural when due allowance is made for hereditary bias and for environment? Where is the ground for accusations of treachery and treason? If anyone can cry "treachery and treason," it is the Southern planter himself, when he realizes, as he does not often do, how the political leaders he trusted lured him onward like so many will-o'-the-wisps into pitfall after pitfall. They were the men who should have studied the economic condition of the South, and seen how far it was falling behind the North on account of slavery. They should have told him that it was slavery that kept his roads bad, that gave him wretched "Oldfield" schools, that prevented his cities from growing, that kept immigrants from his public lands, that, in short, stamped its evil mark on everything he wrote or said or did. They should have kept abreast of the thought of the world, analyzed the relation of master and slave, told him that it rested solely on the doctrine that might makes right, and assured him that this doctrine was abhorrent to civilization and progress.

Instead of this, what did they tell him? They told him that slavery was morally justifiable; and his priests, his bishops, his university professors of moral philosophy, confirmed the falsehood. They told him that slavery was economically and socially a blessing. They told him that the nation which Washington had founded and called a nation was in reality only a league of states, from which it would soon be proper to withdraw. They told him, finally, that he was the happiest, the richest, the bravest, the most intelligent man alive, that the rest of the world envied and hated him, and that all he needed for perfect felicity here below was to shut himself up in his manor house, proclaim cotton king, and leave the mad world to its wicked ways.[15]

This was what they told him; and loyal gentleman as he was (for were they not his chosen representatives, and could he distrust them, since they were Southern gentlemen too?), he believed them, and acted on their advice. Certainly, if anyone has the right to point the finger and cry "traitor," it is the cajoled and betrayed Southern gentleman of the old regime; and next to him it is the nonslaveholding whites of the South, who were led to support a

---

[15] That I have exaggerated or interpolated anything of my own into the above sentences will be affirmed only by that large class of sentimentalists who talk and write about the ante-bellum South, without taking the trouble to study its history.

war whose successful issue could have resulted only in a perpetuation of their pariah-like state. But, after all, were the Southern
politicians traitors?

. . . Whether Calhoun and those who thought and acted with
him were traitors to the Union and to the people they represented
is a question only to those who have not thoroughly understood the
anomalous situation in which the country stood from the time of
the Missouri Compromise to the outbreak of the Civil War.

There was no question as to the legal fact that slavery was acknowledged by the Constitution; there should have been no question as to the moral fact that slavery was not acknowledged as
legitimate by the conscience of the recently awakened world.

But the North, recognizing the constitutional obligation to protect slavery, was conscious also of the moral obligation to suppress
it, and, halting between opinions, proclaimed the doctrine of "a
higher law." The Southerner was in no such dilemma: he knew
that slavery was legal, he could not see that it was immoral; hence
he became righteously indignant at what he was bound to regard
as Northern aggression, and infractions of the Constitution.

But righteous indignation generally leads to extremes; and righteous indignation over the fortunes of an unrighteous institution
was certain to do it. The more fiercely the abolitionist leaders in-
veighed against slavery, the more vehemently the proslavery advocates asserted their own virtue and the baseness of their enemies.
The Northerner began to think all Southerners slave drivers; the
Southerner began to think all Northerners either fanatics or cowardly shopkeepers.

There was not enough travel between the two sections to introduce any real knowledge of either; for the Southerners who went
to Northern watering places were too often vulgar upstarts, who
had no social position at home, and whose loud and boisterous
behavior entirely misrepresented the better elements of the section.
Thus it was that the Northerner began to judge the South through
the spectacles of the abolitionist or the politician, while the Southerner judged the North largely through what his politicians told
him.

These latter were sincere enough in their way. They believed the
North to be engaged in a cowardly war on the South by means of

protective tariffs, Wilmot provisos, *et cetera;* and they retaliated by nullification, commercial conventions, Mexican wars, encroachments on the Territories, Dred Scott decisions, *et cetera.* They believed that the North would talk but not fight; so they indulged in tall talk themselves about drinking all the blood that would be spilt in case the South broke the Union. They indulged in something worse than talk when they resorted to fisticuffs, and fired on the national flag; and they were terribly repaid.

Yet, through it all, they were honest to their constituents and to themselves. Their every action was natural under the circumstances, for were they not unwittingly trying to make wrong right; and has not this attempt, since the beginning of the world, led to evil actions, evil words, evil thoughts without number?

Instead of blaming these men, let us pity them. Let us remember that history teaches us that all abuses die hard, that the worst and most foolish causes have often the most honest and brave defenders. I would no more blame an old-time Southerner for following Calhoun or Jefferson Davis, than I would blame a loyal Highlander for following Prince Charlie. And the leaders themselves, though they wrought woe to their followers, were impelled by destiny as much as by personal ambition; and I, for one, find it difficult to judge them. Of their actions I can speak plainly enough; but of their motives I can say only that the more I study their conduct, the more honest I consider their self-delusion to have been. I will not call them wise statesmen, but I am not going to insult the humanity I have in common with them by calling them traitors and knaves.

Yes; John Caldwell Calhoun, in the seventeen years that elapsed between his debate with Webster on the Force Bill and his death, wrought his country and his section infinite woe, but he did it blindly; he did it, intending all the while to effect only peace and reconciliation. He failed; but so did Webster and Clay fail, and so will any man fail who does not distinguish right from wrong.

Yet it would have needed a statesman with the genius and character of Washington to have seen clearly the South's duty in 1830, and forced her into the right path. She had no such statesman, and slavery accounted for the fact. The section that had led the Union for fifty years, that had developed a dashing type of statesmanship, which, with many faults, had many virtues, that had done much to inculcate and spread democracy through the land, had fallen into the hands of a doctrinaire fanatic, and was soon to pass into worse hands than his. For Calhoun, though utterly and terribly wrong in all that he said and wrote and did for slavery, was nevertheless a dignified and noble figure, whether in the Cabinet or the Senate. Dignity and nobility were far from characterizing most of his successors.

You will hardly expect me, in the brief time that remains to me, to comment with any fullness upon the successive stages of Calhoun's career after he took his stand as the Arch-Nullifier. Those stages are practically the stages of our national history between 1833 and 1850, and they are also stages of the slavery agitation. As each new phase would arise, Calhoun would deliver one of his incisive logical promulgations of states'-rights philosophy, and would utter his prophetic warnings of the doom that awaited North and South alike if the question of slavery were agitated.

He fought manfully and with the courage of despair—of despair that grew greater with the years. On topics unconnected with slavery he was still the weighty, massive Calhoun of earlier days. He fought the spoils system with a noble earnestness that deserves lasting remembrance, even though he did not foresee that Congress would in this matter prove more dangerous and rapacious than the President. With Jackson before his eyes, he naturally feared the executive. But spoils system and subtreasury were mere asides. Strenuous debate on the acceptance of abolitionist petitions, queer political metaphysics on the subject of the admission of new states, violent protests against England's importing her emancipation notions into the law of nations, are much more characteristic of the Senator who owned South Carolina like a pocket borough.

That the Presidential fever should again have taken hold of him is curious, but so it did; and he resigned the Senate in 1842, to be immediately nominated for the great office by his loyal state. South Carolina would stand by her greatest son, whether in defeat or in victory; for he had stood by her, and she was nothing if not loyal. Whether she would have stood by him had he not stood by her "peculiar institution" is another matter, which we need not discuss, since Calhoun was not the man to avow opinions he did not really hold, merely in order to obtain power.

But there was no chance for so able a man in the Democratic ranks; so he abandoned his candidacy, and seemed about to have a chance to rest after a hard-fought life, when Tyler summoned him to the portfolio of state and the invidious task of bringing Texas into the Union. Believing slavery to be a blessing, and believing, furthermore, that the permanence of this blessing depended upon its ever wider diffusion in point of territory, fearing, too, that an independent free state bordering on the extreme South would work damage to his favorite institution, he accepted his appointment, and went about his job—for that it was a political job, though not such in his eyes, no serious student of the times can safely deny.

The methods he and Tyler used to accomplish their purpose deserve all the harsh criticism they have received; but I myself prefer for obvious reasons, in view of much that I have said, . . . to exculpate the men. Calhoun in his sober mind would have repudiated the joint-resolution scheme, but Calhoun the fanatic forgot all his constitutional lore on the subject of the treaty-making power. Calhoun the reserved and courteous gentleman would never have lugged in the slavery controversy in his letters to Pakenham, the British minister; but Calhoun the rampant theorist and controversialist regretted that he could not get another chance at him.

Still, it must be remembered to his credit, that, while he would scruple at little in order to secure Texas for slavery, he would be no party to Polk's schemes for forcing Mexico into a war in order to rob her of more territory. He seems to have been sincere in his claim that he would have secured Texas without bloodshed; but he did not have the wisdom to foresee that he was playing a rash game, at which bolder and more unscrupulous gamblers would soon raise the stakes, and compel him to lay down his hand.

The dream that Polk would retain him as Secretary of State, that he might finish the negotiations he had begun, soon vanished; and he had to content himself with unheeded prophecies of the evil results that must follow the uncontrolled rashness of his own disciples. He was back in the Senate now, Judge Hager having resigned on purpose to restore him his rightful seat; and he could

offer resolutions annulling the Missouri Compromise, and devoting
to slavery soil that even a government like that of Mexico had
devoted to freedom. He could take this step regardless of inconsistency with his past utterances, because he said that only on this
high ground of absolute equality could slavery keep up the struggle
with freedom.

Here, again, he proved a leader, and the next decade worked
out to their logical and bitter results the principles he laid down.
But he was not destined to see the curtain roll up on the last act of
the drama of which he himself had been protagonist.

California with its free Constitution threw itself in the way of
his theories; the crisis of 1850 came, and with it Clay's inevitable
compromises; he made his last great speech, in which he described
his state-veto panacea once more; and at last, on the 31st of March,
1850, his weary and perturbed spirit was at rest.

He had known that his end was near, and, as a dying bequest to
the Union that he loved, had spent a few months that other men
would have devoted to rest, in composing his *Disquisition on Government,* and his *Discourse on the Constitution and Government
of the United States.*

Of these two treatises it will be sufficient to say, that they are in
many respects the most remarkable political documents the student
of American history is called upon to read. He must read them if
he wishes to get a full and well-rounded view of Calhoun's constitutional theories, although it is at once plain that all their important points are covered in the better known speeches.

It is to the *Disquisition* that we must go for the famous praise
of the constitution of Poland, as well as for the fullest explanation
of the doctrine of the concurrent majority. The reader must, however, be warned that it is not safe to approach these books unless
he has thoroughly disabused his mind of the notion that sovereignty
can really be divided and a government founded on compact. If
one start with these notions in one's head, the sure grip of Calhoun's
logic will end by making one a nullifier or a lunatic, it matters
little which.

One must also have one's general knowledge of history in a
shape to use; and one must also be careful to remember that not a
little of Calhoun's munitions of war had been manufactured and

stored away for him by Jefferson, Madison, and John Taylor of Carolina—more especially by the last named, who was in a negative way almost as acute a critic of the Constitution as Calhoun himself. Yet when all is said, Calhoun's masterly analysis of the rights of minorities, and of the best methods of securing them fairly, entitles him to rank as our most original political theorist.

And now, in conclusion, how shall we sum up this man's life and work? The task seems almost hopeless, so beset is it with contradictions. A devoted patriot spends the best portion of his life struggling against the manifest destiny of his country. A profoundly analytical mind fails utterly to grasp the true nature of an institution he has known and studied for nearly a lifetime, in spite of the fact that the wisest of his own forerunners had carefully explained it to him. A practical, level-headed politician and man of affairs turns into a doctrinaire fanatic with a metaphysical theory of politics which would not strike us as out of place if we found it expounded in *Gulliver's Travels*. A loyal, true-hearted gentleman brings himself to write quibbling and almost impertinent letters to the minister of a great power, and lends himself to a sly trick to get around a Constitution he has spent his life in defending from insidious attack. What are we to say of such a man?

I, at least, cannot call him a thoroughly wise and great statesman; but I can admire his strong, subtle intellect, and lofty integrity, and soundness of heart. Mistaken he was often, but he never did anything consciously that he thought was wrong or low. His purposes were too high, whatever the means he used to effect them, for us to be able to do without his example of manly independence. And yet we cannot love him, either for the noble or for the pathetic features of his career. He stands too much apart from his fellows, and the words he speaks are those of prophetic warning rather than those of encouragement or allurement. It is not Cassandra that attracts us in "the tale of Troy divine"; it is winsome Helen, in spite of the fact that she

> Launched a thousand ships
> And burnt the topless towers of Ilion.

✪

A Footnote on John C. Calhoun

Calhoun died in 1850 as Melville was rising to his greatest heights. As a brilliant youngster in the arena of Washington politics, Calhoun, like Clay, was a nationalist, ardent in the defense of American honor against British insults. After the War of 1812, his wide-ranging imagination visioned a union of far-separated sovereign states through a system of military roads constructed by the central government. Long before his death, however, he became to both North and South the principal leader of a section. As an old man he seemed to his enemies to personify sectional intransigence. He forged in the busy smithy of his mind the intellectual weapons with which the champions of the Cotton Kingdom sought to defeat the democratic principle of majority rule. Before Robert E. Lee rose to fame, Calhoun was the greatest of the sectionalists, the most brilliant among the champions of a cause which was ultimately lost. In Washington a few weeks after Appomattox, Walt Whitman overheard a conversation of two Union soldiers discussing a monument to Calhoun in the South. One man remarked that the true monuments to the South Carolinian were to be found scattered over the Confederacy in wasted farms, in broken railroads, in destroyed shops, and in the gaunt chimneys which marked the places where families once had made their homes. This soldier

Ralph Henry Gabriel, *The Course of American Democratic Thought,* Second Edition, pp. 107–114. Copyright © 1956 The Ronald Press Company, New York.

expressed a harsh judgment. But his generation in the victorious North was in a mood to agree with him.

Since 1865 Calhoun's thought almost always has been studied by Americans only against the background of sectional conflict. Among the conventions in the teaching of American history in the schools is one which assigns Calhoun and his theory of nullification irrevocably to the past. Washington, Hamilton, and Jefferson, through their beliefs and admonitions, still speak to the present. The issues which they debated still live. The same is not true of Calhoun. Unlike his contemporaries Webster and Marshall, his words are seldom used by moderns to point an argument. Political scientists have charted his theories, have pronounced them brilliant, and then have tossed them into the scrap heap of discarded ideas. Perhaps the scholars have been too preoccupied with his political devices to consider fully the ideas lying behind them. When his philosophy is analyzed in terms of the American democratic faith, some new insights are achieved both concerning that faith and in the understanding of his thought. The simplest approach is to interrogate the dead Calhoun with respect to the ruling ideas of those decades when he was the champion of the South.

What was his stand on the tenet of the fundamental law? This concept included both the natural law of the Enlightenment and the moral law of the Christians. Emerson in his transcendentalism had united the two in his theory that the moral sense pervaded nature from the center of the cosmos to its circumference. Calhoun, unlike Melville, did not reject such absolutism. The opening sentences of his *Disquisition on Government,* published in the year after his death, state his position: "In order to have a clear and just conception of the nature and object of government, it is indispensable to understand correctly what the constitution or law of our nature is, in which government originates; or, to express it more fully and accurately,—that law, without which government would not, and with which, it must necessarily exist. Without this, it is as impossible to lay any solid foundation for the science of government as it would be to lay one for that of astronomy, without a like understanding of that constitution or law of the material world, according to which several bodies composing the solar system mutually act on each other, and by which they are kept in their respective spheres."

In these somewhat ponderous phrases Calhoun repeated the doctrine of the fundamental law. Whence comes this unwritten constitution or law ultimately governing human life? Calhoun answered simply that the fundamental law of human nature compels men to live in society, and that existence in society requires a government. But of the two, thought Calhoun, society is the more important. "Both are, however," he added, "necessary to the existence and well-being of our race, and equally of Divine ordination." [1] The fundamental law comes of God. Calhoun accepted also the concept of the moral law. In the Senate on February 13, 1840, in discussing the right of petition, he elaborated an argument that if they are to be protected at all, rights must be defended at the first challenge. The individual or group that gives way when a moral issue is raised is, therefore, irreparably weakened in its efforts to maintain the justice of its cause. "The moral is like the physical world," he said, employing an unusual metaphor. "Nature has incrusted the exterior of all organic life, for its safety. Let that be broken through, and it is all weakness within. So in the moral and political world. It is at the extreme limits of right that all wrong and encroachments are the most sensibly felt and easily resisted." [2]

One must understand the application of these generalizations in the affairs of everyday life to comprehend their meaning for the man who during Jackson's administration became the acknowledged and militant leader of a section. Calhoun concurred in the general assumption of Southerners concerning the relation between chattel slavery and the fundamental law. "Negroes are not free," said Calhoun's contemporary George Fitzhugh, "because God and nature, and the general good, and their own good, intended them for slaves." [3] Nature, thought Fitzhugh, had created the races unequal and slavery was the institution through which civilized man gave to the African that share in civilization of which he was capable of making use. Slave owners, moreover, found in Holy Writ

[1] John C. Calhoun, *A Disquisition on Government, and a Discourse on the Constitution of the United States,* 1852 ed., p. 5.

[2] Richard K. Crallé, ed., *The Works of John C. Calhoun,* 1867, III, 445.

[3] George Fitzhugh, *Cannibals All,* 1857, p. 116.

divine sanction for the institution. This premise must be read into all Calhoun's statements concerning the fundamental law and concerning liberty.

What was his stand on the doctrine of the free individual? Calhoun felt himself to be more sensitive than his age to the problems of liberty. "We have had so many years of prosperity," he said in 1848 as the Mexican War was closing, "we have passed through so many difficulties and dangers without loss of liberty—that we begin to think that we hold it by divine right from heaven itself." "It is harder to preserve than to obtain liberty," he added. "After years of prosperity, the tenure by which it is held is but too often forgotten; and, I fear, Senators, that such is the case with us. There is no solicitude now about liberty. It was not so in the early days of the Republic." [4]

The threat of tyranny which Calhoun saw close at hand was that of a numerical majority within the nation seeking to use the power of the central government to build up an agricultural, commercial, and industrial economy based on free labor to the disadvantage of an agrarian economy resting on the institution of slavery. After 1831, the year of the Nat Turner uprising in Virginia and the first issue of William Lloyd Garrison's *Emancipator* [*Liberator*] in Massachusetts, Southerners became a "conscious minority" within the nation. Until his death in 1850 Calhoun remained the chief spokesman in Washington for that minority. For him liberty meant freedom for the Southern people to carry on their lives and to develop their institutions in ways that seemed best to them. He saw in the rising antislavery movement in the North a threat that must be faced and countered. He embodied his proposals in the theories of nullification and of the concurrent majority.

Calhoun proclaimed and insisted upon the rights of the states, thirteen of which were older as independent sovereignties than the Constitution. He described this instrument as a compact among sovereign states to set up a central government to perform certain general functions as an agent of the states. In the midst of Jackson's administration, when the protective tariff became an issue, Calhoun developed the theory of nullification. This theory stated, in brief, that when one of the principals (one of the states) believed that

[4] Crallé, *Works*, IV, 417–418.

the agent had exceeded the authority given it by the compact, the state might nullify the act. South Carolina took such action in 1832 in the matter of a protective tariff. Only South Carolina, however, actively supported so drastic a measure as nullification. This device in Calhoun's mind was merely an aspect of a larger theory, namely, that of the "concurrent majority." Phrased simply, the idea of the concurrent majority meant that each of the major interests—agriculture, commerce, manufacturing—and each of the great sections—North, South, West—should have the power to prevent or halt national actions deemed adverse to its vital interests. On the questions of high policy, unanimous consent among major interests must replace decisions by mere majorities. Calhoun devoted the two final decades of his life to the building up of a set of principles which, if accepted throughout the nation, would protect the Southern minority and permit it to carry on without external coercion its chosen way of life. Calhoun supported his theory with an analysis of the doctrine of the free individual and of the sentiment of nationalism unrivaled in his generation.

Calhoun, in his assumptions concerning human nature, was under an unconscious, but nonetheless heavy, debt to Calvin. Man, thought the South Carolinian, was created to live in society but, paradoxically, his egoistic tendencies outweigh the altruism in his nature. Because of this fact government is necessary to prevent self-seeking individuals from overreaching and exploiting their fellows. The purpose of the state is to enable society to function. Government is the policeman of society. "But government," Calhoun went on, "although intended to protect and preserve society, has a strong tendency to disorder and abuse of its powers, as all experience and almost every page of history testify. The cause is to be found in the same constitution of our nature which makes government indispensable. The powers which it is necessary for government to possess, in order to repress violence and preserve order, cannot execute themselves. They must be administered by men in whom, like others, the individual are stronger than the social feelings. And hence, the powers vested in them to prevent injustice and oppression on the part of others, will, if left unguarded, be by them converted into instruments to oppress the rest of the community. That, by which this is prevented, is what is meant by CONSTITUTION, in its most comprehensive sense, when applied to GOVERNMENT." [5]

Calhoun had Calvin's low opinion of human nature. The lawyers expressed the same attitude in the maxim *caveat emptor*. Upon such assumptions of human fallibility American politics had been founded. It was this skepticism which held in check, in the politics of the United States, the tendencies toward doctrinaire extremism found in the constitutions written during the French Revolution. Calhoun's words were those of the scholar and the theorist, but his thought was that of the run-of-the-mill American democrat. A realism harvested from a life spent in the practice of the political art prevented Calhoun from putting faith in the power of words, even if written on parchment, to restrain the activities of government officials. For him, in spite of the Constitution, the federal Republic was governed by men. The Constitution could not enforce itself. What power it had to restrain public officials must come from its use as an instrument of protection by free citizens. "Power can only be resisted by power,—and tendency by tendency," said Calhoun. "Those who exercise power and those subject to its exercise,—the rulers and the ruled,—stand in antagonistic relations to each other. The same constitution of our nature which leads rulers to oppress the ruled,—regardless of the object for which government is ordained,—will, with equal strength, lead the ruled to resist, when possessed of the means of making peaceable and effective resistance." [6]

Calhoun's was not exactly the doctrine of the malevolent state. It was rather the doctrine that no public official can be trusted unless he knows that he is being watched by citizens who have the power to check usurpations. But, for all his realism, the South Carolinian was an idealist. He believed that he had discovered a political device which, by making constitutional democracy work, would guarantee liberty. Human liberty, the dream of the free individual, was the vision that beckoned him and urged him on. "With me," he said in 1848, two years before his death, "the liberty of the country is all in all. If this be preserved, every thing will be preserved; but if lost, all will be lost." [7]

[5] Calhoun, *Disquisition,* p. 7.
[6] *Ibid.,* p. 12.
[7] Crallé, *Works,* IV, 420.

It is difficult to picture Calhoun outside that small semicircular Senate chamber in the old Capitol which the Supreme Court later occupied for more than half a century. In this almost intimate room he presided in the prime of life as Vice-President. Here, as Senator, he grew old. In this chamber one day, when his failing strength was proclaimed by his pinched features and his sunken cheeks, he spoke of the destiny of America. He had never been more impressive. "It has been lately urged in a very respectable quarter," he said, "that it is the mission of this country to spread civil and religious liberty over all the globe, and especially over this continent—even by force, if necessary. It is a sad delusion. . . . To preserve . . . liberty it is indispensable to adopt a course of moderation and justice toward all nations; to avoid war whenever it can be avoided; to let those great causes which are now at work, and by which the mere operation of time will raise our country to an elevation and influence which no country has ever heretofore attained, continue to work. By pursuing such a course, we may succeed in combining greatness and liberty—the highest possible greatness with the largest measure of liberty—and do more to extend liberty by our example over this continent and the world generally, than would be done by a thousand victories." [8] In such a mood the author of the theory of nullification approached that last doctrine of the democratic faith, that doctrine of destiny which was the essence of the spirit of American nationalism.

Nationalism is a sentiment. It is a thing which is less of the mind than of the emotions. It is a consciousness of the group, a feeling in the heart of the individual that his fate is inextricably bound up with those of his people. It is enhanced by external danger. It deteriorates when the population spreads over an area so wide that communication across the nation becomes difficult. During the decades in which Calhoun urged the adoption of his device of nullification, the American people, with the exception of a brief threat of war with England in 1837, felt secure from attack by foreigners. They did not fear the Mexicans. The civil liberty enjoyed by American citizens was founded upon this sense of security. This liberty, greater than that possessed by any other people in the midnineteenth-century world, became the boast of American nationalism.

[8] *Ibid.,* pp. 416, 420.

It was the trait which was pointed out to distinguish the civilization of the United States from that of other nations.

Calhoun looked deeper than the superficialities of Independence Day orations. As he felt that liberty was a boon easily lost, so also he was convinced that the sentiment of nationalism might under certain circumstances disappear and leave the citizens of the Republic confounded. Almost alone among his contemporaries, Calhoun saw that nationalism in the United States also depends upon security. The loyalty of the individual or of the local community to the national group is primarily the product of the conviction, often unrecognized, that safety lies in merging the life of the locality with that of the nation. As the middle of the century approached, the growing antislavery movement in the North threatened the civilization of the South with disruption. The people of the Cotton Kingdom believed that they had accomplished a practicable solution of that most difficult of all social puzzles, the problem of getting two unlike races to live and work together with a minimum of disorder and a reasonable amount of mutual profit. The solution was the ancient institution of slavery. In communities where Negroes outnumbered the white population by two or three to one, it was impossible in the middle decades of the century for the dominant race to see how civilization could be preserved, if the discipline of slavery were relaxed. The appearance in the North of a vociferous and determined movement to bring African servitude to an end filled the South with apprehension. Calhoun foresaw, what ultimately turned out to be the fact, that this sense of insecurity would erode the sentiment of nationalism until, if measures were not taken to protect the South, the old group loyalty would disappear and the nation would fall apart.

Calhoun saw that the numerical majority offered no security to endangered Southern civilization. A majority is made up of men; and, according to the Calhoun theory of human nature, men in the mass can be as selfish and as tyrannical as they are as individuals. He proposed, therefore, the political doctrine of the concurrent majority. Calhoun thought that the sentiment of nationalism can live only so long as the vital interests of all groups within the nation are equally protected. Guarantee such security to all men, to all interests, and to all sections, argued the South Carolinian, and the sentiment of nationalism will flourish as a garden in the warmth of the summer sun. "The concurrent majority . . . ," he said, "tends to unite the most opposite and conflicting interests, and to blend the whole into one common attachment to the country. By giving to each interest, or portion, the power of self-protection, all strife and struggle between them for ascendency is prevented. . . . Under the combined influence of these causes, the interests of each would be merged in the common interests of the whole; and thus, the community would become a unit, by becoming a common centre of attachment of all its parts. And hence, instead of faction, strife, and struggle for party ascendency, there would be patriotism, nationality, harmony, and a struggle only for supremacy in promoting the common good of the whole." [9] Calhoun defined nationalism in terms of a satisfied and happy minority. He was a nationalist in the sense that he preferred that the Union be preserved. But he made the principle of the concurrent majority the condition of union. Give the South autonomy in matters it deemed vital and "patriotism, nationality, and harmony" would follow.

[9] Calhoun, *Disquisition*, pp. 48–49.

✪

Calhoun: An Interpretation

I

When the bitterly contested subtreasury bill was before the Senate early in 1838, Clay took occasion to upbraid Calhoun for his apostasy. Calhoun replied in kind, and Philip Hone, popular Whig merchant and former Mayor of New York, watching the scene from a seat on the Senate floor, noted a greater "degree of acrimony and ill-nature" than the occasion warranted. Hone was ready to excuse the South Carolina Senator, however, on the ground that he was unusually sensitive, "like all men whose position is doubtful in their own minds." [1]

Hone was a shrewd observer and a good judge of human nature, but he was utterly wrong about Calhoun. Whatever his faults, however great his errors, Calhoun's position was never doubtful in his own mind. He sometimes arrived at his conclusions with baffling rapidity, but the most careful and mature reflection never shook his faith in his own logic. Throughout a lifetime of controversy, as he once confessed with masterly understatement to a friend, he remained "a good deal attached" to his own opinions, and "not so much disposed, perhaps, to take advice" as he ought to be.[2] His insufferable cocksureness made enemies of men who should have

[1] Allan Nevins, ed., *Diary of Philip Hone* (New York, 1927), p. 304.
[2] Calhoun to V. Maxcy, September 11, 1830, Maxcy Papers (New York Public Library).

Reprinted from South Carolina Historical Association, *Proceedings,* 1948, pp. 26–38, by permission of the author.

been his friends; but it was also the measure of his leadership, for in times of stress and turmoil, men who doubt themselves tend to fall in behind those who have no doubts.

The quality of his intellect led Calhoun almost inevitably to generalize from his experience, and to set up his generalizations in the form of universal laws. His unshakable self-confidence, his unquestioning certainty that he was right, led him to evaluate the actions of others and in large measure to determine his own on the basis of these general principles. His own political philosophy, in short, was a framework upon which he hung his reading of history and in terms of which he interpreted the economic and political forces of his time. By the same token it is also a pattern which gives consistency and direction to a career that appeared to his enemies and often to his friends to be erratic and without principle. His course was not determined by simple reactions to people and events, but was rather derived from a system of philosophy into which people and events had first been neatly fitted and arranged. Calhoun's career will become more meaningful if we examine the major tenets of this system, and apply them as he did to the world in which he lived.

Calhoun belonged to an age of revolution, of intellectual ferment, of political and economic experimentation. He was born before the close of the American struggle for independence. When he was a precocious lad of six his father opposed ratification of the new Constitution of the United States, because it gave too much power to a central government. The French Revolution was the overshadowing fact of his youth. He was nearing maturity when Virginia rebelled against the autocracy of the Alien and Sedition Acts, and he had already entered preparatory school when the explosive force of that rebellion carried Thomas Jefferson to the Presidency. He was in college when Bonaparte completed the transition from successful military commander to First Consul to Emperor, and we know from his letters that the young Carolinian watched the process and its aftermath with interest and concern.[3]

Equally suggestive of conflict and upheaval is Calhoun's early

[3] J. F. Jameson, ed., *Correspondence of John C. Calhoun, Annual Report of the American Historical Association, 1899* (Washington, 1900), II, 100.

political career. He entered public life at a time when his country was being forced to choose sides in a world-wide struggle for power. He sat in a war Congress and grappled there with the problems of foreign invasion and internal revolt. He saw, and encouraged, the rise of industry in the northern and middle states, but in the process he had ample opportunity to observe the interaction of economic forces and political events. From the vantage point of a Cabinet seat he witnessed the first sectional rift in the smooth surface of the Union, and he recognized the Missouri Compromise for what it was: an internal balance of power. It was an age of wonderful technological advances, which seemed to go hand in hand with crumbling social institutions; an age when active minds went back to fundamentals, and thinking men sought new interpretations of the world order.

Calhoun's own search for first principles undoubtedly began at an early stage of his career, but it was the fall of 1828 before he reduced his findings to orderly and systematic form in the *South Carolina Exposition.* Thenceforth he weighed every public measure in the same scale. He added illustrations from current politics or from history as he went along, but he found nothing to justify any basic modification in the general thesis. When his theory appeared in definitive form in the posthumous *Disquisition on Government* it was still essentially the same as it had been in its initial version, save for a greater completeness in its presentation. Like the authors of *The Federalist,* Calhoun drew freely from Hobbes and Harrington and Locke, but the significance of the doctrine thus derived lay not in its seventeenth-century skeleton but in its contemporary dress, and in the use to which it was put.

II

Government, for Calhoun, was inseparable from human nature, and with respect to neither was he troubled by any utopian illusions. His major premise, derived from what he called "universal experience," was that man cannot exist without some kind of government. The law of self-preservation requires that we pursue our own interests more assiduously than we pursue the welfare of others. The natural consequence is a tendency to conflict among individuals which would destroy society and make life impossible were it not controlled. The controlling force, whatever form it takes, is government. The powers of government, however, must be exercised by men, and they are therefore liable to abuse because of the same tendency in human nature that makes government necessary. Unless safeguarded in some fashion, the power given to the rulers to prevent injustice and oppression will be used by them to oppress the ruled.

This tendency to abuse of the powers of government could be successfully resisted, in Calhoun's view, only by the internal structure of the government itself. Governments so constructed that the ruled might resist the abuses of the rulers he called limited or constitutional governments. All others were absolute. In neither category did it make any difference whether the ruler was a single individual, an oligarchy, or a majority.

A constitutional government, as Calhoun visualized it, must be based on suffrage; but the right of suffrage alone is not enough to prevent absolutism. By means of popular elections the actual seat of power may be shifted from the rulers to the body of the community, but the abuse of power will not thereby be prevented unless the individual interests of the whole citizen body are the same. Where interests are many and varied, the right of suffrage merely intensifies the tendency to conflict, for each interest strives to gain control of the powers of government as a means of protecting itself. This leads to combinations and arrangements, until the whole community is divided into two hostile parties.

Indeed, the community would be so divided, even if interests were otherwise the same, by the action of the government alone. To fulfill its purpose government must be strong. It must, therefore, employ officers, collect taxes, and spend money in numerous ways. It is difficult if not impossible to collect taxes equally from the whole community, and they are never spent in equal proportions. The community will thus be divided into opposing interests by the fiscal action of the government alone. The majority, moved by the same self-interest as the individuals who compose it, will inevitably seek to aggrandize itself at the expense of the minority. The fact that, by means of the ballot, the two may change places only intensifies the tendency to conflict and disorder.

Suffrage, then, is not enough to prevent the abuse of power. There must be some other provision which will prevent any single interest or combination of interests from gaining exclusive control of the machinery of government. Calhoun's solution of the problem was the theory of the concurrent majority. Where the action of the government might affect the various portions of the community un-equally, he would give to each portion, through its own majority, either a concurrent voice in the making of the laws, or a veto on their execution. To act at all the government would thus require the consent of the various interest groups of which it was composed. Its guiding principle would therefore be compromise, whereas the only principle underlying absolute governments is force.

Such, in broad outline, is Calhoun's system of political philoso-phy. The dogma of state sovereignty, with its correlatives of nullifi-cation and secession, was but an application of this more general doctrine, restated in terms of familiar American institutions. He found a classical basis for his theory in the separate representation of patricians and plebeians in ancient Rome, under a system that gave to each a veto on the acts of government, and a more recent illustration in the balance of classes in British Parliamentary prac-tice. In his own country he found that the basic distinction between interests, though still along economic lines, followed an essentially geographical pattern. They were not stratified as classes or estates, but were localized as sections or regions in terms of the prevalent source of livelihood, this in turn being based on climate and natural resources. The states were most nearly representative of this divi-sion, so it was to the states, in their character as members of a con-federacy, that Calhoun accorded a concurrent veto power.

The controversies of the preceding three decades pointed the way so clearly to this particular application that it would have been the part of political wisdom to use it even if logic had directed oth-erwise. Ever since the Alien and Sedition Acts, and the countering resolutions from the legislatures of Kentucky and Virginia, a debate as to the true construction of the Constitution had been in progress. The Virginia school, for which both Jefferson and Madison had ar-gued, held the instrument to be in fact a compact among independ-ent sovereignties. From this it followed, under accepted principles of international law, that each party to the compact had a right to

judge of its own powers, and to interpose to arrest a patent violation of the agreement. Calhoun's own intensive study during the
summer and early fall of 1828 when he was preparing to write the
Exposition convinced him of the validity of the compact theory,
and served as his point of departure in his subsequent writings and
speeches on the question. The Roman Tribunate had been established by agreement between warring factions. First the temporal
lords and then the commons derived their equal power in Britain
from contracts, signed and witnessed in due form. The concurrent
veto—the great conservative principle of a society—did not just
happen, but came into existence to protect each of the parties to a
compact from violation by the others.

Having fitted the Constitution of the United States into its proper
niche in his political philosophy, it was no difficult matter for Calhoun to reason that the House of Representatives was the organ of
the numerical majority, but that the Senate, with its representation
by states, was intended to give a concurrent voice to the various
interests that made up the body politic. His own function in the
Senate was thus to maintain the interests, economic and political,
of South Carolina, and by extension the interests of the whole region of which the state was a part. He could change sides on major
issues, he could change party allegiance, he could pursue a seemingly erratic course on any phase of public policy, and still be entirely consistent with his own political philosophy. He represented
a minority interest, threatened with extinction by the action of a
government in control of a numerical majority. Nor was it alone for
South Carolina's benefit that he asserted her sovereignty against the
weight of numbers. It was also for the good of the whole; for in that
way alone, so he believed, could the Union endure.

III

The major tenets of this theory of the state—that governments tend
to become absolute, that rulers tend to abuse their powers, that the
honors and emoluments of government are in themselves enough
to fix party lines and precipitate a struggle for power—all of these
propositions were deductions from the nature of man. But they
were far more than that. They were also obvious facts that anyone

could see for himself in the day-to-day operations of the government of the United States. So clear were they to Calhoun that they gave validity to a theory otherwise abstract, and justified extremes that a man of less positive convictions might have hesitated to invoke.

History may be interpreted in many ways, according to the preconceptions of the historian, the material he elects to accept, and the sources he chooses to ignore. The Age of Jackson may, indeed, have been the forerunner of later social movements in which the welfare of the common man was pitted against intrenched privilege and greed. Certainly Amos Kendall and Francis Blair, among the ablest if not the most truthful journalists of the century, strove mightily to provide the contemporary voter (and incidentally, posterity) with just such a picture. But to Calhoun, and unquestionably to a majority of the middle class of his day, Jackson's career was one unbroken march toward despotism. It proved every point in Calhoun's political theory, offered new and pertinent illustrations of the nature of the governmental process, and justified the most vigorous forms of opposition. Let us strip the Jackson era of its supporting propaganda, forget the idealism of the glosses that have been written on it, and look at it as nearly as we may with Calhoun's eyes.

The tools of power were ready to Jackson's hand when that extraordinary man took office, and his political lieutenants were thoroughly skilled in their use. The tools had been thoughtfully provided by unwitting rivals going back for nearly a decade. The four-year tenure law of 1820, conceived by the political genius William H. Crawford, was a potent engine for securing partisans. Under this innocent-looking statute district attorneys, officers of the customs service, registers of the land offices, naval agents, and a few less numerous officials were made removable at the will of the President. Their terms of office, moreover, were specifically limited to four years, so that as each Presidential election rolled around, virtually the entire civilian personnel of the federal government would have to seek reappointment. The more numerous group of postal employees already served for limited periods, defined by the contracts under which the mails were carried.

The four-year law was in fact one element in a closely knit political machine that Crawford had built up on the foundations of the old Jefferson-Burr alliance, and which was expected to make him President in 1824. When ill-health thwarted Crawford's hopes, Martin Van Buren succeeded to control of the machine, which he deftly turned to the service of Andrew Jackson. John Quincy Adams, meanwhile, though he had less than a third of the popular vote, had been elected President early in 1825 by a House of Representatives in which tariff sentiment predominated. Immediately thereafter the leading exponent of the protective policy received the first place in the Cabinet, and the President propounded a legislative program whose maximum benefits would accrue to those states to which he owed his election. He did his best to divert former Crawford partisans to his own cause by judicious reappointments under the four-year law; and in the skillful hands of Secretary of State Henry Clay, the printing and other public contracts were given out with a view to Adams' re-election.

It was not the officeholders, however, but the beneficiaries of the tariff who made up the core of Adams' strength, and shortly before the election of 1828 he prepared to insure their loyalty with still higher duties. Calhoun was already in opposition, since his state and section were the primary victims of the administration policy. He had allied himself perforce with the Jacksonians, even though it brought him into the same camp as the bulk of the Crawford Radicals, his bitter foes of a few years earlier. Calhoun and other Southern followers of Jackson tried to block this new attempt to increase the tariff by introducing provisions deliberately obnoxious to Adams' New England supporters; but when the critical moment arrived Van Buren, Eaton, Benton, and others among the Jackson inner circle voted to pass the measure they had pledged themselves to defeat. The strength of the tariff interest had not been lost upon the Democratic managers, and with the election approaching in the fall, they made their own peace with the manufacturers. They courted both sides and won.

It was at this point that Calhoun wrote the *South Carolina Exposition*. To him, the relation between the dominant economic interest and the partisan majority was clear. In subtle, indirect, but entirely legal ways, the latter had been bought by the former. The government was already in the exclusive control of the stronger interest, and the destruction of the weaker, which was also his own, must inevitably follow, unless Jackson chose to cast the influence of his vast personal popularity into the opposite scale.

Jackson, surrounded as he was by some of the ablest party strategists ever produced in this or any other country, preferred to consolidate his power. His methods were simple, direct, and effective. He began by reappointing to office only known and proven partisans, and by removing those who were not wholehearted in his cause in favor of men whose personal loyalty was undeviating. When the process of patronage distribution was well advanced, in December, 1829, a New York paper devoted to Van Buren's interests announced its support of Jackson for a second term, and of Van Buren for the succession. From the beginning of his campaign, Jackson had been committed to a single term, but before another year was out his candidacy for re-election was acknowledged and a new "official" newspaper had been established in the capital to advance it. The Washington *Globe*, edited publicly by Blair and behind the scenes by Kendall, became thereafter an almost irresistible vehicle for party propaganda. Its financial support came from officeholders, who were required to subscribe for it —and pay in advance—or resign their places to men who would.[4]

Another important milestone on Jackson's march to autarchy was the Maysville Road veto in 1830. The action was received with initial approbation in the South because it appeared to put an end to federal spending for public works. It could therefore be used as an argument for reducing the revenue, which meant the tariff. But it presently appeared, as other internal improvement bills received the President's approbation, that the question was still open. The only real change was that the use of public funds for improvement purposes was made subject in each case to the personal judgment of the executive. The Maysville Road was in Kentucky, whose legislature had sent Henry Clay to the Senate. Highways and canals in more compliant states might perhaps prove to be for national purposes.

Year after year McDuffie introduced into the House bills for tariff reduction in accordance with what he and Calhoun believed to be Jackson's pre-election pledge to South Carolina; and year

[4] B. P. Poore, *Perley's Reminiscences* (New York, 1886), I, 104.

after year they came to nothing. The vote was manipulated by the same economic interest that had elected Adams and now supported Jackson. The cost of manufactured products rose, the price of cotton fell, and Southern leaders, particularly the younger group in South Carolina, threatened revolt. So in July, 1831, Calhoun restated his theory, with embellishments looking to positive action. He pointed out that although a substantial minority believed the tariff to be unconstitutional, the majority continued to pursue that policy to the economic ruin of the cotton states. So he claimed for the interest he represented a concurrent veto, but at the same time expressed his great preference for an adjustment of the point at issue by Congress.

Again the national legislature refused to make concessions, and in that refusal gave further evidence of the validity of Calhoun's premises. For there was actually strong sentiment in many parts of the country for tariff reduction, but to yield to it would have been to concede a political triumph to Calhoun. This neither Jackson nor Clay would do; so at the risk of civil war the Jacksonians and the National Republicans voted together to maintain a prohibitive scale of duties, lest the pretensions of a rival be advanced. Throughout the whole controversy the actions, motives, and purposes of Calhoun and his followers were deliberately misrepresented and distorted by Blair and his satellite editors to arouse public indignation against South Carolina and her leaders.

The issue was joined in the fall of 1832. Calhoun stated the case for state action to arrest the tariff in a letter to Governor Hamilton late in August. It was timed immediately to precede state elections whose outcome would determine whether South Carolina would interpose her sovereignty to restrain the protective system. Calhoun showed how the majority always has an interest in enlarging the powers of government, and how human nature itself would impel the rulers to oppress the ruled, unless they were in some manner prevented from so doing. Majority rule was in fact only rule by the stronger interest, whose cupidity and ambition would inevitably hasten the government along the road to absolutism. The only barrier lay in the original sovereignty of the states.

To those who lost money by the protective policy the argument was convincing. The Nullifiers won their two-thirds majority. The convention was duly called, and the tariffs of 1828 and 1832 were declared null and void within the limits of South Carolina.

Jackson's answer to nullification was a proclamation explicitly claiming for the federal government—which is to say, for the majority—precisely the powers that George III had claimed over the colonies in 1776: the power to judge of its own limits, to pass laws within those limits, and to compel obedience to those laws. The partisan majority then ratified these claims by voting to the President full control over army, navy, militia, and for all practical purpose public treasury, any or all of which might be used to assist in the collection of import duties in the rebellious state. An act, Calhoun called it, to "enforce robbery by murder." He did not doubt that Jackson, like Macbeth, saw in his dreams the vision of a crown.[5]

The compromise of 1833 put an end for the time being to the controversy between South Carolina and the general government, but it impeded not at all Jackson's progress toward undisputed power. In the summer of 1832 the President had vetoed a bill renewing the charter of the Bank of the United States. The bank threw its influence to Clay in the fall election, and for this political opposition, Jackson undertook to destroy the "monster of corruption" without waiting for its charter to expire. In the fall of 1833, with no economic justification and the flimsiest of legal pretexts, the public funds were removed from the custody of the bank and placed with various state institutions where they were directly under executive control. Two Secretaries of the Treasury were dismissed before one who would sign the necessary order was found, and the action was deliberately timed to precede the meeting of Congress, so that it could not be blocked.

In the Senate, where Calhoun and Clay had temporarily joined forces against the administration, the removal of the deposits was denounced as the ultimate act of tyranny. Clay read from Plutarch the description of Caesar entering the Roman Treasury sword in hand. Calhoun showed that whatever the motive, the result in this case was the same. For the Roman had seized the public treasure

[5] Calhoun to Samuel D. Ingham, January 16, 1833, Jackson Papers, 2nd Series (Library of Congress).

to buy partisans with which to consolidate his power; and the public funds in the pet banks were being recklessly loaned out to speculators who were thereby converted into partisans. The Senate voted a resolution censuring the President. Jackson replied with a sharp protest, which the Senate refused to receive.

As of the spring of 1834 the record, in the eyes of Calhoun and those who thought with him, was something like this: First the patronage had been perverted, by instituting the general practice of removal from office without cause—the principle of the Albany Regency that "to the victors belong the spoils." The total number of employees and pensioners of the federal government had doubled since 1825, and expenses, exclusive of payments on the public debt, had likewise doubled, although the population increase was no more than 25 per cent. The revenue had been enormously increased in the same interval, largely through a form of taxation which fell unequally on the different sections of the country, and the President had been given by a subservient Congress the power to perpetuate this inequality by military force. A large and unscrupulous press had been suborned to do the bidding of the party leaders. The public money had been removed without adequate reason or even plausible excuse from the depository established and safeguarded by law, and had been placed in a group of favored banks where it was under the exclusive control of the executive. This money was being used by the banks that held it, not as a deposit but as capital, and the amount of it was loaned out three and four times over, the profits going to the pet banks and the loans going to partisans, present or prospective. Yet when the Senate condemned the final act of power, though it had sanctioned everything that went before, the President, in language skillfully chosen to inflame popular prejudices, accused the Senate of violating his rights. In the Cherokee case two years earlier Jackson had ignored a decision of the Supreme Court. Who but the most blinded partisan could fail to see in this challenge to the Senate the first step toward subverting the legislative arm as well?

All this would have been more than enough to convince men less predisposed in that direction than Calhoun that the Constitution was in fact a dead letter and Andrew Jackson a dictator of unrestrained power. But there was more to come. Jackson decreed that Martin Van Buren should be his successor, and a party convention made up of officeholders and pensioners unanimously ratified the choice. There was no subtlety about it. The President was openly and shamelessly designating his successor, and would use all the vast patronage at his command to insure the election of his favorite. To Calhoun it was as "open and palpable usurpation of the supreme executive power" as though it had been brought about by military force.[6] Force had in fact been threatened for the collection of a relatively trifling debt from France, and that matter still hung fire early in 1836 when Van Buren's cause looked none too bright. So Jackson indulged once more in vigorous saber-rattling, until Calhoun thought him bent upon war to justify himself in accepting a third term.[7] Napoleon was not the first who had risen to imperial estate through successful foreign war, nor was he likely to be the last.

Jackson also decreed that the resolution of censure should be expunged from the Senate Journal, and the faithful Benton, himself designated for the Presidential succession at one remove, undertook the task. He was not "single-handed and alone" for long. The party machinery, reaching down to the smallest hamlet and out to the remotest reaches of a far-flung domain, was set in motion. Senators who had voted to condemn the President were marked for the slaughter, and those members of their state legislatures who had supported them were the preliminary victims. Against each of these local representatives a campaign was waged on his home ground, with all the persuasions that a powerful and wealthy central government could command. In half a dozen states the political complexion of the legislature was changed, and Senators were "instructed" to expunge the hated judgment. Some obeyed, others resigned; but the result was the same. In less than three years the Senate majority was reversed, and Jackson was vindicated in January, 1837. Not without reason Calhoun called

[6] Calhoun to W. F. Gordon, May 22, 1835, A. C. Gordon, *William Fitzhugh Gordon* (New York, 1909), pp. 297–299.
[7] Calhoun to L. W. Tazewell, January 24, 1836, Calhoun Papers (Library of Congress).

it "the melancholy evidence of a broken spirit, ready to bow at the feet of power." [8]

IV

To a generation accustomed to a liberal evaluation of the Jackson era, this picture will seem exaggerated and overdrawn. It was nevertheless the picture that a substantial and talented portion of King Andrew's subjects saw. Calhoun's writings and speeches only add more detail to the skeleton presented here. Substantially the same view will be found in the columns of Duff Green's *United States Telegraph,* of Richard Crallé's Richmond *Jefferson and Virginia Times,* and in many other anti-Jackson papers. It was ably and clearly expressed by many prominent actors on the scene, like John Tyler of Virginia, George Poindexter of Mississippi, Willie P. Mangum of North Carolina, even by Clay and Webster themselves. In literary form Judge Beverley Tucker's novel, *The Partisan Leader,* first published by Duff Green in 1836, traces the same forces through three hypothetical Van Buren administrations, and might have come even closer to prophecy than it did had not the panic of 1837 put an abrupt end, for the time being, to the hand-picked Jackson dynasty.

Calhoun's analysis of the political process was complete long before he gave his own support to Van Buren's program in the special session of 1837. The administration, through the normal reaction of the average man to economic catastrophe, had been thrown into the minority, and Calhoun knew that the interests of South Carolina were no safer in the hands of the Clay-Webster combination than they had been under Jackson or Adams. As the advocate of a special interest it was clearly his duty to go with whichever party was most likely to advance his cause.

The theory, to repeat, was fully matured before Jackson left office, every tenet of it having been in one way or another confirmed by the career of the Hero. It was thereafter a glass through which Calhoun observed the passing scene. The log-cabin-and-hard-cider campaign of 1840 merely showed once more how partisans were lost when the well of patronage ran dry, and were

[8] *Register of Debates,* 24th Congress, 2nd Session, p. 418.

won by promises, however specious. He had reasoned from the start that the struggle for place would tend to become more violent until control changed hands at every election, to be retained at last by force. He saw the partisan majority change with each election from Van Buren's day until his own death in 1850. Believing as he did that the need for new sources of political reward would force the partisan majority to seek new forms of power, he could hardly have been surprised at Polk's venture into aggressive war.

Had Calhoun been less sure of himself, less ready to pursue his own reasoning to the ultimate end, and less ingenious in fitting the facts as he saw them into the pattern as he himself had laid it down, he might perhaps have reached a different explanation of his times, and followed in consequence a different course. Being the type of man he was, and in the environment that was his, like Luther at the Diet of Worms, he could do no other. To him and to a majority of his generation liberty was the most precious possession of mankind. It was for liberty that a revolution had been fought and a new nation established—not to substitute after half a century the absolutism of a successful general for that of a demented British king. History, philosophy, and his own experience taught him that the natural tendency of government was to whittle away the sphere of liberty, and that this tendency could be resisted only by power. Calhoun was simply realist enough to know that the greatest power in any state, next to military might, is the organized power of its economic interests.

GERALD M. CAPERS

✪

A Reconsideration of John C. Calhoun's Transition from Nationalism to Nullification

Like Washington and Lincoln, in the American legend John C. Calhoun is a symbol—a symbol of the Old South which was to be destroyed in the Great Rebellion that began a decade after his death. Unlike Washington and Lincoln, who recently at last have been portrayed as individuals, in the national tradition Calhoun remains a symbol, not a personality, largely because of the treatment he has persistently received from his biographers.

When the Carolinian announced his candidacy for the Presidency in the last days of 1821, his intimate cabinet colleague, John Quincy Adams, regarded the move as deliberate and dishonest treachery. The New Englander had recently received, through a third party, what he considered positive assurance that the Secretary of War had no intention of entering the race. During the bitter months of the Presidential contest which followed, he secretly poured out his venom on the unsuspecting Calhoun in his diary, and in its pages every action of his Southern rival was recorded as that of a self-seeking, hypocritical, and scheming politician. This famous

Reprinted from *The Journal of Southern History,* Vol. XIV, No. 1 (February 1948), pp. 34–48. Copyright 1948 by the Southern Historical Association. Reprinted by permission of the Managing Editor.

diary, published in the 1870's, was used by Hermann E. von Holst as the basis for his hostile biography of the Southerner.[1] Thus in the Reconstruction era Calhoun, seen through Adams' biased eyes, became the personification of the unprincipled and wicked South that plotted rebellion years before she finally attempted it.

Most of his biographers, being Southerners, have in retaliation portrayed him as the symbol of the purity of Southern motives. In their eyes both Calhoun and the South are above reproach, never motivated but by the loftiest incentives. Calhoun the man has remained in the clouds, symbolic of the Lost Cause. As a natural consequence the fiction persists that his great contemporaries, Jackson, Clay, and Webster, were ambitious men who used every means within their power to attain the Presidency. But the Carolinian, willing in his high patriotism to accept that office because he so conspicuously had the interests of the whole nation rather than his own at heart, never stooped to low personal ambition or to the sordid methods of his rivals.

It must be admitted that the letters and papers of Calhoun lend a superficial support to this thesis, but there is a stronger case for a contrary interpretation. Deistic in religion but, like Adams, puritanical in mental habit and temperament, it was a psychological necessity to Calhoun never to admit personal ambition and to rationalize his every political act exclusively in terms of national interest. Such rationalization was not only temperamentally necessary, but his shift in the middle of his career from extreme nationalism to an extreme states'-rights position made it all the more essential. Calhoun apparently was sincere in changing his opinion, and he conveniently used the arguments of his own rationalization in an effort to convince the nation of his intellectual integrity. Confident of his own logic, he regarded those who disagreed as totally in error and frequently considered them positively vicious. Webster made an identical shift in the opposite direction about the same time, yet he was not subject in any such degree to an urge for self-justification. Jackson and Clay, since their appeal was more to men's hearts, never bothered themselves about the matter of consistency. While much of Calhoun's rationalizing

[1] Hermann E. von Holst, *John C. Calhoun* (Boston, 1882).

was unconscious, it satisfied his peculiar complex, and it has generally been accepted by his biographers at face value.[2]

In view of the violent disagreement in every age among contemporaries about the character of many national figures, it is almost impossible to adduce universally acceptable evidence for any specific interpretation of a prominent statesman who has been dead a century, particularly of so complex a personality as Calhoun. But it is unreasonable not to expose him to the same critical philosophy of human behavior with which biographers have approached his distinguished contemporaries. To explain his career in terms of enlightened self-interest and to describe his defense of himself and his actions as rationalization can be regarded as condemnation only to those who persist in identifying the fleshless symbol with the man.

Clay, it is generally agreed, wanted all his life to become President and took practical steps to achieve that objective. His successful efforts at compromise in periods of crisis enhanced as much as they hindered his chances for that high office. Calhoun also wanted the Presidency all his life and, within the limits of his own inhibitions, took what he regarded as practical measures toward that end. That he frequently disagreed with Clay on public matters by no means proved that he was any less desirous of preserving the Union, but rather that he considered his own proposals as the only sure method of preservation. At no stage in his career can it be clearly proven that he consciously placed his own fortunes above those of his nation or section, but Clay and Webster made such a charge against him in the great debate in the Senate in 1838 over the independent treasury bill. They based their charge principally upon his recent return to the Democrats after he had earlier broken with that party and had acted with the Whigs throughout Jackson's second term. Personally, he was always

[2] Besides Von Holst's work, the following are full-length biographies of Calhoun: John S. Jenkins, *Life of John C. Calhoun* (Auburn, 1850); Gustavus M. Pinckney, *Life of John C. Calhoun* (Charleston, 1903); Gaillard Hunt, *John C. Calhoun* (Philadelphia, 1908); William M. Meigs, *Life of John C. Calhoun*, 2 vols. (New York, 1917); Arthur Styron, *The Cast-Iron Man: John C. Calhoun and American Democracy* (New York, 1935); Charles M. Wiltse, *John C. Calhoun, Nationalist, 1782–1828* (Indianapolis, 1944).

able to convince himself that the course most convenient to his own aspirations was also best suited to the general welfare, but his characteristic method of so doing was to begin in his own mind with his conclusion and then select an innocuous premise which would lead irrefutably to it. Those who unwarily accepted Calhoun's premises usually found themselves caught in a locked vise of logic.

As his personal traits differed from those of Clay, so did his methods. Completely lacking the Kentuckian's ability to charm his fellows by warmth of personality, he was by contrast naïve in his views concerning the fundamentals of human conduct. Confident that all men were rational, he assumed that he could win them by the cold force of logic alone. This misconception alienated his contemporaries probably as much as any of his personal characteristics. With Calhoun in the Presidency, said his colleague, Senator William H. Roane of Virginia, he would be in "constant terror, expecting from him some new-fangled scheme or view." [3] A certain Judge Prioleau, a new neighbor of Calhoun's in Pendleton, expressed the general sentiment bluntly when he stated that he never wished to see him again: "I hate a man who makes me think so much . . . and I hate a man who makes me feel my own inferiority." [4]

Pertinent testimony as to Calhoun's belief in the power of reason, as well as to his egotism and his conscious opportunism, comes from the Carolinian himself. "The great ends in his system of life," he wrote in regard to himself in one of the many significant passages in the Autobiography of 1843, "whether public or private, he has ever held to be fixed by reason and general rules; but the time and method of obtaining them he regarded as questions of expediency. . . . Seeing clearly his own ends which . . . he judges with a rare sagacity . . . [he] advances forward and halts when he has taken as much ground as he can occupy, . . . without regard to the remonstrances of his followers, who take their counsels merely from zeal and do not properly ascertain the limits

---

[3] William H. Roane to Martin Van Buren, September 11, 1843, Martin Van Buren Papers (Division of Manuscripts, Library of Congress).

[4] Gustavus M. Pinckney, "Calhoun from a Southern Stand-Point," *Lippincott's Magazine* (Philadelphia, 1868–1915), LXII (1898), 84.

upon human power. . . . This it is which makes him the master-
statesman of his age." [5]

His entrance into the Presidential contest in 1821 and his definite
hope for the Democratic nomination as late as 1848 leave no doubt
of the depth and persistence of his Presidential ambitions. In this
connection certain instances of his characteristic methods of in-
direction should be noted. A highly eulogistic but anonymous
campaign biography, published by Harpers in 1843, was generally assumed at the time to have been written by Robert M. T.
Hunter, a Virginia Congressman. In 1854, however, Robert Barnwell Rhett wrote that Calhoun himself had written all of it but
a page or two and had in vain urged him to accept the nominal
authorship.[6] Similarly, he kept secret his authorship of the *South
Carolina Exposition* in 1828, at a time when the knowledge would
have seriously injured his support from Northern Democratic Republicans as heir apparent to Jackson, and he did not claim it as his
own until several years later.[7] As a member of Monroe's cabinet, he
sought to use patronage in the same backhanded fashion as his
colleague Adams to build up support for his anticipated candidacy
as successor to the Virginian. The instances are not cited as evidence of unethical conduct, but they and other similar cases clearly

[5] Anonymous *Life of John C. Calhoun* (New York, 1843), pp. 52–53.
See also the next note.

[6] "There is but one thing written by Mr. Calhoun that you ought not to
publish as his—and that is—'his life.' He wished me to Father it—but I told
him that it was impossible for me directly or indirectly to allow any one
to understand that I was the author of a publication which I had not written. Hunter and I read it over together in my house in Georgetown. He
inserted about a page and a half, and became the putative author; and it
has done more to lift him to his present position than any thing else in his
public life." Robert Barnwell Rhett to Richard K. Crallé, October 25, 1854,
American Historical Review (New York, 1895–   ), XIII (1907–1908),
311. See also Gaillard Hunt's note on this subject, *ibid.*, pp. 310–311; and for
a contrary argument, Wiltse, *Calhoun*, Appendix A.

[7] In the Charleston *Courier* of August 15, 1831, an anonymous "Civis"
wrote that Calhoun had only recently acknowledged his authorship of the
Exposition. "It is believed," continued Civis, "that Mr. Calhoun was anxious
he should be concealed. It has been frequently denied that he was the author, and both he and his friends indulged a hope that it could not be
fastened upon him." John Quincy Adams was surprised when Joel R.
Poinsett told him late in the summer of 1830 that Calhoun was at the bottom
of the whole agitation. Charles F. Adams, ed., *Memoirs of John Quincy
Adams,* 12 vols. (Philadelphia, 1874–1878), VIII, 237.

reveal that Calhoun did not hesitate to use methods identical in spirit with those for which other public men of the day have been criticized.

Although he was to remain active in national politics until his death, which occurred shortly after his famous speech opposing the Compromise of 1850, actually the crisis of both his political and his intellectual life came in the decade between 1822 and 1832. This was the period of his gradual and reluctant transition from extreme nationalism to equally extreme sectionalism, ending in his open and eloquent defense of state sovereignty in the nullification crisis. It was also a period of an ardent, continuous, and optimistic quest for the Presidency. His conversion to the Southern particularism with which he is identified by posterity was long retarded both by his hopes for the Presidency and his deep-seated nationalism. Not until his fatal break with Jackson in 1831 destroyed his prospects for a future nomination by the Democratic Republican party did he publicly announce his adherence to the doctrine of nullification.

When Calhoun entered the Presidential race in 1821, he ran on a record for arch-nationalism unexcelled even by that of Henry Clay. As the Kentuckian's lieutenant among the War Hawks, he had introduced the bill for the declaration of war in 1812, reporting it in his capacity as chairman of the Committee on Foreign Relations. His labors as leader of the administration forces in the war Congresses led Alexander J. Dallas to single him out as the "Young Hercules Who Had Carried the War on His Shoulders." [8] Striving for national self-sufficiency both to prevent defeat in the third war with England that he believed certain and to avoid the equal danger of disunion sentiment as manifested in the Hartford Convention, he took the lead in the enactment of the nationalistic legislation of the Era of Good Feeling which Clay later named and claimed as the American System. Specifically, he drew up and introduced in Congress both the bill chartering the Second Bank of the United States and the companion "Bonus Bill" providing federal funds for internal improvements. At a crucial point in the discussion of the

[8] See sketch of Calhoun by Ulrich B. Phillips, in Allen Johnson and Dumas Malone, eds., *Dictionary of American Biography,* 20 vols. and index (New York, 1928–1936), III, 412.

Tariff of 1816, he was called in hastily to speak in its behalf, and he argued spiritedly for its protective features as a national necessity. Later, as Secretary of War, he advocated an expensive program of national defense, which the economy drive led by William H. Crawford during the Panic of 1819 eventually doomed to defeat.

His views on the Constitution at this time were as broad as the program which he advocated. "I am no advocate for refined arguments on the Constitution," he said in his speech on the Bonus Bill in 1817. "The instrument was not intended as a thesis for the logician to exercise his ingenuity on. It ought to be construed with plain, good sense." [9] In 1823 he wrote that "the Supreme Court of the Union performs the highest functions under our system. It is the mediator between sovereigns, the State and General Governments, and [draws] the actual line, which separates their authority." [10] A year later he told the son of Alexander Hamilton that he had a "clear conviction, after much reflection and an entire knowledge and familiarity with the history of our country and the working of our Government that his [the elder Hamilton's] policy as developed by the measures of Washington's administration, is the only true policy for this country." [11]

In the same spirit he refused to take alarm at the Tallmadge amendment to exclude slavery from Missouri. He accepted the ensuing compromise with full satisfaction and threw all his influence against the efforts of the Crawford faction to answer the Tallmadge attack by forming a separate Southern party. "We of the South ought not to assent easily to the belief," he argued, "that there is a conspiracy either against our property or just weight in the Union. . . . Nothing would lead more directly to disunion with all of its horrors. . . . If we, from such a belief, systematically oppose the North, they must from necessity resort to a similar opposition to us." [12] This, then, was the younger Calhoun whom

[9] Richard K. Crallé, ed., *Works of John C. Calhoun,* 6 vols. (New York, 1854), II, 192.

[10] Calhoun to Virgil Maxcy, July 11, 1823, Maxcy-Markoe Papers (Division of Manuscripts, Library of Congress).

[11] James A. Hamilton, *Reminiscences: or Men and Events at Home and Abroad* (New York, 1869), p. 62.

[12] Calhoun to Charles Tait, October 26, 1820, in "Tait Correspondence," *Gulf States Historical Magazine* (Montgomery, 1902–1904), I (1902), 98.

Adams characterized as "above all sectional and factious prejudices more than any other statesman of this Union with whom I have ever acted." [13]

Yet within a decade Calhoun began a complete reversal of his earlier program and governmental philosophy. In his later years he incessantly attacked the protective tariff, the bank, and federal internal improvements as unconstitutional and detrimental to the national welfare. Never did a logician exercise his ingenuity more upon the Constitution. It became his dominant theme that only the sovereign states, and not the Supreme Court, could determine which powers had been delegated by that compact to their creature, the federal government. The major effort of his long career in politics after the nullification crisis was his unsuccessful attempt to unite the South in a separate political party.

In considering the circumstances of this amazing transition on his part, the evolution of Calhoun's plans for attaining the Presidency must be kept in mind. When he entered the contest against Adams and Crawford in 1821, against the advice of many of his friends, he undoubtedly expected strong support from all sections in response to his conspicuous nationalism. Two years later a Pennsylvania convention gave a heavy vote to Jackson for President and to Calhoun for Vice-President. Reluctantly he accepted this decision, and though most of his followers allied themselves with the Jackson forces, he kept himself uncommitted until the victorious Adams selected Clay as Secretary of State. Since the Kentuckian presumably would receive the backing of the administration for the succession upon Adams' retirement, his Carolina rival had no choice but to join the Jackson opposition in order to become similarly the General's heir apparent. This meant a delay in Calhoun's elevation to the Presidency until 1832 at the earliest, and then only if the aging Jackson should be elected in 1828 and should stick to his announced intention of retiring after one term. For eight years, meanwhile, he would have to maneuver from the Vice-Presidency, where there was considerable danger that he might be buried.

It was in self-interest, therefore, as well as from conviction, that he endeared himself to the Jackson party by vehement attacks

[13]Adams, ed., *Memoirs of John Quincy Adams*, V, 361.

upon the Adams administration. In order to preserve a convenient ambiguity for Old Hickory on the tariff, Calhoun, in cooperation with Van Buren, devised the strategy which backfired, to his acute embarrassment, in the Tariff of Abominations.[14] A primary purpose of his *Exposition* was to keep South Carolina and the rest of the South loyal to Jackson by holding out the prospect of tariff reduction should he be elected.

But in the end Calhoun's six years of devoted service to the General availed him nothing. Upon their initial success in 1828 the other two wings of the victorious coalition—the northern group under Van Buren and the Tennessee group led by Secretary of War John H. Eaton and Major William B. Lewis—used a variety of personal incidents, particularly the "Eaton Affair," to poison the President's mind against the proud Carolinian. That their conspiracy was successful as early as December, 1829, is evident from a private letter which Jackson wrote to his old Tennessee friend, John Overton.[15] In this he stated in no uncertain terms his loss of confidence in Calhoun and designated Van Buren his choice as his successor in the Presidency. The nation, however, knew nothing of this development until the summer of 1830, when the President used a letter from William H. Crawford, asserting that it was Calhoun who had advocated his court-martial in Monroe's Cabinet because of his violation of orders in the Seminole War of 1818, as a convenient pretext for a formal break with his lieutenant. An involved attempt at reconciliation by the Vice-President failed,[16]

[14] George McDuffie, Calhoun's lieutenant in the House, confessed that "this is what is sometimes called 'fighting the devil with fire,' a policy which, though I did not altogether approve, I adopted in deference to the opinions of those with whom I acted." *Congressional Globe,* 28 Cong., 1 Sess., Part 2 (May 30–31. 1844), p. 747.

[15] "Permit me to say here of Mr. Van Buren that I have found him everything that I can desire him to be, and believe him not only deserving of *my* confidence but the *confidence* of the *Nation.* . . . I wish I could say as much for Mr. Calhoun. You know the confidence I once had in that gentleman. However, of him I desire not now to speak." Jackson to John Overton, December 31, 1829, John S. Bassett, ed., *Correspondence of Andrew Jackson,* 7 vols. (Washington, 1926–1935), IV, 108.

[16] The pamphlet which Calhoun published in his defense in February 1831, is reproduced in *Niles' Weekly Register* (Baltimore, 1811–1849), XL, 11–24 (March 5, 1831).

and it was apparent early in 1831 that he had been read out of the party.

It is perfectly possible that Calhoun had already privately decided that the nationalistic legislation which he had earlier sponsored had subsequently proven injurious both to the nation and to the South.[17] He may also have become convinced that the state sovereignty theory, upon which nullification was based, was the proper interpretation of the Constitution. But the significant fact that he resisted strenuous pressure in his own state to commit himself openly to that doctrine until several months after his break with Jackson had destroyed his chances for the Democratic Republican nomination suggests that his Presidential aspirations were a potent influence upon all his actions during the preceding decade.

Calhoun's opposition to Adams and Clay, in view of the ultra-nationalism of their program, necessitated a discreet retreat from his earlier position after 1825, but the growing opposition to the tariff throughout the South made such a retreat increasingly imperative. The greatly increased production of cotton in the 1820's brought a severe drop in the price of that staple. This, in turn, caused a decline in Southern income that reached the proportions of an acute and continuing depression in the older areas along the seaboard, which suffered from competition of the rich new soils

[17] As early as 1824 Calhoun began to hedge on the question of the tariff and states' rights, as his letter of July 3 to Robert S. Garnett of Virginia clearly reveals. See J. Franklin Jameson, ed., *Correspondence of John C. Calhoun, Annual Report of the American Historical Association,* 1899 (Washington, 1900), II, 219–223. John Taylor had already dismissed Calhoun's careful statement as a quibble, on the grounds that, despite all he said, he believed in "endowing the federal government with a supremacy over the state governments whenever they came in conflict." Taylor to James Monroe, April 29, 1823, "Letters of John Taylor of Caroline, Virginia," *John P. Branch Historical Papers* (Richmond, 1901–1916), II (1905–1908), 348–353.

In 1825 Calhoun was still spiritedly defending his broad national program in South Carolina. Not until 1827, apparently, did he definitely form and act upon the conclusions which thereafter determined his policy. In that year, as president of the Senate, he cast the deciding vote against the Woolens Bill, and on August 26 he wrote a long, confidential letter to his brother-in-law, James E. Calhoun, in which he stated that the "great defect in our system" was the fact that "the separate geographical interests are not sufficiently guarded." Jameson, *Correspondence,* pp. 247–251.

in the Southwest. Yet increased tariff rates were singled out as the sole cause of this economic distress. In the general indignation which followed the passage of the bill of 1828, most Southern legislatures resolved that the protective tariff was unconstitutional, and in South Carolina there was wild talk of forcible resistance to the collection of duties.

It was this situation which led Calhoun secretly to write the *Exposition* in 1828. Surely he realized that the support of his state and his section were essential to his Presidential ambitions and that somehow he must induce the other wings of his party to reduce the tariff. In view of the fact that the heaviest vote for increased rates had come from the Middle Atlantic region and the Northwest, this was to prove an insuperable task. The Vice-President's hold upon his own state, furthermore, had been precarious throughout the 1820's. Its legislature had originally nominated William Lowndes for the Presidency in 1821, and only after his death the following May had it formally approved Calhoun's candidacy. Former Senator William Smith, who led a states'-rights faction in South Carolina which constantly attacked Calhoun as a Federalist, was elected again to the Senate in 1825. In the same year the legislature passed resolutions condemning the tariff and internal improvements as unconstitutional.

Younger Carolina politicos, George McDuffie, James Hamilton, Jr., and Robert Y. Hayne, previously disciples of Calhoun and his nationalism, were becoming ardent states' righters. He was thus forced to follow their lead in opposing the tariff, and in 1827 he cast the deciding vote against the Woolens Bill when Van Buren had contrived a tie in the Senate to embarrass him. Had his tariff strategy in 1828 worked out as he expected, the Tariff of Abominations would never have been passed, and he could not have been unaware of the fact that it was the affirmative vote of the Northern and Western wings of his party for certain protective amendments which caused his plan to miscarry.

A primary purpose of the *Exposition,* therefore, was to exert a subtle pressure upon his own party for tariff reduction. The threat of state interposition and the danger of alienating the South might induce his fellow Democratic Republicans, from motives of political expediency, to support a reduction of duties by Congress. Moreover, the same considerations might influence Jackson to veto the next tariff bill if protective rates were retained. Yet the tone of the document was moderate, and its immediate recommendation was that the state cast its vote for the General in confident expectation that he would restore "the pure principles of our government." [18] Although it argued that nullification was the identical constitutional remedy advocated by Jefferson himself for the protection of a minority against legislation which violated the federal compact and that it was designed to preserve rather than to disrupt the Union, the *Exposition* suggested its use only in the improbable eventuality that more conventional methods should fail. Since Calhoun's authorship was unsuspected at the time outside the state, he in no way endangered his standing in the party, whose initial victory he was thereby assuring.

There can be no doubt that he also sought by the *Exposition* to assure Carolina leaders of his concurrence in their sentiments, and at the same time to avoid positive commitment until he was surer of the outcome of current developments, both in the state and in the nation. While it was not generally known that he favored nullification until his public letter of July 26, 1831, radical leaders in the state knew of his authorship of the *Exposition* from the outset. By this means he hoped, as Frederic Bancroft says, "to obtain secret and at least partial control of the radicals and to retain inconspicuous general leadership in South Carolina." [19] If the tariff should be lowered, he could claim the credit, and particularist sentiment in the state would subside; but if not, he could still claim an early identification with the local movement should he decide in the future upon such a course.

As a matter of fact, both James Hamilton and an anonymous "Sydney," writing in the Charleston *Mercury,* formally outlined the general theory of nullification before Calhoun wrote his more elaborate essay for the committee of the legislature on federal relations. Actually, the legislature refused to adopt the *Exposition* as an official expression of its views, but to save the face of the committee, five thousand copies were ordered to be printed.[20] Not until

[18] Crallé, *Works,* VI, 56.
[19] Frederic Bancroft, *Calhoun and the South Carolina Nullification Movement* (Baltimore, 1928), p. 49.
[20] Meigs, *Calhoun,* I, 382.

the election in the fall of 1830 was it evident that a majority of Carolinians favored formal state action, and even then the Nullifiers failed to control the two-thirds of the legislature necessary to call a convention. Whatever his private and devious relations with Carolina radicals, Calhoun did not become a leader of the nullification movement until the summer of 1831.

In view of the complexity of the situation which he faced in 1828 and the ingenious political methods which he used, it is definitely possible that in writing the *Exposition* Calhoun was also anticipating the potential formation of a states'-rights party under his own leadership. There was universal concern in the South over increasing proposals for compensated emancipation and over indications of a growing abolitionist sentiment, no less than over the injustice of the tariff. If nullification could be established in advance as a certain defense against a frontal attack upon slavery, a grateful and united South would surely follow its author. By thus avoiding the necessity of secession, the cherished Union would be preserved, and the doctrine might well make converts in the West, which had its specific grievances against an Eastern majority. Calhoun appreciated the revolutionary nature of contemporary politics, and while retaining his affiliation with Jackson as his main chance, he seems to have privately encouraged the formation of a states'-rights party as an alternative upon which he could rely in case of necessity. The circumstances of the Webster-Hayne debate lend weight to his hypothesis. If this was Calhoun's game, then the unfavorable response to Hayne's arguments for nullification in the South and in the nation at large was an additional reason for his long delay in committing himself formally to the doctrine.

The climax to Calhoun's plans for the next Presidential election came in 1831 when, despite his final break with Jackson in January, he held high hopes of success. He revealed his aspirations during the spring in a long conversation with James H. Hammond, one of the several leaders of the Carolina radicals.[21] Both Jackson and Clay, he asserted, were rapidly losing followers, who were transferring their support to himself. He outlined in detail to Hammond a plan of sectional compromise which he intended to use as a

[21] See Hammond's Memorandum on the conversation, March 18, 1831, in *American Historical Review*, VI (1900–1901), 741–745.

platform. For the West he would amend the Constitution to authorize internal improvements at federal expense, using the proceeds of land sales for that purpose. For the South he would lower the tariff by reducing purely revenue duties, but for the Northeast he would retain protectionist rates on certain key products manufactured in that region. At the end of May he enthusiastically wrote his friend, Major Christopher Van Deventer: "I will in the coming contest act second to none. . . . I will stand on my own ground, which I know to be strong in principle and in publick support. I do not fear to carry the whole South with me, acting as it becomes my duty, which I will take care to do. I never stood stronger." [22]

During these months Calhoun was pursuing a highly opportunistic policy, but he seems ultimately to have expected nomination by the Anti-Masonic convention, which was to meet in September. Before that date, however, the Carolina radicals forced him to wreck his chances by a public commitment to nullification. Both Hammond and Hamilton had objected strenuously to his compromise and had advised him strongly against entering the Presidential race.[23] To smoke him out, in May, 1831, they opened an intensive

[22] Calhoun to Christopher Van Deventer, May 25, 1831, in Jameson, *Correspondence*, p. 292. What would have been the reception of Calhoun's compromise plan in the rest of the South had he resisted the Carolina Nullifiers is a matter of conjecture. It could be argued that his plan would have been popular, because the South then and later gave indication of its willingness to compromise. The section as a whole voted against nullification in 1833 and for the compromise tariff, which provided for no great immediate reduction. Later, the secession movements of both 1844 and 1850 were defeated, and a working compromise with the West was effected in the 1840's. On the contrary, however, Clay's distribution plan, which was similar to Calhoun's proposals for sectional compromise, was defeated in Congress for ten years. In two instances it was passed, but in the first it was vetoed by Jackson, and in the second it contained an amendment which shortly rendered it inoperative.

[23] When Calhoun told Hammond that he might become a candidate if "things went right," the latter "told him candidly that such a step would be imprudent at this moment both at home and abroad, and should not be thought of at this time. He agreed with me. He said his object was to throw himself entirely upon the South and if possible to be more Southern if possible [*sic*]. . . . He is unquestionably quite feverish under the present excitement and his hopes." Hammond Memorandum, March 18, 1831, *American Historical Review*, VI, 744–745. Soon James Hamilton, whom Duff Green had approached on the same matter, wrote Hammond that he had replied to Green that "in no shape, lot or scot would we be included in the arrangement, that we would take no part in the presidential election,

campaign in the state for nullification. Caught between demands from Nullifiers and Unionists in South Carolina that he express his sentiments, yet fearing to lose support outside the South essential to his nomination, he maintained his silence until July 26, when in a public letter he repeated without reservation the earlier arguments of his *Exposition*.[24] "But for the cry of nullification," bemoaned his ardent lieutenant, Duff Green, "Mr. Calhoun would have been nominated by the anti-Masons." [25]

Thus Calhoun's involved strategy ended in complete failure. Jackson and Van Buren ousted him from the Democratic Republican party, and the formal rejection of nullification by all other Southern states, when South Carolina took her precipitate action in 1832, destroyed all prospects for a Southern party which might support his future candidacy. Worse still, his prolonged delay in joining the Carolina radicals in their campaign for positive state action had seriously endangered his local position. In the crisis produced by the passage of the nullification ordinance, he resigned the Vice-Presidency and went to Washington as senator to defend his native state against the wrath of Andrew Jackson. At the moment he was fighting a crucial battle for his own political future in South Carolina. In this he conspicuously succeeded, but by the same action he doomed himself to a position of isolation in the nation from which he never completely emerged.

---

and that I was quite sure that Mr. C.'s prospects were as hopeless as his ruin would be certain, if he was brought to give his countenance to such a compact." Hamilton to Hammond, June 11, 1831, *ibid.*, pp. 746–747.

[24] Crallé, *Works,* VI, 59–94.

[25] Duff Green to Crallé, October 4, 1831, Frederick W. Moore, ed., "Calhoun as Seen by His Political Friends," Southern History Association, *Publications* (Washington, 1897–1907), VII (1903), 169.

John C. Calhoun: American Portrait

I

Calhoun was born into the system of slavery. Patrick Calhoun had
fixed the destiny of his sons the day that he rode back from a
legislative session in Charleston, with Adam, the first Negro ever
seen in the Carolina up-country, straddling his horse behind. Black
and white faces together had hovered over the baby Calhoun's
cradle. All his life his memory would go back to the woman who
had nursed him, to Adam's son, Sawney, who had hunted and
fished with him. John Calhoun grew up to know the Negroes, not
as abstractions, but as only a farmer could know them who had
plowed in the "brilin' sun," with the black man at his side.

Memories of the system were woven into the fabrics of his
day-to-day living. Mornings with Sawney in the spring, when the
wind was soft and the fishing rods light in their hands. Frantic,
last-minute notes from Floride, reminding him to bring shoes and
medicine for the Negroes—a hectic, last-minute search over Washington, swinging himself up into the stage at last, with the bulky
package under his arm. A Christmas morning at Fort Hill, when
he had called young Cato in to dance, the shaking head, the feet
slapping against the floor—and at the end, the bewildered, almost

Reprinted from Margaret L. Coit, *John C. Calhoun: American Portrait*
(Boston: Houghton Mifflin Co., 1950), Ch. XIX, pp. 284–315, by permission. Full citations for first references in the footnotes to this chapter have
been supplied by the editor.

frightened look on the child's face, when Calhoun had handed him
a shining, new fifty-cent piece, the first coin he had ever seen.[1]

His bewilderment when the black, sleepy-eyed Hector, the coachman, ran away "under the seduction . . . of . . . free blacks";
and his anger when "Alick," the only male house-servant on the
place, gave them "the slip" when Floride threatened him with a
whipping.[2] And never would he forget that swift, stabbing moment
of terror when he had broken the wax on a letter in Floride's small,
cramped hand, and had read the most dreaded words that any
Southern husband and planter far from home could receive: that
the Negroes had been "disorderly," and that measures must be
taken to bring them into subjection.[3]

Details of the system that so horrified outsiders were as natural
to Calhoun as his own breathing. Even in the isolated up-country
of his youth, he might occasionally have seen the tragic spectacle
of Virginia Negroes being herded South for sale: a cart of five or
six children, almost "broiled to sleep"; a cluster of women stumbling forward, their heads and breasts bare, two or three half-naked
men "chained together with an ox-chain"; and behind them always
the white man, his pistol cocked. Familiarity with such scenes did
not destroy their poignance, however; and in his young manhood
Calhoun found consolation only in his belief that slavery was "like
the scaffolding of a building," which, when it had served its purpose, would be taken down.[4]

In his youth, too, walking along the Charleston waterfront, Calhoun could have caught the reeking whiff that to every Southern
man and to every Yankee slave trader meant only the horror of the
slave ship. He could have gone aboard, have peered into that black
hole with its heat and its stench that no white man could describe,

[1] Reminiscences of Cato as told to Mrs. Francis Calhoun, Mrs. Francis
Calhoun Papers (privately owned), Clemson College.
[2] Calhoun to Charles J. Ingersoll, August 4, 1818, J. F. Jameson, ed.,
*Correspondence of John C. Calhoun, Annual Report of the American His-
torical Association, 1899* (Washington, 1900), II, 136–137; and Calhoun
to James Edward Calhoun, August 27, 1831, *ibid.*, p. 301.
[3] Calhoun to John Ewing Calhoun, January 15, 1827, Jameson, *Correspondence,* pp. 240–241.
[4] J. K. Paulding, *Letters from the South,* 2 vols. (New York, 1817), I,
117; see also James Parton, *Famous Americans of Recent Times* (Boston,
1874), p. 119.

have seen the black limbs flailing and coiling like snakes, and the "torpid" body of a child, crushed lifeless against the ship's side. He may have seen the black flood sweep from the hold, pour out across the decks of the ship, men and women, rabid and fighting with one another for a drop of water; or falling limp beside the rail, "in a state of filth and misery not to be looked at." [5]

Whether or not Calhoun ever endured this shattering experience is unknown. It is probable that he did. The changing tide of economics could later make him acclaim slavery as "a good," but, illogically, it never qualified his horror at the "odious traffic," deliberately stealing and enslaving human flesh. As a Southerner, he was sickened and ashamed at his own accessory guilt; as a slaveholder, and conscious of no crime in being a slaveholder,[6] his sincere effort was to see that the slave trade was not only outlawed, but actually abolished.

II

Although his strict conscience was untroubled by slaveholding, it did force Calhoun to face his responsibilities as a master with the utmost seriousness. "Every planter," he said, "must answer, not for the institution—for which he is no more accountable than the fall of Adam—but for his individual discharge of duty." His ideals were high. His severest critics have conceded that he was a "just and kind master to his slaves," and an English guest at Fort Hill noted his freedom from any "vulgar upstart display of authority." [7] Yet, like all Southern men, he was capable of leaping into swift, decisive action when circumstances of the bitter institution demanded it; and as we have seen, in one or two instances had his slaves whipped and otherwise punished if their misconduct was serious. "A perfectly humane man," he yet knew that where slaves were the most indulged, they were the worst servants.[8]

[5] Robert Walsh, *Notices of Brazil,* 2 vols. (London, 1830), II, 477–490, *passim.*

[6] Richard K. Crallé, ed., *Works of John C. Calhoun,* 6 vols. (New York, 1854–1857), IV, 339–349; II, 133.

[7] *Ibid.,* III, 631; Hermann von Holst, *John C. Calhoun* (Boston, 1882), p. 5.

[8] Basil Hall, *Travels in North America,* 2 vols. (Philadelphia, 1829), II, 200.

"The proper management and discipline of Negroes," it was said, "subjected the man of care and feeling to more dilemmas, perhaps, than anything he could find." [9] For plantation Negroes reflected the character of their owners. Ignorant, brutish, and degraded slaves could usually be traced back to a master of the same qualities. As late as the 1850's, there were still isolated plantations where Negroes could be found with no more knowledge of civilization than when they had come out of Africa, fifty or sixty years before. But these were the exceptions. Real as the horrors of slavery were, Southern leaders insisted that cruelty was an abuse and not a part of the system; and that the improvement in the condition of the Negro was as marked as in that of any other laboring class. "I can remember how they were forty years ago— they have improved two thousand per cent," a Virginia planter told the Northerner, Frederick Law Olmsted. "They are treated much better, they are fed better, and they have greater educational privileges." [10]

To sensitive men there could be real pleasure in treating their Negroes, not as animals, but as human beings who could be uplifted and developed. Such a master was Calhoun. Aware of how far economic interest went in compelling masters to do their duty by their slaves, to Calhoun there was another equally important side. "The first law of slavery," said *DeBow's Review*, "is that of kindness from the master to the slave." [11] Calhoun summarized the dual ideal: "Give the Planters Free Trade, and let every Planter be the parent as well as the *master* of his Slaves; that is, let the Slaves be made to do their duty as well as to eat, drink, and sleep; let morality and industry be taught them, and the Planter will have reason to be satisfied; he will always obtain seven or eight per cent upon the value of his Slaves; and need never be compelled to the distressing alternative of parting with them unless he allows them by overindulgence to waste his substance." That Calhoun was personally devoted to many of his Negroes, there is no doubt.

[9] B. MacBride in *The Southern Agriculturist*, III, 175.
[10] Frederick Law Olmsted, *A Journey Through the Slave States* (New York, 1853), p. 106.
[11] *DeBow's Review*, XV, 257–277.

To his friend Maxcy, he wrote his sympathy on the death of a servant whose "character of a slave" was "in a great measure lost in that of a fine, humble indeed, but still a friend." Calhoun's main hope for his slaves, expressed again and again in his unpublished correspondence, was that they be "well and contented." [12]

Just how many slaves Calhoun owned is uncertain. Estimates run all the way from thirty to ninety, and the truth probably lies between those figures.[13] Constantly he strove to mitigate such evils of the system as he could. His son, Andrew, owned a plantation in the hot black lands of Alabama, and for the sake of the Negroes' health and efficiency, the two men worked out an elaborate system of exchange. Andrew would work the slaves for six months, then send them East for recuperation in the vitalizing air of the South Carolina foothills. His father, meanwhile, would have a second group rested and refreshed, ready for another siege in the tropics. In this way, too, the Negroes were kept "in the family," which to Calhoun seemed the most important point of all.[14]

Occasionally Calhoun's solicitude for his servants' family ties would exceed those of the Negroes themselves. Once, when he was sending a family of house servants to live permanently at Andrew's plantation, a mother rebelled, and declared that she would give up all her children if only she could stay with her master and mistress. Said Calhoun: "I could not think of her remaining without her children, and as she chose to stay, we retained her youngest son, a boy of twelve." [15]

III

The "quarters" at Fort Hill—no cluster of whitewashed log cabins, but a single tenement dwelling of stone—stood just past the great

[12] Sarah M. Maury, *The Statesmen of America* (Philadelphia, 1847), p. 378; also Calhoun to Virgil Maxcy, March 18, 1822, Maxcy Papers (Library of Congress).

[13] James Parton, *Famous Americans of Recent Times* (Boston, 1874), p. 120.

[14] *John C. Calhoun,* pamphlet of the State Department of Education, Columbia, S. C.

[15] Mary Bates, *The Private Life of John C. Calhoun,* pp. 20–21.

barn, about an eighth of a mile from the "big house." To reach them, you took the path from the office down the lawn to a tree-shaded lane which wound by the barn, on the left, to the fields and hills beyond. In a shed before the house steamed a kettle, tended by an aging "Mammy," who would take her turn for a week or so minding the children, whose round black heads peered from every window.[16] On some plantations the shouts and giggles might fade into whispers when the master approached, but not at Fort Hill. Calhoun might awe the Senate, but he held no terrors for children, black or white, and they tumbled about his feet, un-afraid.[17]

From the pot would come the smell of vegetables and salt meat, for each family had its own garden patch of greens and yams, corn and turnips, supplemented by allotments of meat and corn meal. On some plantations molasses and rice were also distributed; at Fort Hill, the specialties were fresh meat and "wheaten" bread, which were given out at the Christmas season.[18]

Christmas does not seem to have meant much to Calhoun. Never a "professing Christian," his letters seldom mention the day at all. Away from his family, he had no heart for celebration. But at home he could not resist the holiday spirit. There must have been moments, then, when he envied his servants' capacity for sheer physical enjoyment. A fiddler mounted on a dining room chair! One man beating a triangle; another drumming on wood! A plank laid across two barrel tops with a man and woman at opposite ends, laughing at each other. The shuffling feet, the twisting bodies, the cries to the pair on the barrels: "Keep it up, John! Go it, Nance! Ole Virginny never tire! Heel and toe, ketch a fire!" "The Negroes had a merry-making in the kitchen, the other evening," Calhoun wrote Clemson in 1842. ". . . They danced in the kitchen and kept it up until after midnight." [19]

[16] Mrs. Basil Hall, quoted in *Three Englishwomen in America*, p. 220.
[17] Cato's reminiscences, Mrs. Francis Calhoun Papers.
[18] *Ibid.*
[19] See Frederick Law Olmsted, *The Cotton Kingdom*, 2 vols. (New York, 1861), II, 73; Charles Lyell, *A Second Visit to the United States*, 2 vols. (New York, 1849), I, 263; also Calhoun to Thomas Clemson, December 30, 1842, Calhoun Papers (Clemson College).

IV

Despite Calhoun's ideals as master, slavery at Fort Hill was more typical than ideal. Fifty years after his death, the old men and women who had been boys and girls in the 1840's could remember their joy when their master came home. Why they were happy, they did not know; all they could say was, "just 'kase he were Marse John C." [20]

Fifty years is a long time, long enough for the overseers and the threat of the whip to be forgotten. Out of necessity these evils did exist at Fort Hill. Calhoun had his full share of overseer trouble. Time and again he was compelled to change overseers; often he would complain that they had so neglected things that he had not the least pleasure in looking over the place upon his return from Washington. "It is so important to me," he told his cousin, James, "to have everything satisfactorily arranged before I leave home." [21]

Running a plantation by remote control bore heavily upon both master and slave. For it was on the plantations where the master was absent, and the overseer had full sway, that many of the worst evils of the system occurred. [22]

Even so high-minded a master as Calhoun was compelled to follow existing practices of the slave system. Punishments were necessarily lighter for a Negro than for a white man. [23] A killing was manslaughter; rape was merely a trespass. A few idealists, such as Jefferson Davis, introduced trial by jury among their Negroes, but the experiment usually failed. Punishments would be too severe. "Africans live better under a monarchy," concluded the *Church Intelligencer*. [24]

Without question Calhoun underestimated the mental potentialities of Negroes. Living completely on an intellectual plane himself, unable even to understand white men on a lower level of

[20] Cato's reminiscences.

[21] Calhoun to James Edward Colbourn, October 7, 1835, Calhoun Papers (Clemson College).

[22] Frances A. Kemble, *Journal of Frances Kemble,* 2 vols. (Philadelphia, 1835), II, 338.

[23] Except, of course, when the crime was committed against a white man!

[24] "A Southern Churchwoman's View of Slavery," in *Church Intelligencer,* November 22, 1860.

thought than his own, he was honestly convinced that physical security was the only "freedom" that would have meaning to a slave. Steeped as he was in the philosophy of Aristotle, he could not have felt otherwise. Had not Aristotle differentiated between the injustice of slavery based on "conquest" and "force of law," and the slavery of men who could obey reason, but were unable to exercise it? [25] "Show me a Negro," Calhoun is reported to have said, "who can parse a Greek verb, or solve a problem in Euclid," and he would grant that he was the human equal of the white man. Strange as this statement is, those who judge the ante-bellum slave by the cultivated Negro leaders of the twentieth century, or even the lovable mammies and house servants of history, can have no concept of the mental and moral condition of the semisavage field hands, often but a generation removed from the Congo.[26] Even the most ardent of abolitionists quailed before the Negro slaves of the lower type: Olmsted once declared: "If these women and their children after them were always . . . to remain of the character and capacity stamped on their faces . . . I don't know that they could be much less miserably situated . . . for their own good and that of the world, than they are." [27]

There was nothing in Calhoun's personal experience to alter his opinion. Once he had freed a slave shoemaker and his family, who, cold and starving in the North, returned and begged to be taken back into bondage. "When I told him that I would do all I could for him, he seized both my hands in his, and expressed his fervent gratitude," [28] Calhoun told the story afterward.

It is interesting to speculate on what must have been Calhoun's opinion of a Northern society that could prate of freedom and send starving Negroes back into slavery. Probably, too, the incident did much to confirm Calhoun's belief that to the slave, as

[25] See *The Carolina Tribute to Calhoun,* p. 234.

[26] There were, of course, as many social and intellectual gradings among the Negroes in their native Africa as among any people, and these differences were reflected in the American slaves and their relative status in the slave society. As with all peoples, the ignorant lower classes were, of course, in the majority; and many of these were sold to traders by the ruling chiefs and aristocracy. Individuals of higher type, captured as prisoners-of-war, were often included in these consignments.

[27] Olmsted, *Journey Through the Slave States,* p. 385.

[28] Bates, *Private Life,* p. 21.

to many white men, material security, not political freedom, was the more important.

V

Not the least of the burdens of slavery lay upon the women of the plantation. Men could sit on their porches and argue the virtues of Aristotle and the leisureliness of the Southern way of life by the hour, but women had work to do. Men could sleep like the dead through the black hours of night, when, at a terrified whisper and a damp touch on her shoulder, a woman roused herself, threw a tippet over her nightgown, and hurried down the long hall to the family dining room and the storerooms beyond, searching for medicine bottles in the flickering candlelight—or for a Bible. What did men know of that endless walk to the quarters at two or three in the morning—with that frightened figure at her side, the ruts and rocks that she had never heeded in the daytime cutting into her slippers, and the trees looming up out of the darkness? And then the long hours of watching—the slow smoke of the fire, the tossing, feverish sleep of a sick child, or a dying man. Men had the responsibilities of slavery, or so they said, but what did they know of the work of it? [29]

Floride knew, and for her the day was long. No blessed early morning sleep when her husband's restless stirring roused her at the first pale light of dawn. While he was off, tramping across the fields for exercise, she would dress, seizing a few precious moments of leisure to last her through the hours. A personal maid might attend her, comb out and arrange her long hair, and lace her stays high under her breasts, perhaps even select her dress, for there were slave women of impeccable taste, existing only to wait hand and foot upon their mistresses.[30] But probably no such paragon existed at Fort Hill. There were too few working "hands" for the daily tasks to be easy for anyone.

The instant breakfast was over, work began. Floride might walk down to the quarters to see that the old woman in charge was not

[29] Frances Trollope, *Domestic Manners of the Americans,* p. 199; Caroline Howard Gilman, *Recollections of a Southern Matron,* p. 54.

[30] *Church Intelligencer,* November 22, 1860.

eating the children's share of food, or might have all the children brought up on the lawn and fed before her own eyes.[31] She might stroll down to the chicken yard and listen to tales of "how twenty-five young turkeys had just tottled backward and died *so;* or the minks and chicken snakes had sucked half the eggs"; or it "looked like there weren't *no* chickens that didn't have just one toe nicked, somehow." The question of the chickens was delicate. Originally each Negro family on the place had its own hens, marked by a nicked toe. The Calhouns' own fowls were supposed to strut through their brief life span with toes intact; but Floride soon noted that fewer and fewer chickens were surviving mutilation and more and more eggs were being brought up for purchase by the family. Her ruling was drastic. Chickens were banished at Fort Hill, except for the exclusive use of the Calhouns themselves.[32]

Inspection over, Floride might settle herself in the family dining room, or on whatever porch was shadiest. There she could consult with Cook to "make sure . . . if the day were hot, that dinner would be light and cooling"; broth, fowl, beefsteak, perhaps, with salad, asparagus, claret, good coffee—and ice on the butter plates. She might be called upon to umpire a quarrel between little Lafayette and Venus, who had each staked claims to the same dusting cloth and halted work to roll their eyes and make faces at each other. Uncle Tom, the coachman, would peer around the corner, requesting the key to the storehouse that he might get four quarts of corn for "him bay horse." A woman would shuffle in to report that one of the hands was "fevered and onrestless"; and Floride herself would again hurry to the storeroom to measure out the inevitable calomel, and then to hold the head and slip the spoon into the sick man's mouth, for no slave would take medicine from the hands of anyone but his master or mistress. Home again, Floride could ring for a girl to bring her pocket handkerchief, but five minutes later, she might be running back down the road to the quarters to attend a field hand who had gashed his foot with a hoe. She knew what she would have to do. First, she would tie an apron over her dress; then, with "no shrinking, no hiding of the

[31] Charles Lyell, *Travels in North America,* 2 vols. (London, 1845), I, 157–184, *passim.*
[32] Slave reminiscences in Mrs. Francis Calhoun Papers.

eyes," she would calmly examine the injured foot, dripping with blood and sweat, superintend a bath, prepare a healing application, and bind it on with her own hands.[33]

Did Northern women spend their entire Christmas season standing in the sewing room, a pair of heavy shears in their hands, cutting out dresses and turbans for their servants, until it seemed that their arms and backs would break in two for weariness? Northern women's joy in having servants to answer their merest whim and call might diminish when they discovered that if they wanted so much as a dress pattern cut, they would first have to tell the slaves how to do it, then show them how, and finally do it themselves.[34]

VI

Figures might show that only one-quarter of the Southern whites belonged to the slaveholding class. Undoubtedly the South, like the West, would have produced an agrarian civilization with or without slavery. Yet year by year the tendrils of "the peculiar institution" were entwining themselves more tightly around the Southern roots.

Certainly slavery helped keep the South agrarian, for it was conceded that to change the Negro over from a farm to an industrial worker would involve a process far slower than the rapid expansion of the industrial system had been elsewhere. Slavery forced the South into its demand for a national political system based on states' rights; for otherwise moralists in a nationalistic, consolidated government would have felt themselves legally responsible for the existence of slavery in South Carolina. Slavery was the Southerner's school for statecraft. It produced men trained to command, a breed that for generations controlled over two-thirds of American elective offices. But the strongest effects of slavery were upon those who bore its burdens, the individual Southerners themselves.

As a Southerner and a leader of Southerners, it would have been impossible for Calhoun to have viewed the Negro problem in the

[33] Caroline Howard Gilman, *Recollections of a Southern Matron* (New York, 1852), pp. 181, 50–51, 54, 293; Mrs. Francis Calhoun Papers, and Lyell, *A Second Visit to the United States,* 2 vols. (New York, 1849), I, 265.

[34] *Church Intelligencer,* November 22, 1860; see also Frances Butler Leigh, *Ten Years on a Georgia Plantation, passim.*

abstract. Even in New England, where he tasted the first theories of abolitionism, he could still have seen the last few Northern slaves walking the streets of New Haven. He knew, if the North forgot, the Northern share in the moral responsibility for the system. Still jingling in Northern pockets were the profits of the slave ships and the proceeds from selling the Negro South, upon discovery that the Northern climate and labor system were unsuited to him.

Slavery was an economic question. Outsiders looked with horror on the "forlorn and decaying" villages of the South, on Negro cabins, which a Northern laborer would "scorn to occupy for an hour." They saw the worn-out fields, the sagging, empty plantation houses, and the "poor, degraded white men and women," with neither farming incentive nor industrial opportunity under the slave system. The mere abolition of slavery, concluded one Northern observer, would "whiten those . . . abandoned fields." [35]

There was nothing in history to prove it. Whether slave or free, there would still have remained in the South a huge illiterate population, which might be productive or parasitical, but in either case would have to be provided for. Slavery could be abolished; the problem of Negro labor would still be there. Britain had abolished slavery in Jamaica, but few of the freedmen had chosen to work. They had squatted and starved. What of the great plantations of Santo Domingo, now sinking back into wilderness and jungle—the planters and their families slaughtered in their beds; the former slaves wandering now in poverty and exile—roaming—plundering? Was this dark fate in the Southern stars? [36]

Most important, could the Southern economy stand the financial loss of its "largest item of capital investment"? Or, as it sometimes seemed to the Southerners, was abolition a deliberate Northern trick to wreck Southern prosperity, to reduce the Southern agricultural system to the status of prostitute for Northern industry; to do, under the semblance of outraged "morality," what Northern exponents of high tariffs and centralized banking had, so far, been legally unable to do otherwise? That this picture was grossly exaggerated, if not entirely false, was unimportant. Not the fact, but the Southerner's belief, was what counted.

[35] John S. C. Abbot, *Slavery, South and North,* pp. 142, 154, 161.
[36] Lyell, *Travels,* I, 22.

To Calhoun slavery was a practical question. The Negro was the Southern laborer; slavery, the device by which a semicivilized, alien population had been fitted into the social and economic pattern. Not the relationships of master and slave, but of black and white, was what the system had been primarily designed to regulate. Had slavery not existed in the ante-bellum South, and had the black race been suddenly thrust upon that region, undoubtedly something like slavery would have been created to cope with it.[37]

Not the slave, but the Negro, was uppermost in Southern thinking. Calhoun had thrashed the question over with John Quincy Adams, in Missouri Compromise days, years before. "What of liberty, justice, the rights of man?" Adams had demanded. Did the Declaration of Independence mean nothing at all?

"The principles you avow are just," Calhoun had said slowly. "But in the South, they are always understood as applying only to the white race."

Adams was silent. Slavery, Calhoun had persisted, "was . . . the best guarantee of equality among the whites, producing an unvarying level among them." Under slavery, no white man could dominate another; or, as he pointed out years afterward, "with us, the two great divisions of society are not the rich and the poor, but the black and the white."

Adams might have grunted with disgust. Southerners, he charged, gloried in their indolence, were proud of their masterful dominance.

Calhoun had protested. Slaveholders were not lazy. "I have often held the plough, myself, and so did my father." Mechanical and manufacturing labor was not "degrading." But if he were to hire a white servant in South Carolina, his reputation would be "irretrievably ruined." [38]

For slavery was most of all a social question. What the system actually meant in terms of mores, taboos, and fears, no outsider could ever understand. It was the Negro who set the pattern for Southern living and thinking. If, economically, the question was

[37] Allan Nevins and Henry Steele Commager, *History of the United States,* pp. 214–215.

[38] See Charles Francis Adams, ed., *Memoirs of John Quincy Adams,* 12 vols. (Philadelphia, 1874–1877), IV, 530–531; V, 5–11, 13.

practically unsolvable, socially, it was even more so. For the abolitionists it was enough to blame Southern backwardness on slavery,
to attribute the Southerner's overwrought nerves to the fear of
insurrection and retribution, perhaps even to the guilty conscience
that men who held other men in bondage should have. But a hundred years later, the South was just beginning to emerge from its
backward, poverty-stricken condition as "the nation's number one
economic problem." It was eighty years after the abolition of slavery
that David Cohn, one of the most discriminating of Southern thinkers, would describe the sense of "strain" in the Southern air, "of a
delicately poised equilibrium; of forces held in leash. Here men
toss uneasily at night and awake fatigued in the morning. . . . To
apply patent remedies is to play . . . with explosives." [39]

The most ardent Southern admirers could not deny it. The most
calloused of casual observers could not escape it. What virtually
every Southern woman admitted, every Southern man knew.[40] There
was no peace, no safety in the Southern states. And there was no
hope for escape.

In the white men of the South a common danger had wrought
a common understanding. Taut nerves ran beneath their languid
indolence of pose and gesture. They were quiet men, those farmers
and planters who lounged through long, hot afternoons on the
porches of plantation houses like Fort Hill. Drawling, easy-going,
disarmingly gentle, they might appear to visitors like Charles Lyell
or Captain Marryat, relaxed under the spell of their hosts' charm.
But someone would unwittingly utter a few words, and discover, to
his dismay, that on a subject, which once could be discussed freely
in the South, not a word could now be said. Men, who but a moment
before were urging "indulgence to their slaves," flared up in a
suddenly "savage spirit," speaking of abolitionists in "precisely the
same tone . . . as beasts of prey." Calhoun's Congressional colleague—short, plump, Northern-born Robert Preston, his red wig
askew—would roar that if any abolitionist dared set foot on *his*
plantation, he would "hang him . . . notwithstanding all the interference of all the governments of the earth." Another soft-spoken

[39] David Cohn, "How the South Feels," *The Atlantic Monthly,* January
1944, pp. 47–51.
[40] Kemble, *Journal,* II, 393.

cotton planter, calmly and quietly, but unflinchingly, would announce that should any abolitionist visit his plantation, "I have
left the strictest orders with my overseer to hang him on the spot." [41]

"Fiercely accessory" was the poor white, tobacco-chewing, sweat-
stained, standing on the porch of Fort Hill, confident that his white
skin alone assured him an invitation to dinner. Fear was the unin-
vited guest at his own dinner table; he would hide in the pigpen at
the rumor of an insurrection, and in a back corner of his cabin lay
bags packed for the quickest of getaways if the "Niggers rose." [42]

Fear, too, haunted the clear-eyed yeoman hill farmer, who
worked in the field beside his one or two black men. "I reckon the
majority would be right glad if we could get rid of the Negroes"
was his comment. "But"—and his words were fraught with meaning
—"it wouldn't never do to free 'em and leave 'em here." [43]

Free them! The very idea was enough to enrage the small planter,
the middle-class lawyer, teacher, or doctor, whose ideals, both
economic and social, were closest to those of the great planters.
And as the landed planter might add, it cost nothing to attack slavery, but he could not listen quietly when outside attacks put in
danger "everything we hold dear in the world."

Calhoun's sentiments were similar. "We are surrounded by in-
visible dangers, against which nothing can protect us, but our foresight and energy." The difficulty was in "the diversity of the races.
So strongly drawn is the line between the two . . . and so
strengthened by the form of habit and education, that . . . no
power on earth can overcome the difficulty." [44] And a hundred
years later Cohn would write of "a society kept going by unwritten
and unwritable laws . . . taboos, and conventions. . . . The
Southerner's whole society and way of life is conditioned by the
. . . Negro. If there has never been a free Negro in the South, it
is also true that there has never been a free white . . . the South-

[41] Frederick Marryat, *Diary in America,* p. 193; Lyell, *Travels,* I, 157–
184; A. C. Cole, "The Whig Party in the South," *The Annual Report of
the American Historical Association* (Washington, 1913), and Francis
Grund, *Aristocracy in America,* 2 vols. (London, 1839), I, 30.

[42] Olmsted, *Cotton Kingdom,* II, 111.

[43] *Ibid.,* p. 110.

[44] Calhoun quoted in Hermann von Holst, *John C. Calhoun* (Boston,
1882), p. 141.

erner . . . functions in an environment of which he is a prisoner
. . ." He added: "If segregation were broken down by fiat . . .
I have no doubt that every Southern white man would spring to
arms and the country would be swept by war." [45]

There were sensitive men who writhed under sternness and the
rule of fear, who felt themselves degraded by the degradation of
the Negroes. When administering punishment, they were tortured
by the thought that "I am violating the natural rights of a being
who is as much entitled to the enjoyment of liberty as myself." [46]
Torn by ethical conflict, they were forced to repress their better
natures. Continually they mourned the brutalizing effects of the
system upon their children. They knew that it was among the more
ignorant white classes where "coarse . . . brutal authority" furnished the "disgusting" picture of pretty girls laughing as a cow-
hide whip flicked across the "nasty mouth" of a suffering slave
child, where "power over the males and females" was "most de-
moralizing." [47] But year by year more of the poorer classes were
pulling their way into the slaveholding hierarchy.

The most well-meaning of men were helpless. The more they
hated their responsibilities, the more heavily they weighed upon
them. "We are the slaves, not the blacks," [48] they mourned. Not
for them the easy way of the few, who solved their problem by
turning their Negroes "free" to starve or to beg from their neighbors. They would disdain the spirit of the age, the "judgment of the
world," if necessary, rather than cast the dependent race whom
they were "bound to protect" upon the uncertain mercies of Northern idealism.

Financially the load was staggering. There were the "cotton
snobs" of the Delta, so drowned in acres and slaves that they had
no interest in the sliding scale of their bank accounts. But no man
could fail to read the tragedy of Virginia in the worn-out tobacco
lands, exhausted by two hundred years of crop production for the

[45] Cohn, "How the South Feels," *Atlantic Monthly,* January 1944, pp.
47–51.
[46] William Garnett, July 12, 1805, Papers of Thomas Ruffin, *North
Carolina Historical Commission Publications,* I, 80.
[47] The reference for this footnote is omitted in the original [ed.].
[48] Hall, *Travels,* II, 260.

maintenance of slaves. Slaves had become a crushing burden on the poverty-stricken Virginia masters, who had to feed and maintain them without any work to give them.[49]

All knew that the slave system, as such, gave "the least possible return for the greatest possible expense." In hard times the Northern employer could lay off his hands to shift for themselves; the slaves had "complete insurance against unemployment," and had to be fed and clothed. A man so unlucky as to own a drunkard or a thief was forbidden by law to sell or to free him. He was, however, guaranteed the duty of feeding and clothing him.

With no possibility of discharge, with little hope of advancement, it was to the Negroes' interest "to work as little as they can." Two blacks only do the work of one white, a planter told Charles Lyell. Half the South was employed in watching the other half. Calhoun himself might have seen what the abolitionist Olmsted described— an entire field of women halting work when the overseer had passed, only lowering their hoes when he turned to ride toward them again.[50]

Yet, save for a scattering of yeoman farmers in the hill counties where a black face was never seen, the most difficult of all tasks would have been to convince the average Southerner of the desirability of emancipation. Fear—economic, social, and political—had done its work. Middle- and upper-class planters, and many of the yeomen, were content with the system; and to the arguments of the abolitionists, not even the poor whites gave "a murmur of response." Hinton Helper could marshal proofs that the system was enslaving planter and poor white alike, but not even he could insure the farmer from the competition of free, and cheap, black labor.

Southern whites had been well indoctrinated with the less savory side of Northern industrialism. "A very slight modification of the arguments used against the institutions . . . of the South . . ."

---

[49] Marryat, *Diary,* p. 190; Hall, *Travels,* II, 218.

[50] William Stickney, ed., *Autobiography of Amos Kendall* (Boston, 1872), p. 502; W. H. Sparks, *Old Times in Georgia,* p. 34; Marryat, *Diary,* p. 194; Lyell, *A Second Visit to the United States,* I, 72; Frederick Law Olmsted, *A Journey in the Seaboard Slave States* (New York, 1904), p. 385.

Calhoun had said, "would be . . . equally effectual against the Institutions of the North." [51] Southern poor whites saw no hope in the grinding wheels of industrialism. Temporarily industry might open new jobs, but as more machines took the place of men, both in the factory and on the farm, the day would come when the emancipated Negro and the white workingman would grapple for the few jobs left to the Southerners. Labor-saving machines seemed well named; would they not save employers the necessity of hiring labor? Hence, it was to the interests of the small farmers— and these points were stressed again and again by their leaders—to cooperate with the planter in keeping the Negro out of economic competition, and in preventing industrialism from crushing out agriculture. The pernicious competition of the slave-operated plantations against the small independent farmers was less obvious.

More, even, than economic arguments, the abolitionists' own zeal ripped the problem right out of practical politics. As late as 1828, there were three hundred abolitionist societies *south* of the Mason-Dixon line. As late as 1831, the whole slave question could be openly debated in the Virginia legislature.

It is undoubtedly true that Southerners talked about emancipating far more than they emancipated. Yet so eminent an historian as Albert J. Beveridge has argued that, had it not been for the anger and fear aroused by the abolitionist onslaught, "it is not altogether impossible that there would have been no war, and that slavery would in time have given way to the pressure of economic forces." Allan Nevins, conceding that abolition, gradual or otherwise, was impossible in the Deep South, pronounces it "unquestionably true that the abolitionist madness helped kill all chances of gradual emancipation in the border states of Maryland and Kentucky." In Fredericksburg, Virginia, an active movement for gradual emancipation was under way when the abolitionists stepped in. The ruin was complete. Less than a decade afterward, not a single emancipation society remained south of the Mason-Dixon border. [52]

The abolitionists can, at least, be credited with skill in defeating their own purposes. Not for them the tedious processes of "gradual

[51] *Freedom's Defense* (pamphlet), Worcester Antiquarian Society.
[52] Albert J. Beveridge, *Abraham Lincoln* (Standard Library Edition), II, 19; Allan Nevins, *Ordeal of the Union*, I, 148–149.

emancipation." They would not see the nation's honor stained by truckling to slaveholders through federal reimbursement of the planters for the losses abolition would cause them. To them it mattered not that abolition without compensation would wreck the entire Southern economy and leave the planters destitute. To them the sin of slavery was all that mattered.

It is essential, of course, to keep a sense of proportion in judging both abolitionist and slaveholder. The abolitionists' zeal was, in most cases, a sincere and high-minded moral force. Yet it is easy to understand the attitude of those who were daily told that their financial security, if not their very lives, depended on the maintenance of a system which the individuals of that period found already in effect. Human nature being what it is, and the problem as complex as it was, the Southern attitude toward abolitionists with their inexpensive moral zeal can be readily understood.

"Emancipation, itself, would not satisfy these fanatics," declared Calhoun. "That gained, the next step would be to raise the Negroes to a social and political equality with the whites." [53] The abolitionists dared not deny his words. Early as 1831, incendiary pamphlets were in circulation through the Southern states, demanding the complete political equality of men, many but a generation out of Africa. Openly hot-tongued zealots were calling upon four million slaves to revolt and take over the South for themselves.

Southerners had had more than one grim foretaste of what insurrection might mean. Fresh in memory was "bloody Monday," August 22, 1831, when Nat Turner and his followers ran through a Virginia county, leaving a trail of fifty-five shot and murdered, "but without plunder or outrage," [54] *The Liberator* commented. And at Natchez the mass-murder of Santo Domingo had been escaped only by the white woman who overheard a Negro telling a nurse-girl to murder the child in her charge. Swiftly the planters organized. Negroes and abolitionists alike were rounded up, strapped to tables, and lashed with blacksnake whips until the blood ran inches deep upon the floor. A gigantic plot for the murder of every white man in the Natchez district and the enslavement of their women was uncovered. Never did the planters breathe easily again.

[53] Crallé, *Works,* II, 623; VI, "The Southern Address," 285–313.
[54] See issues of *The Liberator,* August 1831.

Abolitionists could attribute Southern tension to a sense of guilt in enslaving the Negro. However true this may be, Southern recalcitrance was at least, in part, the work of the abolitionists themselves. To a world arrayed against the Southern system, no weakness could be admitted, no word of concession said.

VII

But there were moments when the whole truth was spoken; and men like those who gathered with Calhoun at Fort Hill strove vainly to find a way through the mesh in which they had entangled themselves. With "one opinion for Congress, and another for their private table," they discussed with calm reasoning the evils "which they could not admit in public." [55]

Although a man known to abuse his slaves was punished by law and scorned by his neighbors, all knew of the far-distant plantations in the West and Deep South, which the law and public opinion could not reach. There, in a murky, fever-laden heat, where white men's nerves and tempers were drawn to the breaking point, and black men crouched all day in ankle-deep mud, the rawhide coiling over their backs, slavery existed "in all its horrors." Dark stories seeped in from those swamps, of masters, intemperate, reckless, indulging their own passions on the helpless creatures over whom they held power of life and death; of slaves fed on cotton seed or hung up by their thumbs; of blood-stained whips as much in use as spurs on a horse. A sadistic master, crazed by heat and the power of his authority, could pull out his Negroes' teeth or cut off their hands. [56]

Generally recognized, except in the North itself, was the fact that Northern newcomers were responsible for many of the cruelties which made slavery notorious in the eyes of the civilized world. For Northerners lacked the understanding of the Negroes' needs and weaknesses as individuals. Northerners looked upon the South as a fabulous empire of landed estates with hundreds of acres and

[55] Marryat, *Diary*, p. 194.
[56] Abbott, *Slavery*, p. 74; Olmsted, *Seaboard Slave States*, p. 385; Harriet Martineau, *Slavery in America*, p. 29; Marryat, *Diary*, pp. 190, 193, 195; and Lyell, *A Second Visit*, I, 181–182.

thousands of retainers; Southerners knew that the majority of slave-holders owned but a single Negro family, alongside of whom their owners worked the fields. Calhoun had this heritage. He knew that the Negroes' spirit could be broken by lack of sympathy or over-work; and furthermore, that in the fierce heat of the Southern sun, neither white nor black could expend the energy of a worker in the North. Northern planters, frequently striving for "a rapid for-tune," made no allowances. They drove the Negroes as they would themselves, blamed their failure on the system of slavery, deserted their responsibilities, and returned North to "become very loud-mouthed abolitionists." [57]

Calhoun's own son-in-law, Pennsylvania-born, gave up planting in disgust, with the assertion that "I can do better for my family and myself . . . than . . . spending my life on a plantation." Calhoun, however, was shocked by Clemson's proposals to rent out his Negroes at a profit. Sternly Calhoun reminded him that with rented Negroes it would not be to the interest of the planter "to . . . take good care of them. . . . The object of him who hires," Calhoun sternly reminded Clemson, "is generally to make the most he can out of them, without regard to their comfort or health, and usually to the utter neglect of the children and the sick." Rather than have them thus exploited, if Clemson could not find good masters for them, Calhoun would buy them himself, although to do so would be "financially disastrous" [58] for him.

And always in the background was the "disgusting topic" which lay like a deadweight on the conscience of every thoughtful South-erner—the evil of miscegenation. That it existed was freely ad-mitted; even an abolitionist account of these conditions was ac-knowledged to be "full of truth." Yet no abolitionist so scourged the evil as did the Southerners themselves. No abolitionist could understand the feelings of fathers who, whatever their own youthful follies, lived in constant fear of their sons' promiscuous intercourse with Negro women.[59]

Actually the evil was not as widespread as was claimed. For where

[57] *Church Intelligencer*, November 22, 1860.

[58] Calhoun to Thomas Clemson, September 1846, Calhoun Papers (Clem-son College).

[59] Marryat, *Diary,* pp. 190–191; Thomas Dew, *Pro-Slavery Argument,* pp. 228–229.

the sins were confessed in the color of the progeny, British visitors
were astounded to find that the "mixed offspring" in the Southern
states of ante-bellum days was "not more than two and a half per
cent of the whole population," offering a comparison by no means
favorable to their free country.[60]

To an unhardened observer the slave pen, with its "likely parcel"
of Negroes for sale, on the very spot where horses and cattle had
been auctioned off the day before, seemed the most horrible aspect
of slavery. Yet the "calloused indifference" of many slaves themselves, "very merry, talking and laughing" as they waited to be sold;
and the seeming lack of "offended modesty" was equally repellent.[61]
The deepest tragedy of slavery, however, the separation of husband
from wife, of mothers from their children, happened less often than
Northern visitors believed. Public opinion condemned it. Families
were sold in lots "like books and chairs," but few would buy a
broken-hearted mother without her children. Fathers, however,
were sometimes sold from their families, the husbands and wives
then being free to take other mates.[62]

VIII

Granting the desirability of emancipation, argued the Southerner,
what was to be done with the Negro after he was free? "Singular is
the contempt . . . in which the free blacks are held in . . . free
. . . America," observed Captain Marryat in 1829. Color alone,
the Captain had discovered, made the Negro "a degraded being" in
the land of "liberty, equality, and the rights of man." In the slave
states, the Britisher had "frequently seen a lady in a public con-
veyance with her negress sitting by her," and no "objection . . .
raised . . . but in the free states a man of colour is not admitted
into a stage coach." Segregation in Northern theaters and churches,
Marryat noted, was "universally observed." [63]

As early as 1820, in the very capital of "free" America, Congress had restricted suffrage to white persons. "The crime of a dark

[60] Lyell, *A Second Visit*, I, 271–272.

[61] James Sparks, *Old Times in Georgia*, p. 111.

[62] Lyell, *A Second Visit*, I, 209–210; Mrs. Basil Hall, *The Aristocratic
Journey*, quoted in *Three Englishwomen in America*, p. 210.

[63] Marryat, *Diary*, p. 82.

complexion," declared William Jay, "has been punished by debarring its possessor from all approach to the ballot box." [64] In Philadelphia, a wealthy Negro protested and appealed, but was found to be only white enough to pay his taxes.[65]

Harshest of all were the Northern restrictions against education. One-third of the Southern states had laws prohibiting the Negroes from learning to read, but abolitionists were blissfully indifferent to the fact that in the free states most "academies and colleges" were barred to the Negro, and that colored children were "very generally" excluded from public schools, in deference to the "prejudice of leaders and parents." Only abroad could wealthy young Negroes receive higher education. Connecticut had its Black Act, prohibiting all instruction of colored children *from other states*. In New Hampshire enraged citizens of Canaan passed resolutions of "abhorrence" at the establishment of a subscription school with twenty-eight white and fourteen Negro students, voting that the building be ripped from its foundations.[66]

Even if the freed Negroes were willing to work for wages, what chance would they have with the "protection afforded by their present monopoly of labor withdrawn," and thrown into open competition with the poverty-stricken whites? When a Negro laborer was hired in the North, his fellow workers struck. What would freedom offer the Southern Negro? History would offer the answers.

Actually the Negro of talent sometimes had more opportunity for self-realization in the slave states than in the free. Southerners could point out that exceptional Negroes sometimes made "large fortunes in trade." Hired out as cabinet-makers, builders, and mechanics, they paid a part of their wages to their masters and still were able to save for themselves. In Memphis, Thomas Lowe Nichols, a Connecticut physician, was astounded to find a slave entrusted with the sole care of a $75,000 jewelry store. He was free to escape at any time, and in a moment's theft could have been rich for life, but had no desire to break trust. In New Orleans, Dr. Nichols found another slave the head clerk of a leading book-

---

[64] *Ibid.*, p. 83; also William Jay, *Miscellaneous Writings on Slavery*, pp. 371–394, *passim*.

[65] Marryat, *Diary*, p. 83.

[66] Jay, *Miscellaneous Writings*, pp. 371–394, *passim*.

store, waiting upon "the ladies" with the courtesy of a Creole courtier. He wore gold studs and a diamond ring; on Sundays he made his "promenade" on the shady side of Canal Street, with a young slave woman in a gown of costly changeable silk, a blue bonnet and a pink parasol. He had his seat at the Opera, too, in a section especially reserved for "ladies and gentlemen of color," where no common white trash were permitted to intrude.

Most astounding, a slave was the "head clerk and confidential business man" of one of the largest cotton houses in New Orleans. In New York under freedom, he might have been a whitewasher or a barber, or perhaps have run an oyster-cellar; under slavery, he had his own home, a wife, a family, and all the material comforts he could desire. He could have bought his freedom in an instant, but had no desire to do so.[67] Exceptional as these instances undoubtedly were, they were used by the Southerners to prove that, both economically and socially, even a slave might rise under American democracy.

Northern visitors, however, frequently tempered their moral indignation with telling observations. One was surprised at the "friendly relations" between the blacks and whites of the South, and the interest and kindliness shown by an entire trainload of white passengers toward a group of Negro railroad workers, en route home to their families for Christmas. "I constantly see . . . genuine sympathy with the colored race, such as I rarely see at the North," abolitionist John Abbott was compelled to admit. And he added what Dr. Nichols stood vigorously ready to confirm: "The slaves are much better off than the laboring classes at the North . . . the poor ones." [68]

It is true, of course, that "compulsion to labor" under any system is a violation of human freedom. But what was freedom? asked the defenders of the South. What was slavery? Freedom held a high meaning to Calhoun. To him it meant, not just the absence of tyranny, but the condition which would allow each human being to develop to the highest ends of his nature. And of all varieties of freedom, in the opinion of Calhoun, political freedom was the high-

[67] Thomas L. Nichols, *Forty Years of American Life*, II, 278–280; see also Lyell, *A Second Visit*, II ,71.
[68] Abbott, *Slavery*, pp. 75, 78, 85–86.

est—and the most rare. It was the reward for centuries of striving and growth and unceasing battle against oppression; what would be its fate in the hands of those unused to exercising it? The white man's heritage of liberty stretched back ten hundred years; for untold centuries countless Negroes were slaves in their native Africa.[69] Two races, almost equal in numbers, physically, culturally, and politically at variance, faced each other. Would the white Southerner dare entrust his freedom to the black? He did not dare, and all history, argued Calhoun, was on his side. The safety of the whole, Aristotle had warned, depends upon "the predominance of the superior parts." Calhoun conceded that once the slave had reached a state of moral and intellectual elevation, it would be to the master's interest "to raise him" to the level of political equality, for he would then "be destitute of all power" to "destroy liberty." Henry Clay, too, spoke for the whole South. "I prefer the liberty of my own race," he said. "The liberty of the descendants of Africa is incompatible with the safety and liberty of the European descendants. Their slavery forms an exception . . . from stern necessity, to the general liberty." [70]

Calhoun would have scorned to deny that Southern servitude was slavery. But with equal vehemence, and not without reason, he condemned the "vicious fallacy" of confusing wage labor with free labor. "I like to attend to things as they are, and not the names by which they are called," he said. Carlyle had drawn the distinction. "Free labor means work or starve. Slave labor means work or be flogged." [71]

Even more bitter was the British Sarah M. Maury, representative

[69] The Southern insistence on the "superiority" of the white race was not entirely rationalization to justify the slave system; but was based on an utter ignorance of the Negro in his native Africa. It was not the truth which influenced Southern thinking; but what at that period was thought and reported to be the truth. Twentieth-century research has uncovered African history and culture which was utterly unknown to Calhoun and his time, and which might have made a vast difference in the Southerner's concept of the slave's intellectual potentialities.

[70] Robert Henry, quoted in *The Carolina Tribute to Calhoun*, pp. 234–235; also Henry Clay, Speech on "The Abolition Petitions," February 7, 1839, in *Life and Speeches of Henry Clay*, II, 418.

[71] Crallé, *Works*, IV, 517; William E. Dodd, *The Cotton Kingdom* (New Haven, 1919), p. 63; Vernon L. Parrington, *The Romantic Revolution in America* (New York, 1927–1930), p. 100.

of a race of "freemen," whose women, stripped to the waist, crawled through the coal mines, butting the wains with their balding heads; whose children, "harnessed like brutes . . . tugged and strained in the bowels of the earth" for sixteen or seventeen hours at a time, for months "never even seeing the light of the sun." Said Mrs. Maury: "The sole advantage possessed by the white Slaves of Europe . . . is that they have permission . . . to change each naked, hungry and intolerable bondage for a worse . . . this the white man must call liberty." [72]

Calhoun did not call it so. Liberty held higher meanings for him than freedom for men of superior capacity to exploit the basic inequalities of their fellow men. Was it not more just legally to acknowledge inequalities and to protect men from the selfishness of their fellows? Yes, argued Calhoun, the Northern wage slave was free, free to come South to work in the pestilential swamps at the dangerous tasks at which the life of no valuable slave could be risked;[73] free to hold a job so long as he would vote for the political choice of his employers; free to work fourteen hours a day at seven dollars a week until his health gave way.[74] His earnings were taxed to provide for the paupers and jail-loungers whose "freedom" permitted them the luxury of not choosing to work; but this burden did not weigh upon the Southern slave. "Slavery makes all work and it ensures homes, food, and clothing for all. It permits no idleness, and it provides for sickness, infancy, and old age." [75] Both systems, he insisted, rested on the principle of labor exploitation, but the South had no ugly labor scrap heap; the master was compelled by law to mortgage his acres, if necessary, to provide adequately for old and sick slaves. The master was responsible to society for the welfare of his slaves; no one was responsible for the freeman but himself.

The paradox was, of course, that slavery for the Negro restricted the freedoms of the whites. Freedom could not live anywhere in a slave society. Free speech, for example, was silent on one subject, slavery, in accordance with one of the strangest gentlemen's agree-

---

[72] Maury, *Statesmen of America*, p. 365.
[73] Lyell, *A Second Visit*, I, 82.
[74] *Ibid.*, p. 241.
[75] William J. Grayson, *The Hireling and the Slave*, preface, vii, viii.

ments in all history. Even of Jefferson's Virginia with its liberal, humanistic "free trade" in ideas, Thomas Ritchie could write in 1832 that there had been a "silence of fifty years." [76]

Freedom of the press remained—on the books. A few valiant, fiery, individualistic editors like the fighting Quaker, William Swain, of the Greensborough *Patriot,* and a sprinkling in Kentucky, Tennessee, and Western Virginia, dared denounce slavery to the end, and went unscathed. These were the exceptions. Others, less fortunate, suffered boycotts, cancellation of subscriptions, were even shot down in duels! By 1845 the Richmond *Whig* was openly praising the mob destruction of an abolitionist paper in Lexington, Kentucky; although never in the South were there such crimes against the press as the lynching of Lovejoy in Illinois.

"Letters to the editor" urging abolition of slavery were returned as "too strong for the times." Yet, despite the pressures of wealth and vested interests and the fears of the poor whites, most of the editors "sincerely agreed with their readers on the slavery question." The "lives of the free Negroes in Southern communities" they saw as a demonstration of their "unfitness for freedom."

In Jefferson's time there had been a tolerance toward antislavery doctrines. Virtually every great Virginian of the eighteenth century was on record against slavery. At twenty-one, Henry Clay had been openly urging gradual emancipation on the street corners of Lexington, Kentucky. The Whig planters then, and even later, maintained a tolerance on the question at sharp odds with the newly rich planters of the Democratic persuasion. And in the early years, it was these liberal aristocrats "whom the common people followed." [77]

IX

Restrictions on suffrage were declining rapidly. By the half-century mark, 47 per cent of the white males voted in the lower South and 66 per cent in the upper; figures comparable to those of 47 per cent in Massachusetts, 67 per cent in Pennsylvania, and 62 per cent in

[76] Richmond *Enquirier,* January 19, 1832.
[77] Clement Eaton, *Freedom of Thought in the Old South,* pp. 174–175; 162, 21, 111.

New York. And far from being mere planting aristocrats, the "great majority" of Southerners were "hard-working farmers . . . provincial and conservative, but hardly more so than the people of New England or Pennsylvania." [78]

Not the aristocratic planting society, but the rise of the common man spelled the end of tolerance on the slave question in the South. Jacksonian democracy, with its chants of freedom for the masses, only clamped the Negro the more tightly in his bondage. With the extension of the franchise came contraction of thought. The new-comers had risen too rapidly to assume the patina of a mature culture. They were too closely allied to the lower classes, who, cowering in hatred and in fear, were "pro-slavery almost to a man." And as slavery was the economic foundation of the planter life to which they aspired, they countered any threat to the institution which symbolized their goal. [79]

What was the tyranny of slavery? Out in Illinois, a young Whig named Abraham Lincoln defined the tyrannical principle of the institution as "You work and earn bread, and I'll eat it." [80] What he did not say was that the principle was the same, whether applied to the agrarian capitalism of the South or the industrial capitalism of the North; and that the fact, not the principle, would conquer the world of the present and the future.

Others were more perceptive. From the New York slums rose the great rabble-rouser, Mike Walsh, with his brassy face and out-thrust jaw, youthful, bitter, rebellious. Of birthplace uncertain, of parentage unknown, without money, without education, Walsh was a pioneer of the slums, as was Jackson of the wilderness. For the first time Walsh and his "Bowery b'hoys," were to sound the raucous voice of the city streets in American politics.

It was Walsh's brawling newssheet, *The Subterranean,* which became the first political organ of American labor; and to the horror of the abolitionist idealists, a fervid supporter of the Presidential aspirations of John C. Calhoun. Incongruous the alliance of Southern planters and city slum-dwellers might seem to outside

[78] *Ibid.,* p. 63.

[79] J. D. B. De Bow, *The Interest in Slavery of the Southern Non-Slaveholder,* p. 10.

[80] Quoted in Carl Sandburg, *Abraham Lincoln: The Prairie Years* (Blue Ribbon Books, New York, 1926), p. 403.

observers, but not to the leaders of the two groups. If Walsh, like Calhoun, could declare that the salvation of labor depended upon the preservation of slavery, it was because he and Calhoun each realized that the slaveholding planters formed the last barrier against the protective tariff with its ominous meanings for agrarian and laboring groups alike.

"Demagogues tell you that you are freemen. They lie; you are slaves," [81] was the shout of Walsh to his oppressed followers. No man could be free who was dependent only upon his own labor. The only difference between the workman and the Negro slave of the South was "that . . . one . . . has to beg for the privilege of becoming a slave. . . . The one is the slave of an individual; the other . . . of an inexorable class." Could the abolitionists produce "one single solitary degradation" inflicted on the slave that the Northern laborer did not suffer under "freedom"? Men moralized over the sufferings of the poor Negroes in the South; what of thirteen hundred men in New York City deprived of their liberty, only because they were poor? [82]

Equally disturbing were the caustic truths of the impassioned young preacher-editor, Orestes Brownson of the New York Workingman's Party. Six feet two inches tall and slender, his masses of dark hair thrown back from his face, Brownson was one of the most idealistic of the idealists, one of the most intellectual of the intelligentsia. He had been a Baptist preacher, an admitted agnostic, a dogmatic Unitarian. He had been a supporter of Andrew Jackson, fighting to fit the "economic equality" of the Jackson program to the political liberties of the Jeffersonians. He was a slashing stump speaker, drawing roars from a crowd at every pause for breath; and his writings were acclaimed by Harriet Martineau as nearer "the principles of exact justice" than anything she had ever seen. Now in the Boston *Quarterly Review* Brownson lashed out against the hypocrisy of those who would draw distinctions between the two American capitalistic systems of labor. "Free labor," he asserted, "deprived the workingman of the proceeds of labor most efficiently." Wages were for "tender consciences . . . who would retain the slave system without the expense, trouble and odium of

[81] *The Subterranean,* September 13, 1845.
[82] *Congressional Globe,* 33d Congress, 1st Session, p. 1224.

being slaveholders. . . . If there must always be a laboring population . . . we regard the slave system as decidedly preferable." [83]

Appeals such as this struck terror to the hearts of Northern business leaders. Actually Calhoun was unable to enlist any serious
number of Northern liberals and Northern laborers in his cause;
but the psychological effect, just like the psychological effect of the
abolitionists in the South, was what counted. Threats of abolitionism, Calhoun's followers could match with threats of labor unionism; "chattel slavery" was pitted against "wage slavery." If the
North was a threat to the South, so did the South present a threat
to the North.

It was not to be borne. Slavery, a cheap, competitive laboring
economy, could be tolerated only so long as it functioned under
the kind of tariff and banking legislation that would profit big business. And it was Calhoun, with "a prescience grown by now almost
uncanny," [84] who saw from the first that slavery alone could furnish
the issue which would unite the idealistic antislavery forces of the
North with the manufacturing interests in a "moral" crusade against
the Southern economy.

He had not long to wait.

X

On New Year's Day in 1831 a "pale, delicate . . . over-tasked
looking man" sat down at a pine desk in a dingy room in Boston
where ink had splattered the tiny windows, while from a corner a
printing press roared and shook unceasingly, to read his own words,
starkly black on the first page of the first issue of *The Liberator*.
"Let Southern oppressors tremble—let all enemies of the perse-
cuted blacks tremble. . . . I will be harsh as truth, and as uncompromising as justice. . . . I am in earnest . . . I will not equivo-
cate . . . I will not excuse . . . I will not retreat a single inch
. . . AND I WILL BE HEARD." On the seventeenth, THE PICTURE
appeared, Garrison's concept of a slave auction, incorporating in
one searing message all the evils of the years: the sign, "Slaves,
horses, and other cattle to be sold at 12"; the weeping mother, a

---

[83] Orestes Brownson in Boston *Quarterly Review*, July 1840.
[84] Christopher Hollis, *The American Heresy*, p. 110.

buyer "examining her as a butcher would an ox"; the cluster of dapper young men, carefully eyeing their prospective female purchases.[85]

Men had laughed at William Lloyd Garrison. Calhoun did not laugh. He had seen it all as early as 1819, when he had turned, startled, at John Quincy Adams's dogmatic assertion that "If the Union must be dissolved, slavery is the question upon which it ought to break." Adams was weary of a Union with slaveholders. Let the North separate from the South, he had suggested; have "a new Union . . . unpolluted with slavery . . . rallying the other States by . . . universal emancipation." [86]

Calhoun had agreed with Adams that emancipation was a "great objective," but that it could only come at terrible cost, almost a revolution. And he could not and would not face the thought of disunion "with all its horrors." [87] The abolitionist agitation, he saw, would divide the sections with hatred, strike at the heart of the Union both from the North and the South. If the Union were to be saved, he knew, the agitation must be halted—halted by the insistence and the unity of the slaveholders.

So out of his own knowledge and his own forebodings, Calhoun bid the South to "look to her defenses." To save the values of the Southern way of life within the Union was the standard he raised; and to save these values, the Southern people must unite within a single party and on a single issue. A unit economically, the South was divided politically and socially, with the majority of its great planters members of the Whig Party, and the masses still followers of Jefferson and Jackson.

Slavery was not the issue Calhoun would have chosen. The tariff would have united both the South and the West, but Jackson and nullification had confused the people on that question. Slavery would be the hardest of all issues to defend, but it was the one the North had chosen.

Only through states' rights, through complete autonomy, could

[85] *The Liberator,* January 1 and January 17, 1831.

[86] Oddly enough, twenty-three years later, John Quincy Adams presented to the Senate a petition signed by the citizens of Haverhill, Massachusetts, "for the adoption of measures peaceably to dissolve the Union." (See Carl Sandburg, *Abraham Lincoln: The Prairie Years,* p. 183.)

[87] John Quincy Adams, *Diary,* IV, 530–531.

the South hope to preserve its civilization. Once it allowed a single one of its institutions to be subverted by pressure from the outside, the ground had been surrendered. It was not so much abolition to which Calhoun objected as imposed abolition. Slavery was only a symbol, the most inflammatory of symbols, to be sure, but one upon which the whole South could stand united.

Calhoun well knew that the very name of slavery affronted the latent idealism of humanitarians, not only in the North, but in the world at large. In the face of such opposition, even an orthodox religious defense, such as was summarized by the Reverend John C. Coit, Presbyterian clergyman and friend of Calhoun's, was not enough. The Cheraw pastor cited chapter and verse. There was no moral slavery, he contended. Before God, Negroes' souls were equal with whites'. That "slavery is against the spirit" of Christianity, Thomas R. Dew might insist, but the clergy of South Carolina would not concede even this. How, Coit asked, "could men dare follow, not the letter but the spirit? Who was to know the spirit but through God's word?" [88]

Calhoun went beyond the Bible for his defenses. Slavery could no longer be termed a necessary evil, because the very admission of evil was a concession of justice in the Northern point of view. But to defend slavery unitedly, without giving hope for its ultimate extinction, of course involved a revolution in Southern thinking. To bring about this revolution was the task of Calhoun's mature years. He was incredibly successful. If slavery was the bulwark of Southern agrarian civilization—as Calhoun contended it was—the North knew now that the South could not be forced into abolition. There would be no surrender. From Yale, Calhoun's one-time friend, Benjamin Silliman, wrote sadly of his old pupil's vindication of "slavery in the abstract. He . . . changed the state of opinion and the manner of speaking and writing upon this subject in the South," leaving the region "without prospect of, or wish for, its extinction." [89]

To rest the cause of the South upon the crumbling foundation of Negro slavery was the tragic contradiction of Calhoun's career. With him, as with all Southerners, it was an emotional error. Far from being void of emotion, Calhoun was "a volcano of passion,"

[88] John C. Coit, quoted in *The Carolina Tribute to Calhoun*, pp. 149 ff.
[89] George Fisher, *The Life of Benjamin Silliman*, II, 98.

and it was this which gave him such a hold over the hearts, as well as the heads, of the Southern people. He felt as his people felt, and his feelings blinded him to the facts.

Slavery he could defend with reason, but could not view with reason. The farsighted prophet who detected the disastrous results of the protective tariff with such accuracy was the same short-sighted Southerner, utterly blind to the financial drain of slave labor. He was the bigot who defended human servitude and the philosopher whose system for the protection of minority rights would appear to many, a hundred years after his time, as the salvation of political democracy. The clear-eyed statesman, who could commend Jefferson's denunciation of the Missouri Compromise for its attempt to define the boundary lines of slavery, was the same broken politician who by 1850 could see no hope for the country he loved, save in an artificial restoration of the "equilibrium" which time and history and geography had wrecked forever; an incongruous coupling of the agrarian past to the industrial future.

Yet from the first, Calhoun had seen the basic issue: that the triumph of industrialism would bring "misery to those who lived on the land." That, logically, he knew his fight to be hopeless had no influence upon him. Sustained by his sense of duty, he battled the very future whose inevitability he foresaw, with the same stubborn, hopeless courage of old Patrick Calhoun in his war with the Constitution. "As I know life," he said grimly, "were my head at stake, I would do my duty, be the consequences what they may." [90]

XI

This was the background to the war that opened on the floor of the Senate in December, 1835, never to end until the last "gentleman of the South" had left the Chamber in the winter of 1861. What could be, Calhoun had understood from the first. What would be, it was his task to avert. If the abolitionist agitation continued, he was convinced it would rend the Union apart. And it was as the de-

[90] Gerald Johnson, *The Secession of the Southern States,* p. 61; also George F. Cushman, "John C. Calhoun," *Magazine of American History,* VIII, 612–619.

fender of the Union, not of slavery alone, that Calhoun stood in
the Senate Chamber during those years of the 1830's and 1840's,
hurling back the challenge of the Northern states. And looking on
that taut, erect figure, white with anger, eyes blazing, men might
doubt his prophecies and conclusions, but never his conviction as to
their truth.[91]

"I ask neither sympathy nor compassion for the slave-holding
States," was his proud declaration. "We can take care of ourselves.
It is not we, but the Union which is in danger. . . . We love and
cherish the Union; we remember our common origin . . . and
fondly anticipate the common greatness that seems to await us."
But, "come what will," he warned, with somber prophecy, "should
it cost every drop of blood and every cent of property, we must
defend ouselves." [92]

Strangely enough, it was not Calhoun but Andrew Jackson who
opened the abolitionist fight upon the Senate floor. Much has been
said of Jackson as the great friend of the common man, and of
Calhoun as the great defender of the landed interests. Yet the man
who made democracy a vital and living force in American government never regarded Negro slavery as a violation of that democracy. Not even Calhoun saw the threat of abolitionist agitation any
more clearly than Jackson, nor was he more capable of favoring
thorough and decisive action.

A post office fight aroused the President's wrath. In July, 1835,
the citizens of Charleston raided the post office, stole and burned a
sack of abolitionist pamphlets; then named a committee to meet
with the postmaster to determine what material could not be delivered in the city. The Charleston postmaster promptly notified
the postmaster in New York to forward no more abolitionist mate-

[91] Calhoun's opinions on slavery underwent little change from 1830 to
1850. As the aim of this chapter is to reveal his state of mind on the
entire slave question, his quotations hereafter are not necessarily arranged
chronologically. A question current in 1837 he might have discussed again
more forcibly and effectively in 1848. Through different years, he might
present three or four sides to a question which are here consolidated under
one subject head. The note references clearly indicate the source of the
different quotations; and, of course, in a report of any one specific speech,
this method is not used.

[92] Calhoun, speech on "Abolition Petitions," March 9, 1836, Crallé,
Works, II, 488–489.

rial; and the postmaster in New York laid the matter before Amos Kendall, Postmaster General of the United States.

Nullification had been mild, indeed, compared to the administration's stand. Jackson, four years earlier, had flatly proposed that abolition papers be delivered by Southern postmasters only to those who demanded them, "and in every instance the Postmaster ought to take the names down, and have them exposed thro the publick journals as subscribers to this wicked plan of exciting the slaves to insurrection . . . every moral and good citizen will unite to put them in coventry." So, with the full backing of the President, Kendall declared that he would neither direct the postmaster at New York to forward the incendiary pamphlets nor the postmaster at Charleston to receive them. Even higher than the laws of the United States, declared Connecticut-born Kendall, were the individual's responsibilities to his home community. Meanwhile, Jackson, in his Message to Congress the following December, denounced abolitionists as plotters of a civil war with all its horrors, and recommended passage of a measure absolutely excluding the circulation of "incendiary publications intended to instigate the slaves to insurrection." [93]

The howls with which Northern liberals greeted this proposal have long since been forgotten in latter-day liberal veneration of Jackson. Actually this proposition was too much even for Calhoun. He recognized no "higher law" than the Constitution, with its unmistakable provisions for freedom of the press, and he knew that if he were a party to its violation for measures that would benefit his own people, he could not invoke its protection when the South's rights were violated. "Rights and duties are reciprocal," he said. Such was Calhoun's stand, but there were those who saw in it more than abstract principle. President Jackson's support of a measure, asserted Senator King, was enough in itself to assure Senator Calhoun's opposition. Calhoun protested too much. "I have too little regard for the opinion of General Jackson and . . . his character, too, to permit his course to influence me in the slightest degree." [94]

[93] Jackson to Amos Kendall, August 9, 1835, John S. Bassett, ed., *Correspondence of Andrew Jackson,* 7 vols. (Washington, 1926–1935), V, 360–361.

[94] Crallé, *Works,* II, 515.

Nevertheless, it was Calhoun who moved reference of the President's Message to a special committee, and it was he who was named committee chairman. On February 4, 1836, he brought in a report declaring freedom of the mails essential to freedom of the press, and that Congress could make no law excluding any material whatever from the mails, incendiary or otherwise. Instead, he offered a counter-proposal. He suggested that federal post office agents be required by law to cooperate with state and territorial agents in preventing circulation of incendiary material where such material was forbidden by local law; and that local officials found guilty of violating their responsibilities by declining to examine suspect "literature" be denied the protection of the federal government.[95]

It was Henry Clay who detected the finespun fallacy in this proposition. If Congress had no power to exclude abolitionist documents from the mails, he asked, how then could it exclude their delivery through the mails?

Yet Calhoun's proposition, as well as his objection to the President's, was based on a fundamental constitutional question. Jackson would give the national government the power to regulate the mails; Calhoun would lay on the servants of the national government the obligation to bow to state laws.

The debate dragged on for months, ending in a 25 to 19 defeat for Calhoun's bill. The three-way Southern split served only to open the way for the Northern opposition, who promptly passed a measure, providing fines and imprisonment for any post office official who in any way prevented any material whatever from reaching its destination.

XII

Round two involved the abolitionist petitions. The question was not new. Long agitated in the House, the usual practice had been to receive the petitions and to table them instantly. But this was not enough for Calhoun, who stubbornly insisted that such peti-

[95] See Calhoun's speech on "Deputy-Postmasters," April 12, 1836, Crallé, *Works*, II, 509–533.

tions should be refused from the first. Deliberately he was forcing an issue which, it must be admitted, many of the more moderate slaveholding groups preferred not to force at all. If a petition could term slavery "a national disgrace" in the District of Columbia, why could it not be so termed in South Carolina? If the South had the constitutional right to hold slaves at all, it had a right to hold them in "peace and quiet," Calhoun argued. The fight must be waged on the frontier; for, as he put it, "The most unquestioned right can be rendered doubtful, if it be admitted to be a subject of controversy." [96]

Nor was it a violation of the right of petition to refuse to receive these "mischievous" documents. The First Amendment merely deprived Congress of the power to pass any law "abridging . . . the right of the people . . . to petition the government." It did not require Congress to accept petitions, Calhoun contended. Had not Jefferson himself ruled that before petitions were presented, their contents must be revealed by the introducer, and a motion made and seconded to receive them? Deprived of its right as a deliberative body to determine what to "receive or reject," Calhoun argued, Congress would become the passive receptacle of all that was "frivolous, absurd, unconstitutional, immoral, and impious. . . . If a petition should be presented, praying the abolition of the Constitution (which we are all bound . . . to protect), according to this abominable doctrine, it must be received." If the abolitionist societies should be converted into societies of atheists, and petition that a law be passed, "denying the existence of the Almighty . . . according to this blasphemous doctrine, we would be bound to receive the petition." [97] If Congress was bound to receive petitions to abolish slavery, why then could it not abolish slavery itself?

Why not indeed? Congress listened. With Calhoun few would even attempt debate. His questions went unanswered. Often he would complain that none would reply to his charges. But not

[96] Calhoun, speech on "Reception of Abolition Petitions," February 6, 1837, Crallé, *Works,* II, 627.

[97] Calhoun, speech on "The Abolition Petitions," March 9, 1836, Crallé, *Works,* II, 481–482; see also Thomas Hart Benton, *Thirty Years' View,* 2 vols. (New York, 1854–1856), II, 135, 138.

until Abraham Lincoln would America produce a man to answer
from first principles arguments based on first principles. To such
a man Calhoun would have listened with respect, but to no other.

XIII

On December 27, 1837, Calhoun took the Senate floor. The resolution that he introduced flung the issue right in the teeth of the
Constitution, the North, and the Senate itself. They were far from
watertight, either in logic or practicality. As Benton said, they were
"abstract, leading to no result; made discussion where silence was
desirable, frustrated the design of the Senate in refusing to discuss
the abolition petitions," and promoted the very agitation their
author deplored.

They were penned in sheer desperation. An attack on slavery
anywhere, declared Calhoun, was an attack on slavery everywhere,
an argument true enough in the abstract, but scarcely possible for
a states'-right advocate validly to support. For if "intermeddling"
by the citizens of one state with the "domestic institutions . . . of
the others" violated state sovereignty, how then could it be "the
duty" of the federal government "to give increased security" to
"domestic institutions"? If slavery could not be threatened without
a violation of state sovereignty, how, then, could it be protected? [98]
Calhoun was caught in the net of his own logic. Many of his detractors now saw that if the South could only mind its business
by interfering with the business of the North, then slavery was
intolerable.[99] Were Northerners free only to criticize the laws of
Massachusetts, but not those of South Carolina? Was it possible
for the government to give increased security to liberty in Connecticut and to slavery in Georgia?

But Calhoun's feelings were too wrought up for any possibility
of clear thinking, even in his lucid brain. "Is the South to sit still
and see the Constitution . . . laid prostrate in the dust?" he
demanded furiously.[100] Had the Alien and Sedition Laws been

[98] See text of Resolutions of December 27, 1837, Crallé, *Works*, III,
140–142.
[99] Hollis, *American Heresy*, p. 19.
[100] Crallé, *Works*, III, 145.

defeated by "sitting still and quoting the authority of the Constitution"? Yet he chided Anna Maria for her conclusion that it would be "better to part peaceably at once than to live in the state of indecision we do." He knew "how many bleeding pours [*sic*] must be taken up in passing the knife of seperation [*sic*] through a body politick (in order to make two of one)." Although admitting that "we cannot and ought not to live together as we are . . . exposed to the continual . . . assaults" of the North, he was resolved that "we must act throughout on the defensive, resort to every possible means of arresting the evil, and only act, when . . . justified before God and man in taking the final step." [101] Yet he had long known that difficult as it was "to make two people of one," if "the evil be not arrested at the North," the South would take the initiative. "I, for one," Calhoun declared, "would rather meet the danger now, than turn it over to those who are to come after us." [102]

Day after day, speech after speech, his words poured on. There were those who saw no danger to the Union in the violation of its most sacred principles, but only in the words of those who dared foretell the danger. "If my attachment to the Union were less, I might . . . keep silent. . . . It is a cheap and . . . certain mode of acquiring the character of devoted attachment to the Union." [103] But he saw—and he would speak.

"They who imagine the spirit now abroad in the North will die away of itself . . . have formed a very inadequate concept of its real character. . . . Already it has taken possession of the pulpit . . . the schools . . . the press." He had no patience with Senators who saw in the abolition-disunionists nothing but a "mere handful of females," interested only in abolishing slavery in the District of Columbia, while "they openly avow they are against all slavery." [104]

What were the facts? Fifteen hundred abolitionist societies with an average of a hundred members each, increasing at the rate of

---

[101] Calhoun to Anna Maria Calhoun, January 25, 1838, *Correspondence,* p. 391.

[102] Crallé, *Works,* III, 154; also, *ibid.,* II, 486.

[103] *Ibid.,* III, 154.

[104] Speech on "The Reception of Abolition Petitions," February 6, 1837, Crallé, *Works,* II, 629; *ibid.,* III, 170–171.

one a day, "hundreds of petitions, thousands of publications . . . attacking $900,000,000 worth of slave property and . . . the . . . safety of an entire section of this Union in violation of . . . pledged faith and the Constitution. . . ." And yet, we are told, "if we would keep . . . cool and patient, and hear ourselves and our constituents attacked as robbers and murderers . . . without moving hand or tongue, all would be well." [105]

"We are reposing on a volcano!" Calhoun shouted. The present generation would be succeeded by those taught to hate the people and the institutions "of nearly one half of this Union, with a hatred more deadly than one hostile nation ever entertained towards another." [106] Gone would be "every sympathy between the two great sections," their recollections of common danger and common glory. The abolitionists were "imbuing the rising generation at the North with the belief that . . . the institutions of the Southern states were sinful and immoral, and that it was doing God service to abolish them, even if it should involve the destruction of half the inhabitants of this Union." [107]

"It is easy to see the end. . . . We must become two people. . . . Abolition and the Union cannot co-exist. As the friend of the Union I . . . proclaim it." [108]

Bitterly he ridiculed the belief of the North that "slavery is sinful, notwithstanding the authority of the Bible to the contrary." There was a period, he reminded the Senators with sarcasm, "when the Northern States were slave-holding communities . . . extensively and profitably engaged in importing slaves to the South. It would . . . be . . . interesting to trace the causes which have led in so short a time to so great a change."

What was the Northern concept of liberty? Once it was thought that men were free who lived in constitutional republics. Now all nonslave governments were free, "even Russia with her serfs. . . . The term slave . . . is now restricted almost exclusively to African slavery." Products of the Hindus and the serfs were declared

[105] Calhoun, "Remarks on Resolutions," December 27, 1837 ff.; Crallé, *Works*, III, 159–161.

[106] *Ibid.*, III, 155; II, 629.

[107] *Ibid.*, III, 163–164.

[108] *Ibid.*, II, 629; also *The Carolina Tribute to Calhoun*, p. 361.

free-made, and enjoyed as the products of freedom. "To so low a standard has freedom sunk." [109]

In Northern idealism he saw nothing but sheer fanaticism. The spirit of abolition was nothing more than that "blind, fanatical zeal . . . that made one man believe he was responsible for the sins of his neighbor, that two centuries ago convulsed the Christian world" and "tied the victims that it could not convert to the stake. . . ." [110]

Why, he asked, did the individual Northerner feel himself responsible for slavery? Simply because our government had become nationalized instead of federal, "the States . . . like counties to the State, each feeling responsibility for the concerns of the other." Since the Force Bill passage, in practice, the United States had become "a consolidated government." His resolutions were "test" questions, involving the whole theory of the federal system. [111]

XIV

Calhoun won his battle—on paper. With the specter of actual, practical nullification removed from public view, the Senate, at least, was quite willing to approve the nullification doctrines, and pass five out of six of Calhoun's resolutions, with little material alteration. Whether or not the public would have granted such approval is another matter.

But Calhoun was not content, even with pledging the faith of the federal government toward the maintenance of slavery. His added determination was to secure the safety of the "domestick institution" under international law.

Since 1830, three American ships, the *Creole, Enterprise,* and *Comet,* traveling to and from Latin American ports, had been held with their cargoes of slaves by British authorities. Since 1830, Presidents Jackson and Van Buren had, in Calhoun's words, "been knocking—no, that is too strong a term—tapping gently at the door of the British Secretary, to obtain justice."

[109] Crallé, *Works,* IV, 516–517.
[110] *Ibid.,* III, 148–152, 177.
[111] *Ibid.,* p. 142.

Now Calhoun demanded action. Again he resorted to resolutions, in the bitter words of Adams, "imposing his bastard law of nations" upon the entire Senate, which bowed to his will without a dissenting vote. American property rights had been violated, was his contention. Under the law of nations those vessels "were as much under the protection of our flag" as if anchored in their home ports. Yet England declared the slave that touched British soil to be thenceforth free. Calhoun, with thoughts of India and Ireland bitter in his mind, could sneer at British distinctions between property in persons and property in things. He could warn that "it would ill become a nation that was the greatest slaveholder . . . on . . . earth—notwithstanding all the cant about emancipation—to apply such a principle in her intercourse with others." [112] The British government was obdurate. The greatest maritime power on earth had refused to admit that slavery was recognized by the law of nations, and thus declined the mutual consent upon which all international law rests.

Actually England did release one of the vessels and its human cargo. But the brig, *Enterprise,* which docked after slavery was abolished in the Empire, was never returned. And in 1841 Britain gave freedom to the slaves who had seized the brig, *Creole,* after killing the master in a mutinous uprising. Calhoun was left to the empty victory of having committed the Senate to the stand that a "domestick institution" was recognized by international law; and to the equally empty satisfaction of seeing Secretary of State Daniel Webster appeal impotently to Calhoun's resolutions in his negotiations.

XV

That emancipation, gradual or otherwise, would have been extremely difficult—almost impossible—by 1840 is undeniable. Yet had Calhoun joined with Henry Clay, for instance, in trying to work out a transitional system; had he devoted the same time and thought to a possible solution that he did to his defense of slavery, his claims upon the gratitude of his country would be far greater.

[112] Calhoun, remarks on the "Case of the brigs, Comet, Emporium, and Enterprise," February 14, 1837, Crallé, *Works*, III, 10–12.

For the South the issue would then have been fought in clear-cut terms. For a South sincerely, if hopelessly, attempting to struggle from the morass that engulfed her, the world would have had true sympathy. Against her still would have been ranged the spirit of industrial expansion, the spirit, perhaps, of the entire modern world, but not the outraged moral idealism of the nineteenth century. The North would have lost its issue; and slavery would not have obscured fundamentals.

This Calhoun did not see. Not for him the easy way out of Henry Clay, who could wash his hands of personal responsibility by comforting donations to a pipe dream such as the American Colonization Society. Calhoun had too much intellectual honesty to salve his conscience with lip service to ideals that denied the facts. Boldly and honestly he faced slavery as a fact and not as a theory. Not his own conscience, but the dilemma of the South, was what tortured Calhoun. Historians have shown how, with pitiless clarity, Calhoun saw the doom of his people under the reaped whirlwind of abolitionist agitation, but did not see that a logical doom may not necessarily be an inevitable doom.[113] Although history would prove him tragically right in his somber conviction that abolition superimposed by the North would wreck the South; he could not see that slavery, as such, was not basically essential to the South; and that gradual emancipation by the South itself would have been another matter.

To instinctive Jeffersonians, such as Calhoun was, the dilemma was more than intolerable. Grimly aware of the inequalities of man, Calhoun and his followers were compelled to reduce Jefferson's philosophy to the realities of their own time. Why, if Jefferson believed in emancipation, had he waited until his deathbed to free his own slaves? What if Jefferson had lived until the slave system was so deeply rooted in the Southern soil that its immediate extrication would mean destruction of the entire Southern economy; until attempts at enforced abolition from the North had ruled out all

---

[113] Johnson, *Secession of the Southern States,* p. 61. Marryat, *Diary,* pp. 194–195, points out that slavery was working its way westward; and forecast that within "twenty or thirty years [1860–1870] . . . provided . . . these states are not injudiciously interfered with," the upper South and possibly even Tennessee and South Carolina would "of their own accord, enroll themselves among the free states."

hopes of voluntary abolition from the South? Jefferson had died, haunted with the hopelessness and fear that was creeping like a blight across the Southern people. It is easy to condemn Calhoun for the stain on his otherwise brilliant career; yet, if he had no answer for the most tragic human problem of his time, neither had Thomas Jefferson.

PETER F. DRUCKER

✪

A Key to American Politics:
Calhoun's Pluralism

The American party system has been under attack almost continuously since it took definite form in the time of Andrew Jackson.
The criticism has always been directed at the same point: America's
political pluralism, the distinctively American organization of government by compromise of interests, pressure groups and sections.
And the aim of the critics from Thaddeus Stevens to Henry Wallace
has always been to substitute for this "unprincipled" pluralism a
government based as in Europe on "ideologies" and "principles."
But never before—at least not since the Civil War years—has the
crisis been as acute as in this last decade; for the political problems
which dominate our national life today: foreign policy and industrial policy, are precisely the problems which interest and pressure-
group compromise is least equipped to handle. And while the
crisis symptoms: a left-wing Third Party and the threatened split-off
of the Southern Wing, are more alarming in the Democratic Party,
the Republicans are hardly much better off. The 1940 boom for
the "idealist" Willkie and the continued inability to attract a substantial portion of the labor vote, are definite signs that the Republican Party too is under severe *ideological* pressure.

Yet, there is almost no understanding of the problem—precisely
because there is so little understanding of the basic principles of

Reprinted from *The Review of Politics*, Vol. 10, No. 4 (October 1948),
pp. 412–426, by permission of the author.

American pluralism. Of course, every politician in this country
must be able instinctively to work in terms of sectional and interest
compromise; and the voter takes it for granted. But there is practically no awareness of the fact that organization on the basis of
sectional and interest compromise is both the distinctly American
form of political organization and the cornerstone of practically
all major political institutions of the modern U.S.A. As acute an
observer as Winston Churchill apparently does not understand that
Congress works on a basis entirely different from that of Britain's
Parliament; neither do nine out of ten Americans and 999 out of
a 1,000 teachers of those courses in "Civics." There is even less
understanding that sectional and interest-group pluralism is not
just the venal expediency of that stock-villain of American folklore,
the "politician" but that it in itself is a basic ideology, a basic
principle—and the one which is the very foundation of our free
society and government.[1]

I

To find an adequate analysis of the principle of government by
sectional and interest compromise we have to go back almost a
hundred years to John C. Calhoun and to his two political treatises[2]
published after his death in 1852. Absurd, you will say, for it is
practically an axiom of American history that Calhoun's political
theories, subtle, even profound though they may have been, were
reduced to absurdity and irrelevance by the Civil War. Yet, this
"axiom" is nothing but a partisan vote of the Reconstruction
period. Of course, the specific occasion for which Calhoun formulated his theories, the slavery issue, has been decided; and for the
constitutional veto power of the states over national legislation, by
means of which Calhoun proposed to formalize the principle of
sectional and interest compromise, was substituted in actual practice the much more powerful and much more elastic but extra-

[1] A perfect illustration was the outraged amazement with which most
book reviewers greeted Edward J. Flynn's *You're the Boss*— a simple and
straight recital of facts every American should really have known and
understood all along.

[2] *A Disquisition on Government;* and *A Discourse on the Constitution
and Government of the United States.*

constitutional and extralegal veto power of sections, interests and pressure groups in Congress and within the parties.[3] But *his basic principle itself: that every major interest in the country, whether regional, economic or religious, is to possess a veto power on political decisions directly affecting it,* the principle which Calhoun called—rather obscurely—*"the rule of concurrent majority,"* has become the organizing principle of American politics. And it is precisely this principle that is under fire today.

What makes Calhoun so important as the major key to the understanding of American politics, is not just that he saw the importance in American political life of sectional and interest pluralism; other major analysts of our government, Tocqueville, for instance, or Bryce or Wilson, saw that too. But Calhoun, perhaps alone, saw in it more than a rule of expediency, imposed by the country's size and justifiable by results, if at all. He saw in it a basic principle of free government.

Without this [the rule of concurrent majority based on interests rather than on principles] there can be . . . no constitution. The assertion is true in reference to all constitutional governments, be their forms what they may: It is, indeed, the negative power which makes the constitution,—and the positive which makes the government. The one is the power of acting;—and the other the power of preventing or arresting action. The two, combined, make constitutional government.
. . . it follows, necessarily, that where the numerical majority has the sole control of the government, there can be no constitution . . . and hence, the numerical, unmixed with the concurrent majority, necessarily forms, in all cases, absolute government.
. . . The principle by which they (governments) are upheld and preserved . . . in constitutional governments is *compromise;*—and in absolute governments is *force.* . . .[4]

And however much the American people may complain in words

[3] Calhoun's extreme legalism, his belief that everything had to be spelled out in the written Constitution—a belief he shared with his generation—is one of the major reasons why the importance of his thesis has not been generally recognized. Indeed it is of the very essence of the concept of "concurrent majority" that it cannot be made official and legal in an effective government—the express veto such as the UN Charter gives to the Great Powers makes government impossible.

[4] Quotations from *A Disquisition on Government* (Columbia, S. C., 1852), pp. 35–37.

about the "unprincipled" nature of their political system, by their actions they have always shown that they too believe that without sectional and interest compromises there can be no constitutional government. If this is not grasped, American government and politics must appear not only as cheap to the point of venality, they must appear as utterly irrational and unpredictable.

II

Sectional and interest pluralism has molded all American political institutions. It is the method—entirely unofficial and extraconstitutional—through which the organs of government are made to function, through which leaders are selected, policies developed, men and groups organized for the conquest and management of political power. In particular it is the explanation for the most distinctive features of the American political system: the way in which the Congress operates, the way in which major government departments are set up and run, the qualifications for "eligibility" as a candidate for elective office, and the American party structure.

To all foreign observers of Congress two things have always remained mysterious: the distinction between the official party label and the "blocs" which cut across party lines; and the power and function of the Congressional committees. And most Americans though less amazed by the phenomena are equally baffled.

The "blocs"—the "Farm Bloc," the "Friends of Labor in the Senate," the "Business Groups," etc.—are simply the expression of the basic tenet of sectional and interest pluralism that major interests have a veto power on legislation directly affecting them. For this reason they must cut across party lines—that is, lines expressing the numerical rather than the "concurrent" majority. And because these blocs have (a) only a negative veto, and (b) only on measures directly affecting them; they cannot in themselves be permanent groupings replacing the parties. They must be loosely organized; and one and the same member of Congress must at different times vote with different blocs. The strength of the "blocs" does not rest on their numbers but on the basic mores of American politics which grant every major interest group a limited self-determination—as expressed graphically in the near-sanctity of a senatorial "filibuster." The power of the "Farm Bloc," for instance, does not rest on the numerical strength of the rural vote—a minority vote even in the Senate with its disproportionate representation of the thinly populated agricultural states—but on its "strategic" strength, that is on its being the spokesman for a recognized major interest.

Subordination of a major interest is possible; but only in a "temporary emergency." Most of the New Deal measures were, palpably, neither temporary nor emergency measures; yet their sponsors had to present them, and convincingly, as "temporary emergency measures" because they could be enacted only by overriding the extraconstitutional veto of the business interests.

Once the excuse of the "temporary emergency" had fully lost its plausibility, that major interest could no longer be voted down; and the policy collapsed. By 1946, for instance, labor troubles could be resolved only on a basis acceptable to both labor and employer: higher wages *and* higher prices. (Even if a numerical majority had been available to legislate against either party—and the business group could probably still have been voted down two and a half years ago—the solution had to be acceptable to both parties.)

The principle of sectional and interest compromise leads directly to the Congressional committee system—a system to which there is no parallel anywhere in the world. Congress, especially the House, has largely abdicated to its committees because only in the quiet and secrecy of a committee room can sectional compromise be worked out. The discussion on the floor as well as the recorded vote is far too public and therefore largely for the folks back home. But a committee's business is to arrive at an agreement between all major sectional interests affected; which explains the importance of getting a bill before the "right" committee. In any but an American legislature the position of each member, once a bill is introduced, is fixed by the stand of his party which, in turn, is decided on grounds that have little to do with the measure itself but are rather dictated by the balance of power within the government and by party programs. Hence it makes usually little difference which committee discusses a bill or whether it goes before a committee at all. In the United States, however, a bill's assignment to a specific committee decides which interest groups are to be recognized as affected by the measure and therefore entitled to a part in writing it ("who is to have standing before the committee"), for each committee represents a specific constellation of interests. In many cases this first decision therefore decides the fate of a proposed measure, especially as the compromise worked out by the committee is generally accepted once it reaches the floor, especially in the House.

It is not only Congress but every individual member of Congress himself who is expected to operate according to the "rule of concurrent majority." He is considered both a representative of the American people and responsible to the national interest and a delegate of his constituents and responsible to their particular interests. Wherever the immediate interests of his constituents are not in question, he is to be a statesman; wherever their conscience or their pocketbooks are affected, he is to be a business agent. This is in sharp contrast to the theory on which any parliamentary government is based—a theory developed almost two hundred years ago in Edmund Burke's famous speech to the voters at Bristol—according to which a member of Parliament represents the commonweal rather than his constituents. Hence in all parliamentary countries, the representative can be a stranger to his constituency—in the extreme, as it was practiced in Weimar Germany, there is one long national list of candidates who run in all constituencies—whereas the Congressman in this country must be a resident of his constituency. And while an American Senator considers it a compliment and an asset to be called "Cotton Ed Smith," the Speaker of the House of Commons not so long ago severely reprimanded a member for calling another member—an official of the miners' union—a "representative of the coal miners."

The principle of sectional and interest pluralism also explains why this is the only nation where Cabinet members are charged by law with the representation of special interests—labor, agriculture, commerce. In every other country an agency of the government—any agency of the government—is solemnly sworn to guard the public interests against "the interests." In this country the concept of a government department as the representative of a special interest group is carried down to smaller agencies and even to divisions and branches of a department. This was particularly noticeable during the war in such fights as that between OPA—representing the consumer—and the War Production Board representing the producer, or, within WPB between the Procurement branches speaking for the war industries and the Civilian Requirements Branch speaking for the industries producing for the "home front."

The mystery of "eligibility"—the criteria which decides who will make a promising candidate for public office—which has baffled so many foreign and American observers, Bryce for instance —also traces back to the "rule of the concurrent majority." Eligibility simply means that a candidate must not be unacceptable to any major interest, religious or regional group within the electorate; it is primarily a negative qualification. Eligibility operates on all levels and applies to all elective offices. It has been brilliantly analyzed in "Boss" Flynn's *You're the Boss.* His classical example is the selection of Harry Truman as Democratic Vice-Presidential candidate in 1944. Truman was "eligible" rather than Wallace, Byrnes or Douglas precisely because he was unknown; because he was neither Easterner nor Westerner nor Southerner, because he was neither New Deal nor Conservative, etc., in short because he had no one trait strong enough to offend anybody anywhere.

But the central institution based on sectional pluralism is the American party. Completely extraconstitutional, the wonder and the despair of every foreign observer who cannot fit it into any of his concepts of political life, the American party (rather than the states) has become the instrument to realize Calhoun's "rule of the concurrent majority."

In stark contrast to the parties of Europe, the American party has no program and no purpose except to organize divergent groups for the common pursuit and conquest of power. Its unity is one of action, not of beliefs. Its only rule is to attract—or at least not to repel—the largest possible number of groups. It must, by definition, be acceptable equally to the right and the left, the rich and the poor, the farmer and the worker, the Protestant and the Catholic, the native and the foreign-born. It must be able to rally Mr. Rankin of Mississippi and Mr. Marcantonio of New York—or Senator Flanders and Colonel McCormick—behind the same Presidential candidate and the same "platform."

As soon as it cannot appeal at least to a minority in every major group (as soon, in other words, as it provokes the veto of one section, interest or class) a party is in danger of disintegration. Whenever a party loses its ability to fuse sectional pressures and class interests into one national policy—both parties just before the Civil War, the Republican party before its reorganization by Mark Hanna, both parties again today—the party system (and with it the American political system altogether) is in crisis.

It is, consequently, not that Calhoun was repudiated by the Civil War which is the key to the understanding of American politics but that he has become triumphant since.

The apparent victors, the "Radical Republicans," Thaddeus Stevens, Seward, Chief Justice Chase, were out to destroy not only slavery and states' rights but the "rule of the concurrent majority" itself. And the early Republican party—before the Civil War and in the Reconstruction period—was indeed determined to substitute principle for interest as the lodestar of American political life. But in the end it was the political thought of convinced pluralists such as Abraham Lincoln and Andrew Johnson rather than the ideologies of the Free Soilers and abolitionists which molded the Republican party. And ever since, the major developments of American politics have been based on Calhoun's principle. To this the United States owes the strength as well as the weaknesses of its political system.

III

The weaknesses of sectional and interest compromise are far more obvious than its virtues; they have been hammered home for a hundred years. Francis Lieber, who brought the dominant German political theories of the early nineteenth century to this country, attacked pluralism in Calhoun's own state of South Carolina a century ago. Twenty years later Walter Bagehot contrasted, impressively, General Grant's impotent administration with those of Gladstone and Disraeli to show the superiority of ideological party organization. The most thorough and most uncompromising criticism came from Woodrow Wilson; and every single one of the Professor's points was amply borne out by his later experience as President. Time has not made these weaknesses any less dangerous.

There is, first of all, the inability of a political system based on the "rule of the concurrent majority" to resolve conflicts of principles. All a pluralist system can do is to deny that "ideological" conflicts (as they are called nowadays) do exist. Those conflicts, a pluralist must assert, are fundamentally either struggles for naked power or friction between interest groups which could be solved if only the quarreling parties sat down around a conference table. Perhaps, the most perfect, because most naïve, expression of this belief remains the late General Patton's remark that the Nazis were, after all, not so very different from Republicans or Democrats. (Calhoun, while less naïve, was just unable to understand the reality of "ideological" conflict in and around the slavery problem.)

In nine cases out of ten the refusal to acknowledge the existence of ideological conflict is beneficial. It prevents fights for power, or clashes of interests, from flaring into religious wars where irreconcilable principles collide (a catastrophe against which Europe's ideological politics have almost no defense). It promotes compromise where compromise is possible. But in a genuine clash of principles—and, whatever the pluralists say, there *are* such clashes —the "rule of concurrent majority" breaks down; it did, in Calhoun's generation, before the profound reality of the slavery issue. A legitimate ideological conflict is actually aggravated by the pluralists' refusal to accept its reality: the compromisers who thought the slavery issue could be settled by the meeting of good intentions, or by the payment of money, may have done more than the abolitionists to make the Civil War inevitable.

A weakness of sectional and interest pluralism just as serious is that it amounts to a principle of inaction. The popular assertion "it's better to make the wrong decision than to do nothing at all," is, of course, fallacious; but no nation, however unlimited its resources, can have a very effective policy if its government is based on a principle that orders it to do nothing important except unanimously. Moreover, pluralism increases exorbitantly the weight of well-organized small interest groups, especially when they lobby *against* a decision. Congress can far too easily be high-pressured into emasculating a bill by the expedient of omitting its pertinent provisions; only with much greater difficulty can Congress be moved to positive action. This explains, to a large extent, the eclipse of Congress during the last hundred years, both in popular respect and in its actual momentum as policy-making organ of government. Congress, which the Founding Fathers had intended to be the central organ of government—a role which it fulfilled up to Andrew Jackson—became the compound representative of sections and interests and, consequently, progressively incapable of national leadership.

Pluralism gives full weight—more than full weight—to sections and interests; but who is to represent the national welfare? Ever since the days of Calhoun, the advocates of pluralism have tried to dodge this question by contending that the national interest is equal to the sum of all particular interests, and that it therefore does not need a special organ of representation. But this most specious argument is contradicted by the most elementary observation. In practice, pluralism tends to resolve sectional and class conflicts at the expense of the national interest which is represented by nobody in particular, by no section and no organization.

These weaknesses had already become painfully obvious while Calhoun was alive and active—during the decade after Andrew Jackson, the first President of pluralism. Within a few years after Calhoun's death, the inability of the new system to comprehend and to resolve an ideological conflict—ultimately its inability to represent and to guard the national interest—had brought catastrophe. For a hundred years and more, American political thought has therefore resolved around attempts to counteract if not to overcome these weaknesses. Three major developments of American constitutional life were the result: the growth of the functions and powers of the President and his emergence as a "leader" rather than as the executive agent of the Congress; the rise of the Supreme Court, with its "rule of law," to the position of arbiter of policy; the development of a unifying ideology—the "American Creed."

Of these the most important—and the least noticed—is the "American Creed." In fact I know of no writer of major importance since Tocqueville who has given much attention to it. Yet even the term "un-American" cannot be translated successfully into any other language, least of all into "English" English. In no other country could the identity of the nation with a certain set of ideas be assumed—at least not under a free government. This unique cohesion on principles shows, for instance, in the refusal of the American voter to accept Socialists and Communists as "normal" parties, simply because both groups refuse to accept the assumption of a common American ideology. It shows, for another example, in the indigenous structure of the American labor movement with its emphasis on interest pressure rather than on a political philosophy. And this is also the only country in which "Civics" could be taught in schools—the only democratic country which believes that a correct social philosophy could or should be part of public education.

In Europe, a universal creed would be considered incompatible with a free society. Before the advent of totalitarianism, no European country had ever known anything comparable to the flag salute of the American school child.[5] For in Europe all political activity is based on ideological factions; consequently, to introduce a uniform ideology in a European country is to stamp out *all* opposition. In the United States ideological homogeneity is the very basis of political diversity. It makes possible the almost unlimited freedom of interest groups, religious groups, pressure groups, etc.; and in this way it is the very fundament of free government. (It also explains why the preservation of civil liberties has been so much more important a problem in this country—as compared to England or France, for instance.) The assumption of ideological unity gives the United States the minimum of cohesion without which its political system simply could not have worked.

IV

But is even the "American dream" enough to make a system based on the "rule of the concurrent majority" work today? Can

[5] The perhaps most profound discussion of the American ideological cohesion can be found in the two decisions of the Supreme Court on the compulsory flag salute, and in the two dissents therefrom, which deserve high rating among American state papers.

pluralism handle the two major problems of American politics—
the formulation of a foreign policy, and the political organization
of an industrial society—any more successfully than it could handle
the slavery issue? Or is the American political system as much in
crisis as it was in the last years of Calhoun's life—and for pretty
much the same reasons?

A foreign policy can never be evolved by adding particular interests—regional, economic or racial—or by compromising among
them; it must supersede them. If Calhoun's contention that the
national interest will automatically be served by serving the interests
of the parts is wrong anywhere, it is probably wrong in the field of
foreign affairs.

A foreign policy and a party system seem to be compatible
only if the parties are organized on programmatic grounds, that is,
on principles. For if not based on general principles, a foreign
policy will become a series of improvisations without rhyme or
reason. In a free society, in which parties compete for votes and
power, the formulation of a foreign policy may thus force the
parties into ideological attitudes which will sooner or later be
reflected in their domestic policies too.

This was clearly realized in the early years of the Republic
when foreign policy was vital to a new nation, clinging precariously
to a long seaboard without hinterland, engaged in a radical experiment with new political institutions, surrounded by the Great Powers of that time, England, France and Spain, all of them actually
or potentially hostile. This awareness of foreign policy largely
explains why the party system of the Founding Fathers—especially
of Hamilton—was an ideological one; it also explains why the one
positive foreign-policy concept this country developed during the
entire nineteenth century—the Monroe Doctrine—was formulated
by the last two politically active survivors of the founding generation, Monroe and John Quincy Adams. No matter how little Calhoun himself realized it, his doctrine would have been impossible
without the French Revolution and the Napoleonic Wars which,
during the most critical period of American integration, kept its
potential European enemies busy. By 1820, the country had become
too strong, had taken in too much territory, to be easily attacked;

and it was still not strong enough, and far too much absorbed in the development of its own interior, to play a part in international affairs. Hence Calhoun, and all America with him, could push foreign policy out of their minds—so much so that this is the only country in which it is possible to write a comprehensive work on an important historical period without as much as a mention of foreign affairs, as Arthur M. Schlesinger, Jr. managed to do in his *The Age of Jackson.*

But today foreign policy is again as vital for the survival of the nation as it ever was during the administrations of Washington and Jefferson. And it has to be a foreign *policy,* that is, a making of decisions; hence neither "isolationism" nor "internationalism" will do. (For "internationalism"—the search for formulae which will provide automatic decisions, even in advance—is also a refusal to have a foreign policy; it may well have done this country, and the world, as much harm as "isolationism"—perhaps more.) To survive as the strongest of the Great Powers, the United States might even have to accept permanently the supremacy of foreign policies over domestic affairs, however much this may go against basic American convictions, and indeed against the American grain. But no foreign policy can be evolved by the compromise of sectional interests or economic pressures; yet neither party, as today constituted, could develop a foreign policy based on definite principles.

The other great national need is to resolve the political problems of an industrial society. An industrial society is by nature ultra-pluralistic, because it develops class and interest groups that are far stronger, and far more tightly organized, than any interest group in a preindustrial age. A few big corporations, a few big unions, may be the actually decisive forces in an industrial society. And these groups can put decisive pressure on society: they can throttle social and economic life.

The problem does not lie in "asocial behavior" of this or that group but in the nature of industrial society which bears much closer resemblance to feudalism than to the trading nineteenth century. Its political problems are very similar to those which feudalism had to solve—and failed to solve. It is in perpetual

danger of disintegration into virtually autonomous fiefs, princi-
palities, "free cities," "robber baronies" and "exempt bishoprics"—
the authority and the interest of the nation trampled underfoot,
autonomous groups uniting to control the central power in their
own interest or disregarding government in fighting each other in
the civil conflict of class warfare. And the alternative to such a
collapse into anarchy or civil war—the suppression of classes and
interest groups by an all-powerful government—is hardly more
attractive.

An industrial society cannot function without an organ able to
superimpose the national interest on economic or class interests.
More than a mere arbiter is needed. The establishment of the
"rules of civilized industrial warfare," as was done by both the
Wagner Act and the Taft-Hartley Act, tries to avoid the need for
policies by equalizing the strength of the conflicting sections; but
that can lead only to deadlock, to collusion against the national
interest or, worse still, to the attempt to make the national authority
serve the interest of one side against the other. In other words, an
industrial society cannot fully accept Calhoun's assumption that
the national good will evolve from the satisfaction of particular
interests. An industrial society without national policy will become
both anarchic and despotic.

Small wonder that there has been increasing demand for a
radical change which would substitute ideological parties and
programmatic policies for the pluralist parties and the "rule of
the concurrent majority" of the American tradition. Henry Wallace's Third-Party Movement, while the most publicized, may well
be the least significant development; for third parties are, after all,
nothing new in our political history. But for the first time in a
hundred years there is a flood of books—and by serious students
of American government—advocating radical constitutional reform.
However much Senator Fulbright, Henry Hazlitt and Thomas Fine-
letter disagree on details, they are one in demanding the elimination—or at least the limitation—of the "rule of the concurrent
majority," and its replacement by an ideological system functioning
along Parliamentary lines. More significant even may be Walter
Reuther's new unionism with its blend of traditional pressure tac-

tics and working-class, that is ideological, programs and aims.

Yet all these critics and reformers not only fail to ask themselves whether an ideological system of politics would really be any better equipped to cope with the great problems of today—and neither the foreign nor the industrial policy of England, that most successful of all ideologically organized countries, look any too successful right now; the critics also never stop to consider the unique strength of our traditional system.

Our traditional system makes sure that there is always a legitimate government in the country; and to provide such a government is the first job of any political system—a duty which a great many of the political systems known to man have never discharged.

It minimizes conflicts by utilizing, rather than suppressing conflicting forces. It makes it almost impossible for the major parties to become entirely irresponsible: neither party can afford to draw strength from the kind of demagogic opposition, without governmental responsibility, which perpetually nurtures fascist and Communist parties abroad. Hence, while the two national parties are willing to embrace any movement or any group within the country that commands sufficient following, they in turn force every group to bring its demands and programs into agreement with the beliefs, traditions and prejudices of the people.

Above all, our system of sectional and interest compromise is one of the only two ways known to man in which a free government and a free society can survive—and the only one at all adapted to the conditions of American life and acceptable to the American people.

The central problem in a free government is that of factions, as we have known since Plato and Aristotle. Logically, a free government and factions are incompatible. But whatever the cause —vanity and pride, lust for power, virtue or wickedness, greed or the desire to help others—factionalism is inherent in human nature and in human society. For 2,000 years the best minds in politics have tried to devise a factionless society—through education (Plato), through elimination of property (Thomas More), through concentration on the life of the spirit outside of worldly ambition (the political tradition of Lutheranism). The last great attempt to save freedom by abolishing faction was Rousseau's. But to create the factionless free society is as hopeless as to set up perpetual motion. From Plato to Rousseau, political thought has ended up by demanding that factions be suppressed, that is, that freedom, to be preserved, be abolished.

The Anglo-American political tradition alone has succeeded in breaking out of this vicious circle. Going back to Hooker and Locke, building on the rich tradition of free government in the cities of the late middle ages, Anglo-American political realism discovered: that if factions cannot be suppressed, they must be utilized to make a free government both freer and stronger. This one basic concept distinguishes Anglo-American political theory and practice from Continental European politics, and accounts for the singular success of free and popular governments in both countries. Elsewhere in the Western World the choice has always been between extreme factionalism which makes government impotent if not impossible and inevitably leads to civil war, and autocracy which justifies the suppression of liberty with the need for effective and orderly government. Nineteenth-century France with its six revolutions, or near revolutions, stands for one, the totalitarian governments of our time for the other alternative of Continental politics.

But—and this is the real discovery on which the Anglo-American achievement rests—factions can be used constructively only if they are encompassed within a frame of unity. A free government on the basis of sectional interest groups is possible only when there is no ideological split within the country. This is the American solution. Another conceivable solution is to channel the driving forces, the vectors of society, into ideological factions which obtain their cohesion from a program for the whole of society, and from a creed. But that presupposes an unquestioned ruling class with a common outlook on life, with uniform mores and a traditional, if not inherent, economic security. Given that sort of ruling class, the antagonist in an ideological system can be expected to be a "loyal opposition," that is, to accept the rules of the game and to see himself as a partner rather than as a potential challenger to civil war. But a ruling class accepted by the people as a whole, and feeling itself responsible to the people as a whole, cannot be created by fiat or overnight. In antiquity only Rome, in modern times only England, achieved it. On the Continent, all attempts to create a genuine ruling class have failed dismally.

In this country, the ruling-class solution was envisaged by Alexander Hamilton and seemed close to realization under the Presidents of the "Virginia Dynasty." Hamilton arrived at his concept with inescapable consistency; for he was absorbed by the search for a foreign policy and for the proper organization of an industrial society—precisely the two problems which, as we have seen, pluralism is least equipped to resolve. But even if Hamilton had not made the fatal mistake of identifying wealth with rulership, the American people could not have accepted his thesis. A ruling class was incompatible with mass immigration and with the explosive territorial expansion of nineteenth-century America. It was even more incompatible with the American concept of equality. And there is no reason to believe that contemporary America is any more willing to accept Hamilton's concept, Mr. James Burnham's idea of the managerial elite notwithstanding. This country as a free country has no alternative, it seems, to the "rule of the concurrent majority," no alternative to sectional pluralism as the device through which factions can be made politically effective.

It will be very difficult, indeed, to resolve the problems of foreign and of industrial policy on the pluralist basis and within the interest-group system, though not provably more difficult than these problems would be on another, ideological, basis. It will be all the harder as the two problems are closely interrelated; for the effectiveness of any American foreign policy depends, in the last analysis, on our ability to show the world a successful and working model of an industrial society. But if we succeed at all, it will be with the traditional system, horse-trading, log-rolling and politicking all included. An old saying has it that this country lives simultaneously in a world of Jeffersonian beliefs and in one of Hamiltonian realities. Out of these two, Calhoun's concept of "the rule of the concurrent majority" alone can make one viable whole. The need for a formulated foreign policy and for a national policy of industrial order is real—but not more so than the need for a

real understanding of this fundamental American fact: the pluralism of sectional and interest compromise is the warp of America's
political fabric—it cannot be plucked out without unraveling the
whole.

RICHARD N. CURRENT

✪

John C. Calhoun, Philosopher of Reaction

The shade of John C. Calhoun, who died in 1850, still haunts the
Southern scene. He, after all, was the original architect of the Solid
South. He it was who took Jefferson's liberal doctrine of states'
rights and identified it with a policy of reaction. He, more than
anyone else, made the presence of the Negro an occasion for re-
pressing white men along with black. Wherever contemporary
Bourbons take counsel together, somewhere in their midst hovers
the ghost of the Great Nullifier.

Today the keepers of the reactionary tradition find much to
take counsel about. Fissures are appearing in the masonry of their
Solid South, with all which that implies. The cross winds of the
New Deal have shaken the venerable structure, and the disturbing
currents of the Four Freedoms are giving it another buffeting.
Not that the time has come to predict its early collapse, for it
withstood the disruptive gusts of populism in the 1890's and
recovered quickly enough from the inroads of republicanism in
1928. Indeed, the Solid South was created in the first place as a
windbreak against external storms of popular aspiration—as a
defense, that is, against the threats of "outside agitators"—and the
harder the winds have blown, the more urgent has been the motive
to patch and shore it up. No matter what political realignments
may be in store for 1944 or 1948, such are the repercussions of
the challenge of the new democracy, from Hindustan to Harlem

Reprinted from the *Antioch Review*, Vol. 3, No. 2 (Summer 1943),
pp. 223–234, by permission.

151

and beyond, that reactionary leaders in the South will be bound to maintain some kind of effective solidarity behind the Mason and Dixon front.

The problem they now face is remarkably like the one Calhoun had to contend with in his day, for the vicissitudes of a century have altered the picture only in its details. *Plus ça change, plus la même chose.* The central theme of Southern history has remained the same, but this theme is not what the older school of Southern historians said it was—the maintenance of white supremacy. It is the maintenance of the supremacy of *some* white men, and as a means to this end the fiction of a general white supremacy has been extremely useful. In Calhoun's day the myth took the form of the "proslavery argument," which in truth was inspired not so much by the agitation of Northern fanatics as by the democratic questionings of Southern slaveless farmers. One of Calhoun's own proslavery arguments was this, that simply to turn the Negroes loose without giving them full civic and social rights would not be to free them at all but only to change the form of their bondage: they would cease to be slaves of individual masters and become slaves of the community as a whole. As applied to the group servitude which Calhoun thus foretold, abolition continues to be a live issue in the South. The W.P.A., for example, was abolitionist when it provided alternative employment at unwonted wages for low-paid "colored help." So is the war-time industrial program, wherever Negroes are allowed to compete freely for jobs. So, too, are the world-wide stirrings accompanying this second war for, ostensibly, the establishment of human rights.

The preservation of a South solid against the Negro may well depend on what interests *outside the South* can be enlisted in its defense. This, also, the prophetic Calhoun realized in his day. When he called upon the South to unite, as he did again and again, he was often accused of having "something very sinister," like secession, in mind. He disavowed such aims and assured suspicious Northerners that a "union" of Southerners was a distinct benefit to the larger union itself and to all concerned. It was, in fact, essential to the smooth working of the machinery of the federal Constitution. "The machine never works well when the South is divided," Calhoun declared, "nor badly when it is united." He strove consistently to win Northern sympathy and support for his united South. In these efforts there lurked something really more sinister, in its significance for American democracy, than any thought of disunion.

The true meaning of Calhoun's career has not been clearly understood. In the minds of most students of American history, the South Carolinian stands as the pre-eminent spokesman for the contemporary planting interests of his state and section and, by virtue of that position, also as the chief political foe of the rising captains of industry in the North. He was, of course, the planter champion, yet he himself insisted that he was "no enemy of manufactures or of manufacturers, but quite the reverse," and he was heard to say that the "interests of the *gentlemen* of the North and of the South" were "identical." There is ample ground for taking him at his word. Although he detested the political program of the industrialists, he beheld another danger far greater than what they had to offer. In the rise of a proletariat in the industrial states he foresaw a menace to the security of factory owners and plantation proprietors alike. While, both as a politician and as a theorist, he defended the slave system against the encroachments of the capitalist economy, at the same time he aspired to a grander role as leader of a combined conservatism against the universal forces of revolt.

Historians have completely overlooked the key to Calhoun's political philosophy. That key is a concept of the class struggle. Before Calhoun, other Southern thinkers, notably James Madison and John Taylor of Caroline, had given expression to more or less well-developed ideas of the conflict of social classes, for this was a notion familiar enough to a generation of Americans brought up largely on the history of ancient Greece and Rome. But these others took a liberal view, John Taylor, for one, favoring cooperation of farmers and artisans against their mutual enemy, the moneyed power. Calhoun was strictly the reactionary. Unlike the others, moreover, he used a terminology and treatment which in many respects anticipated the later "scientific" approach of Friedrich Engels and Karl Marx.

He started, as Marx and Engels were also to do, with John Locke's so-called labor theory of value. From that assumption he deduced that in all contemporary and historical societies, except the most primitive, there existed a system of exploitation of a working class. "Let those who are interested remember," he once wrote, "that labor is the only source of wealth, and how small a portion of it, in all old and civilized countries, even the best governed, is left to those by whose labor wealth is created." On another occasion he repeated that "there never has yet existed a wealthy and civilized society in which one portion of the community did not, in point of fact, live on the labor of the other," and that "it would not be difficult to trace the various devices by which the wealth of all civilized communities has been so unequally divided, and to show by what means so small a share has been allotted to those by whose labor it was produced, and so large a share given to the nonproducing classes." Unlike the Marxists, Calhoun did not define the capitalistic producing and nonproducing groups in terms at all precise. He referred to them variously, and loosely, as "the poor" and "the rich," "labor" and "capital," "the operatives" and "the capitalists," "the ignorant and dependent" and "the intelligence of the community," "the needy and corrupt" and "the wealthy and talented," and so forth—terms slightly descriptive but extremely evaluative.

Calhoun anticipated a number of the other Marxist doctrines. Among these were the following: (1) the eventual division of society into only two classes, capitalist and proletarian; (2) the gradual expropriation of the bulk of the population by the capitalists, so that the propertied would become fewer and fewer and the property-less more and more numerous; and (3) the ultimate impoverishment of the masses to a bare subsistence level. All this would come about through capitalist control and use of the powers of the state. Thus, in a conversation in 1831, Calhoun "took the instance of 100 men without a Govt. [and] showed the equilibrium that would prevail. Supposed a Government that would give $5000 to ten of the hundred and then traced the tendency of the Capital to erradicate [sic] the possession of the soil, and to reduce the 90 to a state of simple operatives." There were various fiscal means by which governments might present a bounty to a favored group and so enable it to expropriate the rest, but the chief of these devices (as John Taylor also had pointed out) was the protective tariff. Such governmental "intermeddling" in economic affairs was the cause, in Europe, of the "unequal and unjust distribution of wealth between the several classes or portions of the community." The first effect of the tariff in the United States had been to enrich the North and impoverish the South, but the time would come when it would redistribute property as between the social classes rather than the geographical sections. "After [the planters] are exhausted," Calhoun warned,

the contest will be between the capitalists and operatives; for into these two classes it must, ultimately, divide society. The issue of the struggle here must be the same as it has been in Europe. Under the operation of the [protective] system, wages must sink more rapidly than the prices of the necessaries of life, till the operatives will be reduced to the lowest point,—when the portion of the products of their labor left to them, will be barely sufficient to preserve existence.

As a result of the exploitation and expropriation of the working class, according to Calhoun, there would follow an inevitable social conflict, which would grow more and more severe as the conditions producing it became more extreme, until it must eventuate in a revolutionary crisis. "It is useless to disguise the fact," the gentleman from South Carolina frankly informed his fellow Senators in 1837. "There is and always has been in an advanced stage of wealth and civilization, a conflict between labor and capital." This "tendency to conflict in the North," he said at another time, "is constantly on the increase." And again: "Where wages command labor, as in the nonslaveholding States, there necessarily takes place between labor and capital a conflict, which leads, in process of time, to disorder, anarchy, and revolution, if not counteracted by some appropriate and strong constitutional provision." Calhoun explained this a little more fully when he wrote that

as the community becomes populous, wealthy, refined, and highly civilized, the difference between the rich and the poor will become more strongly marked; and the number of the ignorant and dependent greater in proportion to the rest of the community. With the increase of this difference, the tendency to conflict between them will become stronger; and, as the poor and dependent become more numerous . . . there will be . . . no want of leaders among the wealthy and ambitious, to excite and direct them in their efforts to obtain the control.

Here Calhoun doubtless had in mind the history of the Greek city-states and the Roman republic, but he was nevertheless predicting the defection from the bourgeoisie of leaders to aid the proletariat in its revolutionary struggle. This was an idea to which Marx and Engels attached a great deal of importance in the *Communist Manifesto*.

In his political prognoses Calhoun revealed a rather definite notion of historical determinism. As he watched "the unfolding of the great events" leading to the European revolutionary movements of 1848, he was confident he could predict the outcome, for he had the benefit of "principles . . . drawn from facts in the moral world just as certain as any in the physical." He insisted "it ought never to be forgotten that *the past is the parent of the present*" (he underlined the words). But he did not believe the historical process was always one of continuous growth. Thus "the past condition of Europe," though it had "given birth" to the most advanced civilization hitherto known, might have, "indeed, contained within itself causes calculated to retard or prevent a further progress." The continued advance of material improvement, growing out of the many inventions and discoveries of the preceding century, could be expected only if the changes in means and methods of production and distribution should be accompanied by suitable changes in the organization of society and government.

"What I dread," wrote Calhoun, expressing his own concept of cultural lag, "is, that progress in political science falls far short of progress in that which relates to matter, and which may lead to convulsions and revolutions that may retard or even arrest the former." When he took a long-run view, however, he was optimistic. The myriad discoveries and inventions, particularly "the application of steam to machinery of almost every description," though they would "cause changes, political and social, difficult to be anticipated," must in the end accrue to the good of mankind.

It is, however, not improbable, that many and great, but temporary evils, will follow the changes they have effected, and are destined to effect. It seems to be a law in the political, as well as in the material world, that great changes cannot be made, except very gradually, without convulsions and revolutions; to be followed by calamities, in the beginning, however beneficial they may prove to be in the end. The first effect of such changes, on long established governments, will be, to unsettle the opinions and principles in which they originated,—and which have guided their policy,—before those, which the changes are calculated to form and establish, are fairly developed and understood. The interval between the decay of the old and the formation and establishment of the new, constitutes a period of transition, which must always necessarily be one of uncertainty, confusion, error, and wild and fierce fanaticism.

The chief of the "erroneous opinions" characterizing this transitional period would be the belief in rule by the "numerical majority," a belief based upon the "false conception" that men had once lived in a state of nature and could therefore claim liberty and equality as natural rights. It was this error—the Four Freedoms of that time—which was "upheaving Europe" in 1848. The falsity of the democratic dogma would soon become apparent, because, according to Calhoun's dialectic, an overextension of liberty must lead to "a contraction instead of an enlargement of its sphere." Unlimited democracy would be followed by anarchy, and then an "appeal to force," and finally dictatorship, "monarchy in its absolute form." Out of the contradictions in society that produced the chaos, however, an entirely different synthesis might emerge through the application of political science. And by "political science" Calhoun meant of course his theory of "concurrent majorities" with all its paraphernalia, including some scheme of federation and the power of "interposition" by the member states, that is, nullification or its equivalent. Hence, in 1848, he cherished some hope for Germany, where there already existed the elements of a federation out of which the "dread" of French radicalism might produce "a federal system somewhat like ours." About the fate of France herself he was pessimistic and, accurately enough, predicted that she would soon "find herself in the embrace of a military despotism."

In no single writing did the Carolina philosopher-statesman systematically develop his views on the class struggle and his materialistic interpretation of history. He gave fragmentary expression to these ideas on scattered occasions—in private letters, public reports, conversations, and speeches, and in one of his two treatises on government. From these various sources the parts must be extracted and rearranged if they are to make a systematic whole. For Calhoun was interested less in composing a well-rounded statement of the theory than in using it for the practical purpose of defending the property of the planters.

On behalf of the planter class he appealed again and again to fellow conservatives among the bankers and manufacturers of the North. As each great sectional issue came to a head between 1828 and 1850, he was ready with a new instalment of his class-struggle argument. He made the first public statement of his thesis (anonymously) in the famous South Carolina *Exposition* itself, in which he denounced the tariff of 1828 and proposed his nullification procedure as a remedy for the South, but in which he also warned that protectionism would ruin the planter class and leave Northern employers to fight alone the coming battle with their employees. In 1834, when the bank issue was intensified by a sharp financial crisis, he took occasion to point out that a banking system with power to swell and shrink the money supply was as dangerous as the protective system in causing an uneconomic distribution of wealth and hastening the day of revolution. In 1836, reporting to the Senate on "incendiary" abolition literature, he told the propertied classes of the North that they ought to be as much concerned in this matter as the Southern slaveholders themselves, because "a very slight modification" of the arguments used to attack property in slaves "would make them equally effectual" against property of all kinds. In 1841 he criticized Henry Clay's distribution bill (for dividing among the several states the proceeds from the sale of public lands) by asserting that its effect would be to array "one class against another." And during the Mexican War he took his stand against the conquest of *all* of Mexico (large areas of which were unsuited to slavery) on the ground that the creation of an American empire would lead to dangerous social changes within the older union.

The main point in Calhoun's case against abolition—that the elimination of slavery in the South would prepare the way for social revolution in the North—was a distinctive contribution to the text of the proslavery argument. The Carolinian reasoned that the conflict between capital and labor, with all its "disorders and dangers," could have no place in the Southern scheme of life. "The Southern States are an aggregate, in fact, of communities, not of individuals.

Every plantation is a little community, with the master at its head, who concentrates in himself the united interests of capital and labor, of which he is the common representative." Naturally, according to the reasoning of the planter mind, this arrangement made slavery "a good—a positive good" for both the master and the slave, a creature better fed, clothed, and housed, and happier than the Northern workingman. But Calhoun emphasized that it made slavery a positive benefit for the Northern capitalist as well. "The blessing of this state of things," he said, "extends beyond the limits of the South. It makes that section the balancer of the [constitutional] system; the great conservative power, which prevents other portions, less fortunately constituted, from rushing into conflict." For this reason, the capitalists should not oppose the extension of slavery into the West; they ought to realize that they had as much to gain as the planters themselves in preserving an "equilibrium" of slave and free states. And if the quarrel over the territories should threaten to end in disunion, the Northerners and not the Southerners were the ones who ought to count the cost of that event. The South could live safely to itself, for the very need of defending its peculiar institution would "bind its various and conflicting interests together." The North, however, possessed no such "central point of union," and if deprived of the stabilizing influence of the "conservative" section, would soon be torn apart as a result of social conflict.

Not only American capitalists but also the British ruling classes had a stake in the preservation of Southern slavery. According to Calhoun's logic, there was no real difference between the subjection of one man to another, as in the South, and the subjection of one class to another, as in the British Isles, or the subjection of one nation to another, as in the British Empire. Hence, in encouraging abolition, the rulers of the Empire were attacking the very principle upon which their own position rested, and were giving rise to such "convulsive" movements as chartism in England and socialism in France.

Calhoun's appeal to the Northern capitalist before the Civil War was like Marx's appeal to the Northern workingman after the war had begun: both the great reactionary and the great revolutionary, though for exactly opposite purposes, contended that the destruction of capitalism would come only after the destruction of the slave economy.

Calhoun believed it was possible to find a basis for the resolving of planter-capitalist quarrels, for he thought their causes less fundamental than those which provoked the labor-capitalist conflict. Between the planter and the manufacturer there was no ineradicable antagonism of economic interest. From no such contrariety had abolitionism arisen: it originated in "fanaticism" and gained strength only because of the close division of parties in the North, which gave politicians a motive for catering to antislavery sentiment. Nor would protectionism, once the tariff question was rightly understood, remain a barrier to cooperation between the cotton grower and the textile maker. Calhoun would advise the manufacturers —"if they would hear the voice of one who has ever wished them well"—that the domestic market was entirely "too scanty" for their resources and their skill. They should abandon the protective system, which limited exports in proportion as it checked imports, and "march forth fearlessly to meet the world in competition." Once they had "commanded" the foreign market, "all conflict between the planter and the manufacturer would cease." Upon such a policy of commercial imperialism, with cotton going out of the country not as raw stuff but as yarn and fabric, millowners and plantation proprietors might unite in mutual prosperity.

Or so Calhoun averred, at any rate. And if he had thus found an economic basis, he was even more confident that he had discovered a political basis for the alliance—his familiar doctrine of states' rights and nullification. This was his "common constitutional ground, on which the reflecting and patriotic, of every quarter of the Union, might rally to arrest the approaching catastrophe" of social revolution. His scheme of polity, as outlined in many reports and speeches and summed up and reformulated in *A Disquistion on Government* and *A Discourse on the Constitution and Government of the United States,* provided for "State interposition" to veto acts of the federal government and for secession by the individual state as a last resort. But he himself minimized these negative aspects and emphasized the positive, constructive, "conservative" features of his system. The arbiter, in case a disaffected state interposed to challenge the validity of a federal law, was to consist of three-fourths of the whole number of states. A group of commonwealths comprising one more than a fourth of the whole, Calhoun admitted, could negative the interpretation of federal powers made by the rest. This very requirement of widespread unanimity among the "concurrent majorities," however, would tend to make the leaders in all the states less demanding, more conciliatory. It would create union and strength, not division and weakness. It would ameliorate, not worsen the relations between the sections. And thus it would enable the planters of the South and the capitalists of the North to act together harmoniously in the face of a wave of revolution that threatened to engulf them both.

Presenting as he did a common ground for planter-capitalist collaboration against the class enemy, Calhoun intended his theory not merely as a bogey with which to frighten the manufacturers into yielding on the sectional issues of the day. Anyhow, he was not so naïve as to suppose that his words, by themselves, could induce the capitalists to see the light. "That any force of argument can change public opinion . . . ," he wrote in 1831, "I do not expect; but I feel assured that the coming confusion and danger, which I have long foreseen, will." Though the revolutionary movements then under way in Europe failed to have the repercussions which he anticipated for the United States, the time of confusion and danger finally seemed at hand when the financial crisis of 1834 beset the nation. Calhoun now persuaded himself that his doctrines were rapidly growing popular among the well-to-do in the North. Thousands were beginning to look to the South for protection not only against the "usurpation" of Andrew Jackson, but also against the "needy and corrupt" among their own population. "They begin to feel," Calhoun congratulated himself, "that they have more to fear from their own people, than we from our slaves." A year later, though the financial crisis had passed without fulfilling his expectations, he still nourished a hope that the capitalists would be converted sooner or later through fear of a mass uprising. "The first victims would be the wealthy and talented of the North," he thought.

The intelligence of the North must see this, but whether in time to save themselves and the institutions of the country God only knows.

But whenever their eyes may open, they will be astonished to find that the doctrines which they denounce as treason are the only means of their political salvation, while those which they so fondly hugged to their bosom were working their certain destruction.

In 1848, when Calhoun was completing his *Disquisition on Government,* he similarly felt that he could win Northern converts only after the "failure and embarrassment of the French experiment" should have "prepared" the "publick mind" by putting the capitalists in a receptive mood. Not his persuasions, then, but a crisis in the class struggle itself would bring the Northern capitalists into an alliance with the Southern planters.

Thus Calhoun supposed that, in the United States, the decisive clash between proletariat and bourgeoisie would appear before the decisive clash between bourgeoisie and landed aristocracy—an order of events that in Marxian theory was to be reversed. If his anticipations had been met, the American Civil War would have been a class war in which Northerners and Southerners fought together against a common foe. To explain why it was actually otherwise would involve a retelling of ante-bellum history, but in part what happened seems to be this: Just as the plantation politicians had succeeded in solidifying Southern opinion through the proslavery argument, so the politicians of Northern business eventually unified the diverse interests of their section with antislavery propaganda. In both parts of the country domestic discontent, or much of it at least, was deflected upon objects away from home, on the other side of Mason and Dixon's line. The point to be made here, however, is that, though Calhoun did his part in creating a sectional patriotism in the South, he persisted in hoping it would be impossible for labor and capital to achieve a similar unity in the North. Eventually, he thought, the harassed men of business would be only too glad to meet the plantation leaders on the latters' terms.

After Calhoun's death some of the apologists for a solid, proslavery South went much farther than he had gone. Jefferson Davis, horrified at the spread of strikes throughout the free world, made more explicit the parallel between abolitionism and socialism as twin attacks upon property. George Fitzhugh took a very different but even more extreme stand. In his *Sociology for the South, or the Failure of Free Society,* published at Richmond in 1854, he admitted the accuracy and justice of the socialist case against capitalism but asserted that the socialists overlooked the need for a master at the head of each of their ideal communities—a need which the Southern plantation system, or something like it, alone could meet. Fitzhugh praised slavery as the only workable form of socialism and urged the whole world to adopt it, at once, as the sole cure for class conflict and the other ills of competitive society! The pro-slavery propagandists were firm believers in what was later to be known as the *Führerprinzip,* at least insofar as it could be applied to local affairs.

But it is the spirit of Calhoun, not that of his more forthright followers, which lives on. It is a spirit that may be about to materialize in new and startling forms. Now, if ever, is the time for right-wing Republicans to join with Bourbon Democrats in the sort of reactionary alliance that Calhoun envisaged. The shibboleths of these allies will be not nullification, indeed, but certainly states' rights; not the Four Freedoms exactly, but liberty with the connotations it had for Calhoun and for the American Liberty League. The real objects of their attack will be the social controls which liberals will seek to maintain in the interests of world peace, and the democratic aspirations which have been let slip with the cry of havoc but which cannot be chained up again with the dogs of war. The leaders of the new movement will no doubt point with pride to Thomas Jefferson. But the Sage of Monticello is not their man. Let them look, instead, to the political metaphysician of South Carolina, John C. Calhoun.

The Constitution: Calhoun and Fitzhugh

When we examine more closely the inner tensions of Southern thought, the inability of the Southerners to emancipate themselves from the liberal ideas they were in the process of destroying, we find a record of turmoil as vivid as one might expect it. It is not easy to live at the same time in the dark world of Sir Walter Scott and the brightly lit world of John Locke. The contrasts are blinding, confusing, and in the end they drive a thinker mad. Calhoun, it seems to me, is our clearest proof of this.[1]

One makes such a remark about Calhoun with some trepidation, for he is the philosophic darling of students of American political thought, the man who is almost invariably advanced when a thinker of European stature is asked for in the American tradition. And yet, despite the outward literary appearance of "rigor" and "consistency" in Calhoun's work, one is bound to affirm that the man is a profoundly disintegrated political theorist. What is "rigorous" about grounding the state in force and Providence after the fashion of Maistre and then creating a set of constitutional gadgets that would have staggered even Sieyès? What is "consistent" about destroying Locke's state of nature and then evolving a theory of minority rights that actually brings one back there for good? There

[1] The interpretation of Calhoun which follows is essentially a much abbreviated version of one that I have developed in an essay on the Nullification Act of 1832, Daniel Aaron, ed., *Crisis in American History* (New York, 1952), pp. 73–89.

are more impressive thinkers to whom the American historian can point. Fitzhugh . . . must be ranked as one of these, for if on the surface he seems like a cracker-barrel commentator, at bottom he has a touch of the Hobbesian lucidity of mind. He, more than anyone else, sensed the awful way Calhoun betrayed the Reactionary Enlightenment when he based the sectional defense of the South on the ancient liberalism it tried to destroy. He fought continuously to substitute the concept of "organic nationality" for the concept of state "sovereignty," and there was the keenest logic to this substitution. By extracting a traditionalist type of Southern nationalism from the conservative theory of slavery itself, he was able to give up all of the compacts and all of the checks on which Calhoun relied.

We have to concede, however, that without this approach there was really no alternative to riding the two horses Calhoun tried to ride. For the theory of the reaction grounds itself on the divinity of existing coercions, and while this may serve a purpose for the defense of Negro slavery, it hardly serves a purpose for the liberation of the South from regional "slavery" to the North. The second type of slavery, if we take the Southerners at their word, was just as existent as the first, and if Calhoun's God ordained the one, how could he have failed to ordain the other? The irony of the Burkian position, even in Europe, was that it became articulate at precisely the moment it became untenable, at the moment when God had introduced a new reality to challenge his old one, which meant that when Burke denounced the French Revolution he had to become something of a rationalist himself. Under these circumstances, lacking Fitzhugh's faith in the South's romantic nationalism, it is not hard to see why Calhoun in his battle against the North kept applying the ethos of the Kentucky-Virginia Resolutions. After all an inconsistency is better than a logical surrender.

But let us make no mistake about the fact of inconsistency: it is not merely striking, it is doubly and triply striking. Had Calhoun merely maintained an ordinary faith in the mechanics of the American Constitution at the same moment that he grounded government in force and tradition, this would have been one thing. But his faith is not an ordinary one. There is a weird quality about Calhoun; he has a wild passion for the conclusions his premises nullify, as if a pang of guilt made him redouble his affection for the things that he destroyed. The idea of state "sovereignty" shatters a meaningful American union, and yet he insists with the most anguished repetition that this alone can serve as a national "preservative." The idea of a fixed Southern minority and a fixed Northern majority amounts to civil war, and yet the scheme of the "concurrent majority" he builds upon it he describes in terms of compromise that are nothing short of idyllic.[2] The best example of this mounting love in the midst of murder is the one that I have mentioned: the attempt to ground both of these mechanical schemes on the organic naturalism that his social defense of slavery inspired.

For surely the idea that the Constitution is a "compact" among "sovereign" states, that states may therefore nullify federal legislation, and that the proof of this is to be found in a diligent study of ratification procedures in 1787, is about as far away as you can get from the spirit of "Divine ordination." This not only makes the American system of government a rationalistic instrument of extreme delicacy but it pins its origin to a decisive moment in historical time just as Condorcet, misunderstanding American constitutionalism, pinned it in the eighteenth century. If the Southerners usually had to distort American liberalism in order to denounce it as "metaphysical," they would not, ironically enough, have had to distort Calhoun's version of its constitutional embodiment in order to denounce it in that way. That version met all of the "metaphysical" standards. It left nothing to tradition, nothing to force, and nothing to God. Nor is it the only thing we have to consider. There is also Calhoun's theory of the "concurrent majority," which supplemented state nullification with the nullification of individual "interests." When we pile the one on top of the other, we have a scheme of man-made political instruments which the French Enlightenment in its palmiest days never dared to develop.

It is here, in his passionate defense of the minority interest, that Calhoun goes back to Locke's state of nature after having destroyed it in a blaze of organic glory. For there are of course minorities

---

[2] Note the words in the *Disquisition:* "And hence, instead of faction, strife, and struggle for party ascendency, there would be patriotism, nationality, harmony, and a struggle only for supremacy in promoting the common good of the whole." R. K. Crallé, ed. (New York, 1943), p. 49.

within minorities—as Unionists like Hugh Swinton Legare did not fail to remind Calhoun in South Carolina in 1832—and since Calhoun offers no reason why these should not be given a policy veto too, the idea of the "concurrent majority" quickly unravels itself into separate individuals executing the law of nature for themselves. When Locke accepted majority rule, in other words, he accepted more force in politics than Calhoun, the great theorist of force and slavery, was ready to accept. When Locke accepted majority rule, he was more pessimistic than Calhoun, the great pessimist, would permit himself to be. What could be worse for the logic of the Southern position? Here are grim traditionalists denouncing Northern liberalism as a code of "anarchy," and Calhoun supplies them with a political theory that even Daniel Webster can denounce as a theory to "anarchy." Here are ardent corporatists denying that a natural harmony of interests can ever exist—and Calhoun advances a logic of harmony that one would have to go to Godwin to duplicate.

Since Calhoun's mechanical suggestions were a failure, it is interesting that his newfound organic philosophy did not suggest the nature of their failure to him. One might say, as has often been said, that Calhoun was here merely extending the checking-and-balancing ethos of the Founding Fathers. If this is true, then his wild rationalism has a curious logic to it. Adams and Morris, instead of grounding their hope for America on a liberal unity that could support even their clumsy scheme of checks and balances, grounded it on the capacity of those checks and balances to contain and control frightful social conflicts that did not exist. In the only time in American history when such conflicts did appear, what was more reasonable than for a disciple of theirs to multiply passionately all of the checks and balances that were about to be exploded? But in his role as an antagonist of American liberalism, why didn't Calhoun see the futility of this reasoning? Why didn't his organic sense for the importance of social solidarity make him realize that however much you compounded "interest" checks with other checks none of them would work if the social fabric was actually torn apart? There was at least this relevance of traditionalism to the liberal cement of American life: that by concentrating on the solidarity that comes from "prejudice" it might have exposed the

liberal prejudices that had held the country together to the view
of "realistic" thinkers who had managed not to see them. Some
Southern organicists actually caught this point, but Calhoun himself did not: the lesson of Adams ran too deep for a sudden correction by Burke.

And yet it would be unfair, after all of this has been said, not to
notice that Calhoun was aware of the basic contradiction he faced.
In his famous *Disquisition* he drew a distinction between "government" and "constitution." Governments were rooted in force and
inspired by God even as Negro slavery was, but constitutions were
a different thing entirely. They controlled government, and being
the product of a later age, when "invention" replaced "superstition," they could be used to abolish the South's regional enslavement to the North. Here was a straightforward effort to deal with
the problem of Maistre and Sieyès. But it reminds us alas, for all
of its ingenuity, of a man carefully placing a match on top of a
stick of dynamite. For clearly if "constitution" and "government"
ever come together at any point, if it is ever established that the one
has any of the characteristics of the other, an explosion is bound
to occur which wipes the Southern position off the face of the philosophic earth. Not only does the South become validly enslaved
to the North, but the whole structure of "compact" and "concurrent
majority" is swept away in a fierce tide of irrationalism. What difference then does it make whether a genuinely "American people"
did or did not exist in 1787? God could have created one in the
interval. What difference does it make whether minorities are
coerced? Coercion is a law of life. What difference does it make
whether the Southern "interest" is consulted? Interests can never
work together freely and harmoniously anyway. This was a great
deal to stake on a tenuous distinction between "constitution" and
"government." And to say that the distinction was tenuous is putting the matter mildly. There are some who would argue that the
control of government is actually the highest form of the governmental task.

Fitzhugh, then, was rightly terrified at the doctrines of the
"Calhoun school." His theory of blood and solid nationalism, of
"organic nationality," avoided all of the inner turmoil and the
brink-of-destruction gyrations that the Calhounian position in-

volved. Romantic, grounded in the claim of slave culture itself, it could never be assailed by the conservative theory that slavery produced. Nor should we assume that Fitzhugh was here a voice crying in the wilderness. Many Southerners, as the sense of their separateness was forced upon them and as the appeal of Scott and Disraeli grew, became attached to the principle of traditionalist nationalism with a genuine and ardent feeling. Of course, few of them became attached to it so much that they were ready to give up constitutional apologetics entirely, which meant that their original dualism of Burke and Locke was simply duplicated again on the plane of nationalism. But under the circumstances what is striking is not how little romantic nationalism there was in the political thought of the South but how little there was of it in the political thought of the "nationalistic" North. Daniel Webster remained as legalistic as Marshall, despite the fact that had he adopted some form of romantic nationalism (it would, of course, have to be a Rousseauan or a Mazzinian type in his case), he would have been able to explode against Calhoun much of the dynamite that he was playing with. There was much romanticism in the North, but with the exception of a few men like Barlow and Emerson, it spent itself in a Thoreauan individualism or a Garrisonian cosmopolitanism. Garrison denounced constitutional lawyers as fervently as Fitzhugh did, but he put on the masthead of *The Liberator,* "Our country is the world."

Thus, oddly, the South, the "sectionalist" South, became the real originator of romantic nationalism in American political theory. But one thing has to be said about that nationalism: it radicalized the whole Southern position. For it is hard to control the claim of nationalism, and especially the claim of Scott's nationalism, with its love of chivalry, its faith in force, its ethos of blood and soil. Implicitly the solution that Fitzhugh offered called for independence and beat the drums of war. And here the "Calhoun school," at least until 1860, might have offered a reply: it did not want independence and it did not want war. If it clung to Enlightenment contractualism because it wanted to defend the South against the North, it clung to it also because it wanted them both to live together. Its inconsistency pointed in two directions. This is the larger secret of Calhoun's intellectual madness: he appears at a moment when the South's fear of the North and its love of the Union hold each other in perfect balance, so that starting with explosive premises like sovereignty and conflict and force he drives himself somehow to avert the explosion with conclusions like nullification and the "concurrent majority." He was caught in the classic agony of the brink-of-war philosopher.

But the main point I want to emphasize is the coexistence in the Southern mind of its new Burkian traditionalism and its old Jeffersonian rationalism. Calhoun exemplifies it perfectly, a man whose thought is cut in two by the tug of the liberal past and the pull of the reactionary present. He slays Jefferson only to embrace him with a passion in the end, he destroys the Founding Fathers only to carry their work forward. Under such circumstances why should Garrison bother to reply to the elaborate Providential organicism of the South? The South was doing a good enough job of replying to it itself. The point illustrates again the basic dilemma the Southerners faced: their liberalism was so traditional that even they could not get away from it: Garrison the "jacobin" had the power of their own historic irrationalism on his side, and they, the historic irrationalists, could not even be decent "jacobins." They were, in a sense, outside of time and space, carrying on a reactionary conversation with themselves in a kind of Alice-in-Wonderland world where nothing was what it seemed to be, where nothing was what it ought to be, where liberalism was oddly conservatized and conservatism oddly liberalized. Or, if one prefers Stevenson to Carroll, they were a set of Dr. Jekylls constantly becoming Mr. Hydes—their own worst enemies and their own executioners.

WILLIAM W. FREEHLING

✪

Spoilsmen and Interests in the Thought and Career of John C. Calhoun

Over a century after his death John C. Calhoun is still considered one of America's outstanding political theorists. In a culture which has usually exalted the doctrine of majority rule, he stands out as an entrenched defender of minority rights. The South Carolinian's political theory has been equally renowned for its emphasis on economic interests, and even detractors heap praise on his insight into the economic roots of political events. Political scientists term him a founding father of pressure group theory, while historians point to him with pride as an American counterpart of the great European theorists of economic determinism. Recently, two leading historians have suggested that Calhoun anticipated Marx in his contention that the struggle between classes determines political controversy. In a more traditional interpretation the Carolinian's overriding theme remains the conflict between the great geographical subdivisions in a nation. But whether viewed as a theorist of class or of sectional interests, Calhoun is usually considered a leading American exponent of a consistently economic theory of politics.[1]

[1] For a representative sampling of the extensive Calhoun literature, see Charles M. Wiltse, *John C. Calhoun*, 3 vols. (Indianapolis, 1944–1951); Wiltse, "Calhoun and the Modern State," *Virginia Quarterly Review*, XIII (Summer 1937), 396–408; Richard Nelson Current, "John C. Calhoun, Philosopher of Reaction," *Antioch Review*, III (June 1943) 223–234; Cur-

Reprinted from *The Journal of American History*, Vol. 52, No. 2 (June 1965), pp. 25–42, by permission.

172   WILLIAM W. FREEHLING

No one would deny that the clash of pressure groups alarmed
Calhoun. But he was far from a thoroughgoing economic determin-
ist. The crucial reason why his political philosophy is hopelessly inconsistent is that he had only a sporadic commitment to an economic interest theory of history.

First of all, Calhoun had a morbid appreciation of the political
power of antislavery ideology. For the last two decades of his life
the abolitionist campaign was Calhoun's master concern, and he
feared the antislavery "fanatics" not because they appealed to
Northern pocketbooks but because they engaged the nation's conscience. Calhoun often reiterated his conviction that "a large portion of the northern states believed slavery to be a sin," and he
always dreaded the moment when the Yankees would feel "an
obligation of conscience to abolish it." [2] The notion that ideas can
be the decisive force in politics makes Calhoun a rather milk-toast
Marxist, and marks his first important step away from a thoroughly
economic conception of history.

The dangers wrought by corrupt spoilsmen, Calhoun's second
deviation from an economic interest theory of politics, is even more
significant in his political thought. To a Marxist, or to any consistent believer in economic determinism, the politician's quest for
the spoils of office is of minor importance. Politicians are the tools
of the interests they represent, and the commands of the interests—
not the intrigues of the spoilsmen—form the driving force of the
historical process. But Calhoun always believed that demagogic
spoilsmen could delude the rabble, control popular elections, ignore the desires of the great communal interests, and turn the political scene into a mere scramble for patronage. As a disdainful
patrician in the age when the two-party system first became an
American fixture, he feared that democracy could not survive the
race for the spoils. This alarm about emergent spoilsmen is the
neglected theme in the thought and career of the Carolinian.

rent, *John C. Calhoun* (New York, 1963); Richard Hofstadter, "John C.
Calhoun: The Marx of the Master Class," *The American Political Tradi-
tion and the Men Who Made It* (New York, 1948), pp. 67–91; August O.
Spain, *The Political Theory of John C. Calhoun* (New York, 1951); Peter
F. Drucker, "A Key to American Politics: Calhoun's Pluralism," *Review
of Politics*, X (October 1948) 412–426.
   [2] Richard K. Crallé, ed., *The Works of John C. Calhoun*, 6 vols. (New
York, 1854–1857), II, 483, 628.

Calhoun's concern with corrupt politicians is particularly evident in *A Disquisition on Government,* the most systematic statement of his political philosophy.[3] The *Disquisition* has long been regarded as Calhoun's definitive formulation of, and solution to, the problem of warring economic interests. However, to read the *Disquisition* in this way is to miss half of Calhoun's intention. The *Disquisition* presents a picture of democracy gone to seed. Corruption in government has been a prime cause of its swift decline; spoilsmen feuding over patronage will soon bring on anarchy and revolution; the unscrupulous political boss will emerge the despotic victor. Calhoun's concern with the war of selfish economic interests is no more acute than his very different concern with the clash of scheming political spoilsmen. These twin obsessions, inseparable yet irreconcilable, produce a political theory which can best be termed a mass of contradictions.

For the purpose of analysis the two theories which are intertwined in the *Disquisition* have been termed the "theory of interests" and the "theory of spoilsmen." The theory of interests designates Calhoun's contention that the leading interest groups—the different classes, separate sections, various economic groups—dominate political events. The theory of spoilsmen deals with his contention that corrupt demagogues control the democratic process.

The theory of interests is the well-known portion of the *Disquisition,* and hence a brief summary will suffice. Calhoun began with the assumption that man "is so constituted, that his direct or individual affections are stronger than his sympathetic or social feelings." It follows that a group of men with similar concerns is more

---

[3] *A Disquisition on Government* was partially intended as an introduction to *A Discourse on the Constitution and Government of the United States,* Calhoun's long essay on American constitutional history. However, the *Disquisition* was also intended to stand on its own as a theoretical "foundation for political science." John C. Calhoun to Mrs. T. G. Clemson, December 31, 1849, J. F. Jameson, ed., *Correspondence of John C. Calhoun, Annual Report of the American Historical Association, 1899* (Washington, 1900), II, 777. This article will focus on the *Disquisition* as a statement of theoretical philosophy rather than as an introduction to constitutional theory. The author will discuss Calhoun's constitutional theory at length in a forthcoming volume on the nullification controversy. For a preliminary statement see William W. Freehling, "The Nullification Controversy in South Carolina" (Doctoral dissertation, University of California, Berkeley, 1964), pp. 222–241.

self-interested than disinterested. Therefore, in a democracy, if one interest group contains a numerical majority, it will "pervert its powers to oppress, and plunder the other." If no pressure group can muster a majority, "a combination will be formed between those whose interests are most alike." In both cases minority riches will soon be transferred into majority pockets by legislative edict, a form of legal plunder which rivals the exactions of the most despotic prince. Neither a separation of powers nor a written constitution can relieve the plight of the hapless minority. The numerical majority will elect the President and the Congress; the majority President will appoint majority judges; and the appointed judges will interpret the Constitution, stripping away minority rights by judicial decree.[4]

A government of the concurrent majority, on the other hand, will end the danger of majority tyranny by giving each pressure group a veto on all legislation. Since each interest will have to concur for any law to pass, successful selfishness will become impossible, and the various social interests will be forced to send disinterested compromisers to the legislative chambers. There remains the possibility that the constant use of the veto power will lead to governmental paralysis and to social anarchy. Calhoun confessed that an impotent government would be an intolerable evil. But he presented two crucial reasons why the concurrent majority will produce creative compromise rather than a permanent stalemate. First, since anarchy is "the greatest of all evils," the various interests will have every selfish reason to cooperate whenever pending legislation becomes an "urgent necessity." [5] Secondly, this desire to seek compromise will inspire the leading pressure groups to elevate to power the very statesmen who are most able to find grounds for conciliation.

Under the numerical majority, argued Calhoun, each interest elects unscrupulous and designing politicians, since such men are best equipped to devise means of plundering other interests. These sordid schemers are incapable of seeking the common good through disinterested compromise. But in governments of the concurrent majority, interests will realize that they must cooperate instead of compete, and hence the politician's craft will give way to the statesman's art. Calhoun held that "each portion, in order to advance

4 Crallé, *Works*, I, 3, 16, 31–34.
5 *Ibid.*, pp. 38–39, 65.

its own peculiar interests, would have to conciliate all others, by showing a disposition to advance theirs; and, for this purpose, each would select those to represent it, whose wisdom, patriotism, and weight of character, would command the confidence of the others." [6]

This combination of interests determined to compromise and statesmen dedicated to conciliation will insure the success of the concurrent majority. Thus the pack of selfish interests will be forced to maintain a disinterested government and to elevate its handful of selfless men to power. Calhoun waxed lyrical at the beneficent prospect: "instead of faction, strife, and struggle for party ascendency, there would be patriotism, nationality, harmony, and a struggle only for supremacy in promoting the common good of the whole." [7]

Before turning to the theory of spoilsmen, it would be well to underscore the assumptions upon which the theory of interests is based. The problem posed by warring interests and the solution achieved by the concurrent majority both assume that the legislators perfectly represent the desires of their constituents.[8] Discord in Congress merely reflects conflict between economic interests. When the pressure groups are neutralized, the legislative feuds will cease. The new objectives of the economic interests even produce the growing quality of political leadership. As the pressure groups' thirst for plunder gives way to the necessity for compromise, statesmen inevitably replace politicos at the head of the state. The major economic interests are the guiding, primal force in the political drama. The men who sit in the halls of Congress are mere servants who speak, maneuver, and vote as their constituents direct.

The theory of spoilsmen, like the theory of interests, is based on the primordial selfishness of human nature. However, the focus shifts from the economic interests to their politicians, and the servants become masters. Spoilsmen, breaking free from the control of the interests which selected them, emerge as the primary historical force. This time, the pot of gold which turns men into plunderers is the spoils of office rather than the riches of minorities. Since nations

[6] *Ibid.*, pp. 68–69.
[7] *Ibid.*, p. 49.
[8] *Ibid.*, pp. 14, 28.

—like individuals and economic interests—are primarily selfish, governments must maintain "vast establishments" to deter aggressive enemies. The politicians who are elected to the higher offices in the government control the hiring, paying, and firing of the thousands of employees which such huge military preparations require. Since politicians—like almost everyone else—are self-interested, they will employ every effective method to gain a monopoly of the spoils.[9]

The spoilsmen have the supreme weapon of demagoguery at their disposal. Calhoun assumed that the average voter is a greedy and gullible creature who will respond to inflammatory appeals to his passions. Demagogues bent on securing patronage need only make full use of "cunning, falsehood, deception, slander, fraud, and gross appeals to the appetites of the lowest and most worthless portions of the community." Soon the nation will be "thoroughly debased and corrupted." Demagogic spoilsmen will completely control their depraved constituents.[10]

Meanwhile the party structure will be refined and extended. Patronage will be used to control wayward legislators, and the party boss will demand absolute obedience from his immediate subordinates. As Calhoun's dirge unfolds, politicians forget their constituents and engage in the most violent struggle for patronage. Those "seeking office and patronage would become too numerous to be rewarded by the offices and patronage at the disposal of the government"; the disappointed would shift their allegiance causing the control of the government to "vibrate" between the factions until "confusion, corruption, disorder, and anarchy" become so destructive that all social interests seek peace from their politicians by turning to a military despot.[11] Thus in the imminent destruction of democracy spoilsmen rather than interests will tear down the last walls of the republic.

Nothing better shows the extent of Calhoun's fear of spoilsmen than the historical examples he developed in the *Disquisition*. Calhoun believed that the Romans and the English had experimented with the concurrent majority, and he employed their histories to

[9] *Ibid.,* p. 18.
[10] *Ibid.,* pp. 41–42.
[11] *Ibid.,* pp. 40–44. See also pp. 17–24, 37–39.

demonstrate his principles. The resulting narratives bear little resemblance to historical truth, but they supply an excellent illustration of Calhoun's own logic and fears. With both Rome and England, Calhoun viewed his historical material through the perspective of his social theory. And in each narrative the war of spoilsmen poses the greatest threat to the concurrent majority.

In ancient Rome, argued Calhoun, two distinct classes of interests existed, the patricians and the plebeians. A violent conflict between the two classes was at last resolved by giving the Tribune, controlled by the plebeians, the power to veto all laws that the Senate, controlled by the patricians, passed. But the concurrent majority soon broke down. The enormous wealth gained in conquest caused

the formation of parties, (irrespective of the old division of patricians and plebeians,) having no other object than to obtain the control of the government for the purpose of plunder. . . . Under their baneful influence, the possession of the government became the object of the most violent conflicts; not between patricians and plebeians,—but between profligate and corrupt factions. They continued with increasing violence, until, finally, Rome sank, as must every community under similar circumstances, beneath the strong grasp, the despotic rule of the chieftain of the successful party;—the sad, but only alternative which remained to prevent universal violence, confusion and anarchy.[12]

Thus the concurrent majority, introduced to end a bloody conflict of class interests, was itself overturned by the equally violent strife of political spoilsmen. However, the concurrent majority wins its vindication in Calhoun's panegyric on the political genius of the English. For in Calhoun's England the concurrent majority successfully ends the supremacy of spoilsmen.

The miraculous success is gained by totally ignoring the conflict of pressure groups. Calhoun's visionary England is undisturbed by controversies between classes or occupations or sections. The sole problem revolves around the spoils of office. The prime contestants include the citizens who pay the taxes, the monarch who dispenses the patronage, and the lords who receive the offices. Each of the disputants controls a segment of the government, and each segment has a veto on all legislation. The House of Commons repre-

[12] *Ibid.*, pp. 92–95, 97.

sents "the great tax-paying interest by which the government is supported." The King is "the conduit through which, all the honors and emoluments of the government flow." The conflict between Commons and King would necessarily "end in violence and an appeal to force" were it not for the stabilizing influence of the House of Lords. Whereas the King dispenses the patronage, the Lords receive the spoils. Since the members of the House of Lords are "the principal recipients of the honors, emoluments, and other advantages derived from the government," their most profound desire is to preserve the system. Thus the Lords interpose to maintain the equilibrium between Commons and King.[13]

The genius of the system, continued Calhoun, is most evident when the British kingdom expands. Rome collapsed because the bounty gained in conquest inspired a resurgence of spoilsmen. But in England an increase in patronage only adds stability to the system: "the greater the patronage of the government, the greater will be the share" which the House of Lords receives; "the more eligible its condition, the greater its opposition to any radical change" in governmental form. No matter how lush the spoils become, the Lords, Commons, and King will go on checking each other, thus preventing a war over patronage and demonstrating the supreme virtue of the concurrent majority.[14]

In both the Roman and English narratives, then, corruption in government emerges as Calhoun's prime concern. In Rome, the concurrent majority checked the clash of interests and then succumbed to a conflict of spoilsmen. In England, communal pressure groups are nowhere to be found, and the system is devised to avert a war over patronage. These historical fantasies reveal once again how profoundly Calhoun was disturbed by the intrigues of the spoilsmen.[15]

[13] *Ibid.*, pp. 102–103.
[14] *Ibid.*, pp. 105–106.
[15] Calhoun's discussion of the problems of minority interests also superbly illustrates the central importance of his theory of spoilsmen. Calhoun sometimes assumed that the principle of periodic elections would be of no help to minority interests, for the numerical majority would simply reelect the same representatives at subsequent elections. But in the *Disquisition* Calhoun admitted that minority interests could become part of a new majority coalition when the polls reopened. The problem is that the war between spoilsmen will lead to a revolution which will close the polls

Calhoun never really explained how the success of the concurrent majority in England points the way toward a cure for the disease of spoilsmen in a democracy. As Calhoun described it, the alleged absence of spoilsmen in England depends as much on the principle of monarchy as on the doctrine of the concurrent majority. Spoilsmen do not develop in England, he wrote, partly because the dispenser of patronage is an hereditary king rather than an elected politician, which prevents "in consequence of its unity and hereditary character, the violent and factious struggles to obtain the control of the government,—and, with it, the vast patronage which distracted, corrupted, and finally subverted the Roman Republic." [16] Calhoun was hardly proposing that a democratic nation save itself by adopting a king. The question remains, how could the concurrent majority cure the disease of spoilsmen in a democracy?

First of all, Calhoun believed that governmental revenues would inevitably shrink when each minority interest could veto any tax bill. Reduced taxes would result in diminished patronage, thereby removing the cause of the clash between spoilsmen. On the other hand, under a government of the numerical majority, the minority interests would continually be forced to pay higher taxes, thereby increasing patronage and stimulating spoilsmen. [17]

But, as Calhoun indirectly admitted, minority veto would never reduce patronage enough to discourage the spoilsmen for long. Calhoun is remembered today more for his later years as a determined sectionalist than for his early career as an ardent nationalist. Yet the fundamental premise of the early Calhoun, the assumption that strong national military preparations alone insure lasting peace, is what destroys his later political theory. Calhoun could legiti-

---

forever. "It is true," Calhoun conceded, "that . . . the minor and subject party, for the time, have the right to oppose and resist the major and dominant party, for the time, through the ballot box; and may turn them out, and take their place. . . . But such a state of things must necessarily be temporary. The conflict between the two parties must be transferred, sooner or later, from an appeal to the ballot box to an appeal to force." *Ibid.*, pp. 39–40. See also pp. 23–24.

[16] *Ibid.*, p. 106.

[17] This is never directly expressed in the *Disquisition* but it is often reiterated elsewhere. See, for example, Calhoun to Armistead Burt, December 24, 1838, Jameson, *Correspondence*, pp. 422–423.

mately expect that minority veto would remove one of the two
causes of huge bureaucracy, a majority's systematic perversion of
the power of taxation to exploit the minority. However, the South
Carolinian hoped and believed that no interest would veto the
necessary expenses for national defense—the second reason for
vast government—and he maintained that legitimate appropriations
for military survival would alone produce a government large
enough to stimulate violent conflicts between spoilsmen.[18]

Thus Calhoun's first solution to the problem of spoilsmen fails
because, even under the concurrent majority, patronage will be
extensive enough to attract demagogues. But Calhoun did not rely
solely on reducing the spoils to put down the politicians. He also
believed that the very nature of government under the concurrent
majority would elevate to power men of enlarged and enlightened
views. Since pressure groups would have to cooperate instead of
conflict, they would elect disinterested statesmen rather than scheming politicians. The concurrent majority would effectively force
interests to destroy the spoilsmen.

The difficulty with this solution to the problem of spoilsmen is
that it rests on the premises of the theory of interests; it assumes
that pressure groups control their politicians. But the theory of
spoilsmen assumes that demagogues can delude the rabble and
break free from all control. If the concurrent majority would force
interests to elect statesmen, the spoils of office would continue to
call forth the demagoguery of the spoilsmen. Since the "vast"
military establishments would still offer rich patronage harvests,
corrupt politicians would have no reason to cease their electioneer-
ing. And since the masses would remain as gullible as ever, statesmen would still have little chance of defeating demagogues in a
popular election.[19] Thus the need for disinterested compromisers,

18 Crallé, *Works*, I, 17–18.
19 At one point in the *Disquisition* Calhoun claimed that demagogues
would pose no threat to a government of the concurrent majority. His
reasons, however, are unconvincing. Under the numerical majority, he
argued, "the wealthy and ambitious" would inevitably "excite and direct"
the "more ignorant and dependent portions of the community." Thus suffrage would have to be severely restricted. But under the concurrent
majority, continued Calhoun, suffrage could be well nigh universal. "Mere
numbers" would no longer control the government, and hence demagogues
"would have neither hope nor inducement" to delude the masses "in order

like the reduction in the size of government, may slow down but cannot stop the rise of spoilsmen. In both cases the "vast" military establishment remains to invite the resurgence of demagogues. Under the concurrent majority in the future, no less than under the numerical majority in the past, the supremacy of spoilsmen will continue to threaten the republic.

The concurrent majority's failure to end the disease of spoilsmen is serious enough in itself. The race for patronage alone leads to revolution and dictatorship. However, the continued supremacy of political spoilsmen also has a disastrous effect on an ultimate reconciliation of economic interests. Critics of the *Disquisition* have always maintained that minority veto would destroy a democratic system by completely paralyzing the governmental process. As has been seen, Calhoun conceded the overriding importance of this consideration, but he countered with the assertion that the concurrent majority would inevitably produce compromise because enlightened statesmen would be elevated to power. With "representatives so well qualified to accomplish the object for which they were selected," argued Calhoun,

the prevailing desire would be, to promote the common interests of the whole; and, hence, the competition would be, not which should yield the least to promote the common good, but which should yield the most . . . herein is to be found the feature, which distinguishes government of the concurrent majority so strikingly from those of the numerical. In the latter, each faction, in the struggle to obtain the control of the government, elevates to power the designing, the artful, and unscrupulous, who, in their devotion to party,—instead of aiming at the good of the whole,—aim exclusively at securing the ascendency of party.[20]

---

to obtain the control." *Ibid.,* pp. 45–46. Of course Calhoun is right that the concurrent majority would prevent the masses from passing laws detrimental to a propertied minority. But this would not affect the motivation of the spoilsmen. The spoils of office would still give demagogues every "inducement" to debase the mob in order "to obtain the control." And as Calhoun readily conceded, whenever "party triumph and ascendency" is placed "above the safety and prosperity of the community," the combined force of "falsehood, injustice, fraud, artifice, slander, and breach of faith," will "overpower all regard for truth, justice, sincerity, and moral obligations of every description." *Ibid.,* pp. 49–50.

[20] *Ibid.,* p. 69.

It is hardly necessary to trace the ultimate defect in Calhoun's theory. The concurrent majority, to be successful in conciliating interests, must result in compromise; statesmen are likely—but by Calhoun's own admission, spoilsmen unlikely—to seek the general interest; the concurrent majority fails to stop the war of spoilsmen; hence politicos, not the wise and virtuous, will be elected; thus governmental deadlock and social anarchy are likely to ensue; therefore the concurrent majority cannot successfully end the clash of interests.

The failure of the concurrent majority is the result of the fundamental contradiction in Calhoun's political philosophy. The concurrent majority, expressly designed to end political strife by preventing clashes between different portions of the community, assumes that the interests control their politicians. The theory of spoilsmen rests on the premise that demagogues control their constituents. The concurrent majority, in curing the disease of the interests, will not affect the intrigues of the demagogues. Even a completely disinterested government will supply enough patronage to whet the appetites of the spoilsmen. Thus corrupt demagogues will still use the rabble to obtain high office and use high office to enrich themselves. And the continued success of unscrupulous politicians will undermine the chance of a disinterested compromise between communal interests. In the end, Calhoun's attempt to unite in one theory two irreconcilable conceptions of political causation topples the entire logical structure.

The central importance of the theory of spoilsmen in the *Disquisition* leads to the obvious question, why was Calhoun so distressed about political corruption? The answer comes from two directions. First of all, as a political philosopher well versed in the ideology of the Founding Fathers, Calhoun inherited that strain of late eighteenth-century thought which considered democratic politics the pursuit of gentlemen and disdained legislative cabals and mass parties. Secondly, as the political leader of the South Carolina planters during the Age of Jackson, Calhoun had special reasons to deplore the emerging spoils system. A brief consideration of Calhoun's intellectual heritage and his political career will help to explain the emphasis on corrupt politicians in his formal political theory.

To the men who led the American Revolution and founded the federal Republic, the possibility of party conflict always seemed one of the great dangers which beset a democracy. The Founding Fathers were upper-class republicans, and they sought "to refine and enlarge the public view" by insuring that a propertied elite would rule. If political parties developed, corrupt demagogues might "first obtain the suffrages, and then betray the interests, of the people." [21] As John Taylor of Caroline put it, "all parties, however loyal to principles at first, degenerate into aristocracies of interests at last; and unless a nation is capable of discerning the point where integrity ends and fraud begins, popular parties are among the surest modes of introducing an aristocracy." [22]

The Founding Fathers' distrust of political parties received its classic expression in George Washington's famous "Farewell Address" of 1796. Washington could not take leave of his countrymen without warning them "in the most solemn manner against the baneful effects of the spirit of party generally." Party agitation, he declared, "is seen in its greatest rankness" in republican governments "and is truly their worst enemy." The spirit of party "serves always to distract the public councils and enfeeble the public administration. It agitates the community with ill-founded alarms; kindles the animosity of one part against another; foments occasionally riot and insurrection." Only "a uniform vigilance," said Washington, can "prevent its bursting into a flame." [23]

During the early years of the Republic the Founding Fathers' political practices often belied their antiparty principles. The election of 1800, in particular, was a bitterly fought contest between two aggressive political parties. However, the Jeffersonian and Federalist parties remained only half developed; they had all but dissolved by 1820. More important, the new nation's early Presidents were usually enlightened aristocrats, philosopher statesmen who spent less time than their midnineteenth-century successors perfecting partisan political organizations.

During the Age of Jackson more systematic national political

[21] Benjamin Fletcher Wright, ed., *The Federalist* (Cambridge, 1961), p. 134. See also pp. 111, 271–272, 441, 459, 487–488.

[22] Quoted in Hofstadter, *American Political Tradition*, p. 13 n.

[23] James D. Richardson, ed., *A Compilation of the Messages and Papers of the Presidents*, 11 vols. (Washington, 1897–1914), I, 210–211.

parties emerged, requiring a different style of political leader and making the struggle for the spoils of federal office of high importance. A plentiful supply of patronage could knit together the diverse factions which made up a national party. Moreover, leading this hybrid of local factions required flexibility, tact, and political maneuver. By 1850 the Founding Fathers' vision of a republic without political parties had been rendered hopelessly obsolete, and the age of the philosopher statesman had given way to the age of the political manager.[24]

Calhoun's career spanned the years of transition. Educated at Yale College and the Litchfield Law School at the beginning of the nineteenth century, the South Carolinian studied under Timothy Dwight, James Gould, and Tapping Reeve, three high priests of the Federalist faith. Calhoun remained a Jeffersonian in spite of his mentors. But Jefferson himself prayed that popular majorities would select "natural aristocrats" to govern, and the young Calhoun probably raised few objections to the elitist side of the dogmas handed down at Litchfield and Yale. Calhoun emerged from his encounter with the Federalists steeped in the eighteenth-century conviction that democracies could best survive if enlightened aristocrats continued to rule.

Throughout his ensuing national career Calhoun fought to preserve the Founding Fathers' principles against the onslaught of the emerging political managers. In his brilliant early years as Secretary of War under James Monroe, Calhoun opposed the Presidential aspirations of William H. Crawford partly because the Georgian hoped "to attain favor, not by placing himself on principles and policy . . . but by political dexterity and management." [25] Calhoun's crusade against John Quincy Adams' administration was also partly motivated by growing concern with base political methods. Adams had risen to power, according to Calhoun, by a "corrupt bargain" with Henry Clay in which Adams bought the Presi-

[24] This shift in the nature of American political leadership is particularly well chronicled in William Nisbet Chambers, *Old Bullion Benton, Senator from the New West: Thomas Hart Benton, 1782–1858* (Boston, 1956). For Calhoun's own analysis, see Calhoun to Duff Green, February 10, 1844, Jameson, *Correspondence*, pp. 568–569.

[25] Calhoun to Charles Fischer, August 1, 1823, Fischer Papers (Southern Historical Collection, University of North Carolina Library).

dency by paying Clay with the appointment as Secretary of State.[26] In late 1829, when the political craftiness of Martin Van Buren had begun to drive Calhoun to the rear of the Jackson movement, the South Carolinian wrote John McLean that "I deeply apprehend, that the choice of the chief magistrate will finally be placed at the disposition of the executive power itself, through a corrupt system to be founded on the abuse of the power and patronage of the government." [27]

Thwarted by Van Buren and isolated from Jackson in 1831, Calhoun became a leader of the South Carolina Nullifiers. One of the many reasons for his action was the belief that South Carolina's veto of the tariff would lower governmental revenues and thereby reduce executive patronage.[28] By 1835 the South Carolinian was obsessed with the notion that Jackson's use of the patronage to promote the ascendancy of his own handpicked candidate was turning democracy into dictatorship.[29] Arguing in his "Report on the Extent of the Executive Patronage" that the executive corps was becoming "so strong as to be capable of sustaining itself by the influence alone, unconnected with any system or measure of policy," Calhoun urged Congress to enact controls on "King Andrew's" manipulation of the spoils.[30] Thereafter, in every major policy decision, from distributing the surplus revenue to enacting the Independent Treasury, from lowering the tariff to entering the Mexican War, the "Cast-Iron Man" from South Carolina carefully weighed the effect on executive patronage. For a time, in the late 1830's and early 1840's, Calhoun believed that patronage could be successfully dried up.[31] But by 1848 an embittered Calhoun had almost admitted defeat. He did not see "how any man who has the ability and the disposition to correct abuses and reform the government can in the present state of politics be elected. The

[26] Calhoun to Micah Sterling, August 12, 1827, Calhoun Papers (South Caroliniana Library, Columbia).

[27] Calhoun to John McLean, September 22, 1829, McLean Papers (Manuscript Division, Library of Congress).

[28] Calhoun to the Committee of Arrangements, September 16, 1836, *Pendleton Messenger*, September 30, 1836.

[29] Calhoun to Francis Pickens, May 19, 1835, Calhoun Papers.

[30] Crallé, *Works*, V, 148–190, esp. 163.

[31] Calhoun to Armistead Burt, December 24, 1838, Jameson, *Correspondence*, pp. 422–423.

governing, I might with truth say, the exclusive object of both parties, in electing the President, is to obtain the spoils. They are both equally ready to sacrifice any other consideration to it." [32]

In denouncing Crawford's use of the Congressional caucus, in castigating the "corrupt bargain" between Clay and Adams, in thundering against Jackson's distribution of the spoils, Calhoun was not merely echoing the antiparty rhetoric of the Founding Fathers. He was also voicing the typical disdain of a South Carolina patrician for the new political methods in the Age of Jackson. Throughout the first half of the nineteenth century the South Carolina planters remained solidly committed to a quasi-aristocratic version of democracy, and no other group in American society clung more tenaciously to the eighteenth-century ideal of a nation ruled by gentlemen. In his campaign against the spoilsmen, as in so much else, Calhoun can only be understood against the background of the state whose cause he made so peculiarly his own.

The South Carolina patrician was a democrat with the brakes on; he had faith only in the right kind of democracy. If the natural aristocracy was allowed a free hand to govern, the Carolina planter could afford to be a democrat. He conceded that the people should choose which aristocrats would rule. As James Hamilton, Jr., put it, "The people expect that their leaders in whose . . . public spirit they have confidence will think for them—and that they will be prepared to *act* as their leaders *think*." [33]

The South Carolina Constitution of 1790 as amended in the early nineteenth century institutionalized this qualified faith in democracy. Any adult white male who had resided in South Carolina for two years could vote for state legislators. However, the legislators elected almost all other state officials from the Governor to the tax collectors, as well as United States Senators and Presidential electors. A high property qualification for the legislature kept lower-class opportunists outside the statehouse. Finally, the apportionment of legislative seats gave the small minority of low-

[32] Calhoun to Elwood Fisher, February 14, 1848, Calhoun Papers.
[33] Hamilton to Stephen Miller, August 9, 1830, Chesnut-Manning-Miller Papers (South Carolina Historical Society, Charleston). See also John Belton O'Neall, *Biographical Sketches of the Bench and Bar of South Carolina*, 2 vols. (Charleston, 1859), I, 180 ff.; *Edgefield Hive*, April 6, 1830.

country aristrocrats control of the senate and a disproportionate influence in the house. Political power in South Carolina was uniquely concentrated in a legislature of large property holders which set state policy and selected the men to administer it.[34]

The characteristics of South Carolina politics cemented the control of upper-class planters. Elections to the state legislature—the one control the masses could exert over the government—were often uncontested and rarely allowed the "plebeians" a clear choice between two parties or policies. Even in the state legislature, the Carolina gentry eschewed organized parties. Leaders of a well-disciplined legislative party might organize a state-wide popular ticket and encourage the "mob" to overreach themselves by debating issues. Unscrupulous demagogues would subsequently seize control from disinterested patricians by bribing and deluding the rabble. Political parties would overturn the rule of the rich, well born, and able, and would thus upset the precariously balanced, qualified democracy which alone won the approbation of the South Carolina patricians.[35]

Although sensitive souls throughout the country were disgusted with the emerging spoils system in the Age of Jackson, the South Carolina aristocrats shrieked the longest and the loudest. The rise of the political manager upset their delicately balanced, limited democracy and produced some of the evils they most feared— a passion for federal patronage, the rule of party hacks, the rise of inferior demagogues.[36] South Carolina's participation in the political parties was occasional and superficial. The Calhounites,

---

[34] J. M. Lesesne, ed., *The Constitution of 1790* (Columbia, 1952).

[35] The Carolina statesmen did indulge in extensive public debates during moments of high excitement. However, these political methods were always used with the most revealing misgivings. For example, during the nullification controversy, the Nullifiers created state-wide political "Associations." But they defended these political clubs only as an extraordinary response to an unusual crisis and disbanded them immediately after the tariff was lowered. The more conservative unionists feared the demagoguery and corruption of parties so deeply that they refused to form rival political clubs, and thereby handed the Nullifiers a decisive advantage. For extended discussion see Freehling, "Nullification Controversy," pp. 352–359.

[36] William J. Grayson, the leading planter and proslavery poet, gave classic expression to South Carolina's hatred for the new political brokers in his verdict on the causes of the Civil War. William J. Grayson, *Autobiography* (typecopy in South Caroliniana Library), pp. 225–226.

quickly disillusioned by their bitter experience with the early Jackson movement, usually remained aloof from national coalitions. And when Calhoun sporadically and suspiciously rejoined the Democratic party, he always insisted that taxes should be lowered so that the party would be based on principles rather than spoils.

However, Calhoun's attempt to reform the Democratic party was not solely the disinterested campaign of a South Carolina patrician to re-establish the ideals of the Founding Fathers. His rhetoric on executive patronage also probably reflects the bitter disappointment of a brilliant and supremely ambitious young man who climbed with incredible speed to the higher ranks of federal power and then never achieved his ultimate goal. Political maneuvering had destroyed his Presidential prospects of 1832 and threatened to produce a life of personal frustration. Calhoun may well have realized that his marked superiority at political reasoning was somewhat offset by his notorious failings as a practical politician. In this sense, he may have hoped that reduced executive patronage would produce a nation where the Calhouns rather than the Van Burens, the philosopher statesmen rather than the party managers, would once again have a chance to be President of the United States.[37]

But Calhoun's obsession with political corruption was more than a response to unfulfilled ambition, more than a patrician's distrust of the new political managers. It was also one expression of that violent South Carolina radicalism in the crisis of the 1830's which produced both the nullification crusade against the tariff and the gag rule fight against the abolitionists. The South Carolinians, morbidly aware of their own weaknesses—depressed economically, frightened by recurrent slave conspiracies, able to

[37] This is not to say that Calhoun always shunned the methods he deplored. The South Carolinian enthusiastically directed his own Presidential campaign in the early 1820's, and—as Charles G. Sellers has pointed out to the author—the Calhounites tried to use Van Burenite methods to defeat Van Buren himself in the contest for the Democratic nomination in 1844. But even at such times, Calhoun was somewhat uneasy about using partisan political techniques. See, for example, Calhoun to Duff Green, June 7, 1843, Jameson, *Correspondence,* pp. 537–538. Calhoun's disdain for the new style of democratic politics may have been an important reason for his ineptness as a practical politician. For an illuminating discussion see Gerald M. Capers, *John C. Calhoun—Opportunist* (Gainesville, 1960).

defend slavery only with the doctrine that bondage was a "necessary evil" (and secretly believing that necessary or not the evil
was grave)—found themselves faced for the first time with a
mounting abolitionist attack and a high protective tariff, both of
which seemed to threaten slavery and the future of Southern white
civilization. The planters devised (and tried to believe) a proslavery argument, developed a closed, rigid, restrictive society,
and even endeavored (a bit lamely) to acquire some of that
Yankee spirit of commercial enterprise which they held in such
contempt. But for their ultimate salvation they turned to national
politics. Convinced that their only hope lay in the most rigid
adherence to principle, the South Carolina aristocrats were made
desperate by the apathy of natural allies throughout the nation.
Many Southerners seemed content to compromise with the abolitionists. Most Democrats, both North and South, refused to engage
in an uncompromising fight against Clay's American System. There
could be only one explanation. Politicians were compromising with
abolitionists and monopolists to keep their party together and to
increase their chances of grabbing a share of the spoils of office.
If the American System could be destroyed and patronage reduced,
the South might be brought to defend itself in time and the Democrats brought to stand steadfast on the only principles which could
save the union.[38] And surely Calhoun's belief that politicians often
ignore their constituents in their race for the spoils originated in
part with what he considered the shame of the spoilsmen in the
1830's.

Thus, in his practical career as in his political theory, Calhoun's
concern with spoilsmen was as important as his fear of interests.
By exorcising the new political brokers Calhoun could hope to
bring the Republic back to the enlightened rule of disinterested
patricians, fulfill his Presidential ambitions, and develop national
political movements based on principles rather than spoils. When
statesmen replaced spoilsmen, the clash between fundamental interests over the American System and over abolition could also
be resolved.

[38] Crallé, *Works*, I, 375; Calhoun to James Hammond, January 25, April
2, 1840; Calhoun to Thomas G. Clemson, June 7, 1845, Jameson, *Correspondence*, pp. 443, 452, 663–664.

Yet Calhoun's practical program was vitiated by the same logical contradiction between the theory of interests and the theory of spoilsmen which destroyed his political philosophy. The South Carolinian was again unable to decide whether pressure groups or politicians caused historical events. On the one hand, Calhoun held that the Democratic party would be run by spoilsmen rather than statesmen until the American System ceased to supply patronage. On the other hand, he maintained that the American System would only be destroyed when statesmen replaced spoilsmen at the head of the Democratic party. If interests could be neutralized, spoilsmen would disappear. Yet spoilsmen must disappear before interests could be neutralized. The reformer hardly knew where to begin. As Calhoun saw the dilemma in a more practical situation, Jackson's Democratic politicos—although elected by interest groups opposed to Clay's brainchild—compromised with an American System which fed them patronage, thereby frustrating their constituents.

Nullification was, among other things, a desperate way out of the vicious circle. South Carolina, by nullifying high duties, could at once neutralize interests and reduce patronage. For a time in the late 1830's Calhoun was almost sanguine. But even nullification was no real escape, for by Calhoun's own admission the unnullified military establishments remained to invite the resurgence of spoilsmen. More important, in the 1840's, with nullification discredited, the South Carolinian was again trapped in his own logical nightmare. Thus when Democrats like Thomas Ritchie and Van Buren compromised a bit with the American System and with the abolitionists, Calhoun's profound bitterness was the logical culmination of the inconsistencies in his own political program.

The *Disquisition,* written in the late 1840's, reflects Calhoun's despair as his career drew to a close. The increasingly angry controversy between Northern and Southern interests seemed disastrous enough in itself. But in addition the vast federal patronage seemed certain to perpetuate the regime of the spoilsmen. With unscrupulous politicians in power the North and South would never find grounds for reconciliation. Thus the *Disquisition* represents one of Calhoun's last desperate attempts to restrain the interests and spoilsmen which together seemed destined to break up the republic.

In one sense, the *Disquisition* is a justly celebrated contribution to the American democratic tradition. Calhoun was a political realist who ranks with James Madison and John Adams in his mordant analysis of the defects of a democracy. As Calhoun endlessly reiterated, entrenched majorities can ignore constitutional restraints and pay little heed to minority rights. The South Carolinian was also clearly right that the clash of interests and the intrigues of spoilsmen often threaten the efficiency of a democratic government.

The problem with the *Disquisition* lies not in its diagnosis but rather in its exaggeration of the weaknesses in a republic. Calhoun's critics have often argued that the theory of interests overstates both the helplessness of democratic minorities and the selfishness of economic interests. It must now be added that the theory of spoilsmen magnifies the threat posed by scheming politicians. Ambitious demagogues may sometimes exert more political influence than the economic determinists like to think. But Calhoun surely overestimated the spoilsmen's capacity to delude the masses and overthrow the system. Indeed Calhoun's rhetoric on the evils of patronage often sounds suspiciously like that of a late nineteenth-century mugwump, fighting his curious crusade to save democracy by enacting civil service reform. The combination of this exaggerated fear of spoilsmen and Calhoun's exaggerated fear of interests simply posed problems too grave for the concurrent majority, or any constitutional reform, to solve. The resulting inconsistencies in the *Disquisition* must create renewed doubts as to whether Calhoun deserves his reputation as America's most rigorous political logician. It would be closer to the truth to call the author of the *Disquisition* one of the more confused political philosophers in the American tradition.[39]

The contradictions in Calhoun's *Disquisition* provide a particularly revealing illustration of that ambivalence toward democratic principles which so often marked the political thought of the more aristocratic Southern slaveholders. As historians have often reminded us in the past two decades, the clash between American

---

[39] Louis Hartz reaches a similar conclusion from a different direction in his brilliant comments on Calhoun. See Hartz, *The Liberal Tradition in America* (New York, 1955), pp. 145–177.

politicians has characteristically taken place within a consensus of belief in democratic government. Calhoun paid his personal testimonial to this pervasive American consensus by straining to remain both a statesman and a theorizer of the democratic persuasion. But the deeper significance of Calhoun's tragic career is that despite his fascination with abstract political argument he could not put together a consistent democratic theory. The key to Calhoun's thought is not just his concern with class or any other kind of economic interests, not just his concern with moral fanatics, not just his concern with demagogic spoilsmen. Rather, the secret of his political philosophy—the reason why it is inevitably inconsistent —is that Calhoun distrusted democracy for so many exaggerated and contradictory reasons. An eighteenth-century elitist increasingly disillusioned with the emerging political order in the Age of Jackson, Calhoun by the end of his career no longer quite believed in American democracy.

RALPH LERNER

✪

Calhoun's New Science of Politics

John C. Calhoun's *Disquisition on Government* is that rarity in American political thought—a work that explicitly declares itself a theoretical study of politics. By purporting to give a comprehensive and systematic account, by claiming to have explored new territory beyond the range of American discoveries, Calhoun in effect put his *Disquisition* in a class of which it is almost the sole example: an American political theory. But this claim to esteem and originality has been disputed; and in the subsequent debates among his interpreters, we have yet to find a satisfactory solution to the problem that Calhoun represented in such clear shape. Those who have rated him as a statesman and thinker—be that assessment high *or* low—and those who have accepted *or* denied his claim to originality have all failed to solve the peculiar problem of how to study and interpret the writing of a man of theory-and-practice. Until that problem is met, our understanding of the *Disquisition* is not clear and we remain without a way of evaluating Calhoun's merits and originality.

How, then, ought Calhoun's *Disquisition,* or his high theoretical pretensions in general, best to be understood? Reducing his theory to practice, or saying in effect that the *Disquisition* was only another string to his proslavery bow, forecloses the question of what Cal-

I am indebted to my colleague Herbert J. Storing and to Marvin Meyers (Brandeis University) for their discerning criticism of this essay.

Reprinted from the *American Political Science Quarterly*, Vol. LVII, No. 4 (December 1963), pp. 918–932, by permission.

houn can teach us. Reducing his practice to theory places what is almost a superhuman burden upon a man who was at or near the center of the national political stage for forty tumultuous years. A more moderate procedure would seem to be indicated. First, the *Disquisition* should be examined as the work of political theory it claims to be. At the same time, free use ought to be made of the practical political arguments and positions he adopted over a lifetime of political activity as further indications of his intention and meaning. Following this procedure may help in assessing Calhoun's stature as a political theorist.

In advancing his claim to the rank of political theorist, Calhoun proposed not only to transcend the practical, but to transcend conventional political theory as well. He would make of politics a science modeled after astronomy: the solid foundation must be some fundamental law, standing in relation to human nature as gravitation does to the material world. This astronomical political science is concerned with facts, with the way in which humans actually behave. In fact, humans behave in a manner that testifies to the primacy of interest or selfishness or self-preservation.

That men behave in such a manner is for him the decisive consideration; the praise or blame that we may attach to this behavior is, strictly speaking, beside the point. We legislate, not for man in the abstract or for men in general, but for a particular portion. The guide for the legislator is not what he thinks men ought to do, but rather his shrewd perception of what actually moves these men. "We must take human nature as it is, and accommodate our measures to it, instead of making the vain attempt to bend it to our measures." [1] It is, above all, in his *Disquisition,* wherein he hoped to "lay a solid foundation for political Science," that Calhoun strove hardest to emulate his avowed models: New-

---

[1] References are to Richard K. Crallé, ed., *The Works of John C. Calhoun,* 6 vols. (Columbia, S. C., New York, 1851–1855), hereafter cited as *Works.* Volume I consists of *A Disquisition on Government* and *A Discourse on the Constitution and Government of the United States,* two posthumously published writings on which Calhoun worked intermittently during the last few years of his life. Where the reference is to the other five volumes of this edition, I have added the year of publication or delivery, since Crallé's order is not strictly chronological. Unless otherwise noted all italics in quotations are in the original. *Works* I, 1, 3; II, 182 (1817), 648 (1837).

ton, Laplace, Galileo, and Bacon. Calhoun's science is not to be mistaken for an ethics or a particularistic empiricism or an arid "scholastic refinement"; but it may be called metaphysics, if by that we mean as he did the mind's power of reducing a complexity to its elements and of combining these into one harmonious system. The test of a theorist that Calhoun would have applied to himself is the extent to which he can prepare the way for a *science* of politics, one that goes beyond "a mere observation of insulated facts." He will have met the severest test—and, incidentally, have laid claim to "the highest attribute of the human mind"—if, heedless of the "senseless cry of metaphysics," he succeeds in formulating scientific laws adapted to "the high purpose of political science and legislation."

But what precisely is that purpose? The analogy to astronomy fails us. Calhoun spoke of the latter as "that noble science which displays to our admiration the system of the universe." But for Calhoun, as for any man not utterly removed from the stuff of political life, the end of his theorizing about politics was not a theory that displays to our admiration the system of the political universe, but rather a theory that directs itself to political practice. It is without any sense of self-contradiction or confusion that Calhoun could begin with a political science, patterned after astronomy or chemistry and whose first premise is the self-interested behavior of men, and end by asserting that enlisting "the individual on the side of the social feelings to promote the good of the whole, is the greatest possible achievement of the science of government." [2] How did he move between these two points?

I

The beginning of political science lies in a fundamental understanding of the "matter" of politics—human nature. Calhoun began by making two assumptions; he regarded both as incontestable. First, that man's "inclinations and wants, physical and moral, irresistibly impel him to associate with his kind; and he has, accord-

[2] *Ibid.*, I, 70; II, 232 f. (1833). J. Franklin Jameson, ed., *Correspondence of John C. Calhoun, Annual Report of the American Historical Association, 1899* (Washington, 1900), II, 768 (1849). (Hereafter cited as *Correspondence.*)

ingly, never been found, in any age or country, in any state other than the social." Second, that "while man is so constituted as to make the social state necessary to his existence and the full development of his faculties, this state itself cannot exist without government. The assumption rests on universal experience." Calhoun suggested that man's association with his fellows is due at least in part to a subrational drive. In any event, neither society nor government is a matter of choice for man. Both are necessary for the bare existence, let alone the perfection or full development, of the human kind; they are "equally of Divine ordination." Man's natural state is social or, rather, political.[3]

The question remains: why is the existence of society and government no more a matter of volition than is breathing? How does the nature of man dictate such arrangements? Calhoun does say that man has natural feelings of sympathy for his fellows, but these social feelings are subordinate to his selfish feelings. In the *Disquisition* (though not in the *South Carolina Exposition* of 1828), he avoided the expression "selfish feelings" because, "as commonly used," it carries an inference of "something depraved and vicious."

For Calhoun, however, "selfish" did not connote vice. Like the framers of the American Constitution, who "understood profoundly the nature of man and of government," Calhoun recognized that our nature remains "unchanged by change of condition." Selfishness, like gravitation, is one of the facts of the world and hence part of that science which would explain the world. There are, to be sure, exceptions—"few," "extraordinary" exceptions—but these only prove the rule. A mother's subordination of her individual feelings to those of her infant is due to one of those "peculiar relations"; then, again, there are "peculiar constitutions" over whom education and habit have singular effect. A science may admit of such exceptions without undermining the generality and force of its most fundamental law: the predominance of "the selfish passions of our nature," which are "planted in our bosom for our individual safety." We have, in fact, arrived at a law not merely of human life,

[3] Crallé, *Works,* I, 2, 5, 8; IV, 509 f. (1848).

but of all animated existence, throughout its entire range, so far as
our knowledge extends. It would, indeed, seem to be essentially connected with the great law of self-preservation which pervades all that
feels, from man down to the lowest and most insignificant reptile or
insect. In none is it stronger than in man.[4]

The fundamental fact of human life is not distinctively human;
the law upon which a science of politics will be erected points to
man's subrational part, to the part that makes him brother to the
beast. If man has foresight, its effect is to enable him to fear more
and hence to be more, and more intelligently, concerned with self-
preservation than any lower animal could be.

Calhoun allowed that, given certain preconditions, men's social
feelings might grow. In no case, however—even assuming safety,
abundance, and "high intellectual and moral culture"—could this
"all-pervading and essential law" of self-preservation be over-
powered. The social feelings, as indeed the very conditions in which
they thrive, are of only limited effect. There is a passing suggestion
that Calhoun found it easier to conceive of a human devoid of
any social feeling than to imagine one in whom sympathy for his
fellows outweighed or perhaps even equaled his selfish feelings.
The predominance of selfishness is seen as necessary for the preservation of a being such as man with "limited reason and faculties."
Of this, at least, Calhoun was certain: that "self-preservation is
the supreme law, as well with communities as individuals." In
developing both his theoretical teaching and his practical program,
he always bore in mind what he took to be "the strongest passions
of the human heart,—avarice, ambition, and rivalry." [5]

In the course of a long digression that interrupts the *Disquisition*'s discussion of liberty and governmental power, the argument
is made that a presocial state is "purely hypothetical." "Instead
of being the natural state of man, it is, of all conceivable states,
the most opposed to his nature—most repugnant to his feelings,

---

[4] *Ibid.*, I, 2–4; II, 63 (1814); VI, 53 (1828).
[5] *Ibid.*, I, 4 f. 10, 47; VI, 202 (1832). However, there appear to be such
things as "too concentrated" affections and too predominant a regard for
self-interest. See Calhoun's condemnation of Webster and of the Northern
states. *Ibid.*, III, 287 (1838); IV, 386 (1847).

and most incompatible with his wants." [6] We are hardly surprised, however—considering Calhoun's "psychology"—to find many, if not all, of the inconveniences of the state of nature appearing in the social, pregovernmental stage of human development. Our natural inclination to give greater weight to our selfish feelings than to "what affects us indirectly through others" [7] produces "the tendency to a universal state of conflict, between individual and individual; accompanied by the connected passions of suspicion, jealousy, anger and revenge,—followed by insolence, fraud and cruelty." Unchecked, the result of such a tendency can only be the destruction of social life and of the "ends for which it is ordained."

For Calhoun, we may say, society was intended to secure not mere life, but a fully human life. In analogous, but subordinate, fashion, government seeks not only to "preserve" or "protect" society, but to "perfect" it. Both society and government, as already noted, are divinely ordained, and in the assignment of such states to man, Calhoun saw another manifestation of the Creator's "infinite wisdom and goodness." [8] But if the easy necessity that impels man to seek his own kind and to form government is a sign of God's goodness, the difficult option of controlling the governors through some kind of constitution is perhaps a sign that God's goodness is incomplete.[9] The governors are no better than those they govern and for that very reason require a check upon their tendency to aggrandize themselves at the expense of their

[6] *Ibid.*, I, 58. See also *ibid.*, IV, 509 f. (1848); VI, 221 f. (1843); *Correspondence*, p. 758 (1848).

[7] Crallé, *Works*, I, 2 f., 4. Such is Calhoun's careful circumlocution for sympathetic or social feeling. Our regard for others is ultimately a regard for self.

[8] The emphatic distinction of social and political states replaces the "state of nature—civil society" dichotomy of the modern natural rights teachers. At this stage of the argument one can only suspect that Calhoun wrought this change less with a view to building a doctrine that vested associations of men with a right of revolution than to avoiding the premise of natural egalitarianism.

[9] Calhoun used such terms as "the Creator" or "the Infinite" or "Providence" in the *Disquisition*. The sole mention of "God" there occurs when the concurrent voice of a people is called "*the voice of God.*" *Works*, I, 39. On Calhoun's avoidance of this name, see Gerald M. Capers, *John C. Calhoun—Opportunist: A Reappraisal* (Gainesville, Fla., 1960), p. 17 n.

fellows. The ultimate perfection of God's handiwork lies in the hands of man.

On first thought, we might suppose that the need for this ultimate perfection is limited. Savages require government, but hardly stand in need of that government which perfects society, namely constitutional government. Simple societies, with the requisite political intelligence and while still in a relatively natural and undifferentiated condition, can control their governors through the operations of simple majorities. What "has thus far exceeded human wisdom, and possibly ever will"—a perfect constitution holding the government to its proper ends—does not appear to be a need of every place and every age.

This supposition, however, is undermined by Calhoun's reexamination of the problem. Governmental powers necessarily entail opportunities for private aggrandizement. Men's finite capacities and great diversities,[10] and various other causes, lead to the formation of independent communities. Among these communities there is the same "tendency to a universal state of conflict" that Calhoun discovered in the ungoverned human association. For Calhoun, as for Publius, it was "a sort of axiom in politics, that vicinity, or nearness of situation, constitutes nations natural enemies." [11] Because war is always a possibility, domestic aggrandizement is always a possibility. The community's self-preservation takes precedence over "every other consideration." A government that must be strong enough to ward off foreign dangers, by that very fact forms a domestic danger. The need for constitutional government is one that necessarily develops out of human society.[12]

However persistent the need for constitutional government might be, its founding and perpetuation are matters of the greatest difficulty and rarity. Calhoun never tired of reiterating his contention that chance and circumstances are of decisive importance. An insufficient regard for the prerequisites of constitutional government might lead to the subversion of such a government as had been formed "by some good fortune." There is no suggestion that

[10] In this connection Calhoun mentioned "language, customs, pursuits, situation, and complexion." This is the only direct reference to color in the *Disquisition. Works*, I, 9.
[11] *The Federalist*, No. 6 (Modern Library ed.), p. 33.
[12] Crallé, *Works*, I, 2, 4–10, 42 f., 52.

a sufficient regard for the prerequisites of constitutional government would suffice of itself to establish such a government. This is not to maintain that theoretical understanding is superfluous. Indeed, we would be hard put to understand the intention, form, and style of the *Disquisition* on any such premise. But it is to maintain that Calhoun's highest political teaching rests on or presupposes "some fortunate combination of circumstances." Two of the hallmarks of constitutional governments, setting them apart from the various absolute forms, are "complexity and difficulty of construction." In even more marked form than Burke—"the wisest of modern statesmen"—Calhoun belittled the efficacy of human understanding in meeting and solving major political problems.

He saw but two ways in which constitutional governments, of whatever form, might be constructed, and in neither instance was as much due to wisdom and patriotism as to "favorable combinations of circumstances." In most cases, constitutional governments are the unforeseen result of the struggles of warring interests; thanks to "some fortunate turn," an unremitting civil war is avoided and each of the belligerent parties is given "a separate and distinct voice in the government." Necessity prevails where human sagacity fails. The other, less frequent way in which such governments have been formed is not essentially different from the first: "fortunate circumstances, acting in conjunction with some pressing danger," have compelled men to adopt constitutional governments with their eyes open as a desperate move to avoid chaos. Even if we grant that it is within the grasp of the human mind or human minds to know thoroughly the character, needs, and interests of a particular advanced community and to construct a suitable constitutional government for that people, its adoption by that people is problematic. Necessity prevails where the persuasive power of wisdom fails. The conclusion remains: "Such governments have been, emphatically, the product of circumstances." [13] If Calhoun, like a proud Bacon, now grasped a truth that others had only on occasion

---

[13] *Ibid.*, I, 13, 31, 77–79; III, 591 (1841). For similar judgments of the American Constitution, see *ibid.*, I, 199; IV, 99 (1842), 417 (1848). The establishment of the Roman tribunate is called both "wise" and "fortunate." In neither Rome nor Britain did the warring interests have "any conception of the principles involved, or the consequences to follow, beyond the immediate objects in contemplation." *Ibid.*, I, 96, 104.

stumbled upon, he also, like an unpresumptuous Burke, ultimately had to rely upon the workings of fortunate historical accidents.

Not only is Fortune's realm expanded, but there is also some contraction in the task assigned or assignable to education. We have already noted Calhoun's judgment that it is only in men of "peculiar constitutions" that education and habituation have sufficient force to enable social feelings to overpower selfish ones. The general rule is unshaken. The deepest stratum of human nature remains unchanging and unchangeable, beyond the reach of education or, indeed, of civilization. A free press, for example, may do much to enlighten men and meliorate society; "far less power" may be needed for governing as men learn that they can safely enlarge their social feelings and restrain their individual feelings. But men would not be changed in the most fundamental sense: men still would need governing, and governing still would require power. It is this power over men that forms the core of the political problem. In the absence of a constitutional check to the exercise of political power—that is, in the absence of some form of concurrent majority rule—the mere use of such power is corrupting. "Neither religion nor education can counteract the strong tendency of the numerical majority to corrupt and debase the people."

Calhoun developed an elaborate argument in support of a system of peaceable and effective resistance to the abuse of power. Not the least part of that argument is the attempt to show the whole train of consequences for public and private morals that follows from the alternative modes of organizing government. Calhoun looked forward to a governmental structure that would reinforce, or at least not undermine, the formation of good character. "For of all the causes which contribute to form the character of a people, those by which power, influence, and standing in the government are most certainly and readily obtained, are, by far, the most powerful." The "talented and aspiring" crave for these objects, take due note of the means of securing them, and "assiduously" cultivate those means. The alternative paths to the desired respect and admiration are marked with Calhoun's favorite colors—white and black. Knowledge, wisdom, patriotism, and virtue contend with cunning, fraud, treachery, and party devotion. There is no indication that the "youths who crowd our colleges" would find anything as convincing as a formula for success that works. Virtue appears to be almost entirely imitative; its utility may be persuasive, but hardly its beauty.[14] "The great principle of demand and supply governs the moral and intellectual world no less than the business and commercial." [15] What the science of politics has to teach is not so much edifying as useful. Calhoun's science takes men as they are and then proceeds to lead them, indeed not directly to the goal of an enlightened and civically virtuous populace actively laboring for the public good, but indirectly—through a balance of powers—to the regulated actions and controlled consequences that to some extent free men from their baser impulses.

The clearest evidence that Calhoun thus deliberately narrowed the scope of political science merits full quotation here:

. . . By what means can government, without being divested of the full command of the resources of the community, be prevented from abusing its powers?

The question involves difficulties which, from the earliest ages, wise and good men have attempted to overcome;—but hitherto with but partial success. For this purpose many devices have been resorted to, suited to the various stages of intelligence and civilization through which our race has passed, and to the different forms of government to which they have been applied. The aid of superstition, ceremonies, education, religion, organic arrangements, both of the government and the community, has been, from time to time, appealed to. Some of the most remarkable of these devices, whether regarded in reference to their wisdom and the skill displayed in their application, or to the permanency of their effects, are to be found in the early dawn of civilization;—in the institutions of the Egyptians, the Hindoos, the Chinese, and the Jews. The only materials which that early age afforded for the construction of constitutions, when intelligence was so partially diffused, were applied with consummate wisdom and skill.

---

[14] Compare Alexis de Tocqueville, *Democracy in America* (New York, Vintage Books ed.), II, bk. ii, Chap. 8, p. 129.

[15] Crallé, *Works*, I, 3, 50 f., 74 f.; III, 116 f. (1837). In the context of the last citation, the banking system is attacked for "concentrating in itself most of the prizes of life—wealth, honor, and influence—to the great disparagement and degradation of all the liberal, and useful, and generous pursuits of society. The rising generation cannot but feel its deadening influence."

To their successful application may be fairly traced the subsequent advance of our race in civilization and intelligence, of which we now enjoy the benefits. For without a constitution, . . . there can be little progress or permanent improvement.

In answering the important question under consideration, it is not necessary to enter into an examination of the various contrivances adopted by these celebrated governments to counteract this tendency to disorder and abuse, nor to undertake to treat of constitution in its most comprehensive sense. What I propose is far more limited,—to explain on what principles government must be formed, in order to resist, by its own interior structure,—or, to use a single term, *organism*, —the tendency to abuse of power. This structure, or organism, is what is meant by constitution, in its strict and more usual sense. . . . It is in this strict and more usual sense that I propose to use the term hereafter.[16]

Calhoun kept his word: the other four devices are not themes of the *Disquisition*. The core of Calhoun's science of government —indeed, by far its largest part—is what he called an organic arrangement. Let us return, however, to the quoted paragraphs, some of whose most striking features are also the most puzzling. We had at first entertained the supposition that a perfect constitution was a luxury of sorts, that only men in a highly civilized, that is, "artificial," condition stood in need of it. That suggestion seemed to be untenable in view of the accumulation of power— and hence possibilities for the abuse of power—made necessary by the omnipresent threat of external danger. Now we learn that the concern with a perfect constitution has occupied the thoughts of the wise and the good "from the earliest ages." The devices and applications most worthy of note are located in the "early dawn of civilization," before the darkness of barbarism had been dissipated and while intelligence was the preserve of a few. We marvel at these ancient lawgivers, whose names Calhoun either did not know or would not disclose.[17] Their success may have been partial, but they apparently were successful. We are puzzled by their success. Did the founders of these "celebrated governments" succeed

---

[16] *Ibid.*, I, 10 f.

[17] Calhoun went to some lengths to avoid using any individual's proper name in the *Disquisition*. Consider, *e.g.*, the highly abstract account of English history. *Ibid.*, I, 99 f.

because of, or despite, the rude character of their people? If the latter, there are perhaps some valuable lessons yet to be gleaned from their institutions.[18] If the former, we owe them a nod of thanks and little more.

Calhoun's procedure in the *Disquisition* leaves us in no doubt of what his answer was. He did not find it necessary to even "enter into an examination" of these "remarkable" devices of remote antiquity. The success of the ancient legislators depended as much upon the general backwardness of the times as upon the legislators' wisdom and skill. Accordingly, our interest in them can be little more than antiquarian. True, our progress beyond those ancient peoples is due in no small part to them, but the very success of the early lawgivers has made obsolete most of the devices to which they had recourse.[19] Today's man-in-the-street is more knowing than his forefather in the woods. Superstition, ceremonies, education, and religion cannot deter him from the shrewd perception of his selfish interest in the market place of ambition. His manners are less rude, but he is cagier.

For Calhoun, no less than for Publius, the science of politics was susceptible of great improvement. Publius saw that progress in the moderns' understanding of various principles, "which were either not known at all, or imperfectly known to the ancients." At the same time, he was far from rejecting the use of devices that Calhoun seemed to consider as no longer of consequence.[20]

[18] *The Federalist* reached back to Minos (see No. 38); Calhoun cast his net wider, but never mentioned the Greeks in the *Disquisition*. The Romans, from whose institutions lessons *are* drawn, apparently belong to a later stage.

[19] Now, as always, a disproportionately large share of wealth is given to the nonproducing classes. But the "brute force and gross superstition of ancient times" have been supplanted by the "subtle and artful fiscal contrivances of modern." *Works*, II, 631 (1837). A reversion to barbarism is out of the question for Calhoun. While commerce diffuses the blessings of civilization and printing preserves and diffuses knowledge, the military applications of steam and gunpowder have "for ever" assured the ascendancy of civilized communities. *Ibid.*, I, 62, 87 f. On the relation of manufacturing to the moral and political progress of civilization, see *ibid.*, IV, 103 (1842), 184 (1842), 283 f. (1846); VI, 92 (1831). One of the two examples of impiety mentioned in the *Disquisition* is doubting that the discoveries and inventions of technology will "greatly improve the condition of man ultimately." *Ibid.*, I, 89.

[20] *The Federalist*, No. 9, p. 48; No. 49, pp. 328 f.

For Calhoun, man's progress consists less in the discovery of wholly new principles of political life than in the outgrowing of some old devices of governance and the adaptation of another. What first appears as a sloughing off of outmoded and outgrown restrictions turns out to be a more complex and artificial elaboration of the "old and clumsy, but approved mode of checking power, in order to prevent or correct abuses." [21]

This mechanistic device of resisting power by power and tendency by tendency, on which Calhoun's entire system rested, cannot be instituted in a mechanical fashion. There are prerequisites to the formation of constitutional government, and of these Calhoun held the principal to be the right of popular suffrage. "When this right is properly guarded, and the people sufficiently enlightened to understand their own rights and the interests of the community, and duly to appreciate the motives and conduct of those appointed to make and execute the laws," suffrage may suffice to control the governors. [22] The psychological premises of the *Disquisition* do not require that the degree of popular enlightenment be very great. It suffices that the people understand that irresponsible rulers endanger what affects them directly (private rights) and what affects them indirectly through others (community interests).

But while suffrage is effective in holding rulers to account, it does not even begin to solve the problem of oppressive government for any but "small communities, during the early stages of

[21] *Works*, I, 10 f., 42; VI, 85 (1831).

[22] Calhoun's firm adherence to the language of rights deserves at least passing notice. While he denied that a numerical majority could conclude for an entire people, he was far from denying the "rights, powers, and immunities of the whole people" or that "the people are the source of all power; and that their authority is paramount over all." *Ibid.*, I, 30; VI, 226 (1843). If one regards man in "what is called the state of nature," he will be found to have rights and duties deduced from the faculties and endowments common to the human race as a whole. "All natural rights are individual rights, and belong to them as such. They appertain neither to majorities nor minorities. On the contrary, all political rights are conventional." This is the teaching of "Locke, Sydney, and other writers on the side of liberty," whose doctrines "fortunately for us . . . became the creed of our ancestors." When *"the right of revolution"* is properly invoked, it is a case of individuals resuming their natural rights, "which, however restricted or modified they may be, in the political state, are never extinguished." *Ibid.*, VI, 138 (1831), 221 f. (1843), 226 (1843), 230 (1843), 269 (1846).

their existence," while these are still in a relatively natural—that is, poor, unrefined, simple—condition. In all other cases, where the motives for the oppressive use of governmental power are considerably enhanced, the "organism" of concurrent consent is needed to complete, or rather to form, constitutional government.[23] Such an organism presupposes "the different interests, portions, or classes of the community, to be sufficiently enlightened to understand its character and object." The *Disquisition on Government* might be said to be a work of popular enlightenment in this sense. It is hardly farfetched to surmise that Calhoun believed the United States of 1850 to stand in "some pressing danger" that might force the adoption of what he defined to be constitutional government.[24] If his estimate of the shortcomings of human sagacity in coping with chance and circumstance was correct, it nonetheless did not preclude his own desperate efforts. Fortune seemed most apt to smile on men standing at the precipice's edge.

II

The *Disquisition on Government* consists of a critique and a proposal. The full dimensions of the proposal can be perceived only in the light of the critique. In its barest formulation, the critique is this: that representative government, when most perfectly realized, partakes of all the vices of a pure democracy. This is precisely the point denied by the defenders of the American Constitution; indeed, the contrary proposition was, in their eyes, one of the Constitution's most considerable advantages. "The true distinction between [the ancient republics] and the American governments, lies *in the total exclusion of the people, in their collective capacity,* from any share in the *latter*. . . ."[25] One senses the full measure of Calhoun's undertaking when one recognizes that he

---

[23] "The numerical majority, *perhaps,* should *usually* be one of the elements of a constitutional democracy. . . ." *Ibid.,* I, 45 (Italics supplied.) In the Senate, Calhoun said that he did not object to the preponderance of the numerical majority in the American government, but to its "subjecting the whole, in time, to its unlimited sway." *Ibid.,* IV, 92 (1842). The *Disquisition's* argument, though cautiously stated, spells out the implications of these earlier remarks.

[24] *Ibid.,* I, 12 f., 26, 42 f., 78 f.

[25] *The Federalist,* No. 63, p. 413.

was calling not so much for the reform of constitutional government in America as for its refounding. Stated most radically, the United States have not yet had a fully constitutional government. If such a government, strictly understood, would once have been an unnecessary complication, that hardly could be said to be the case today (1850). The critical fact of political life is the diversity of interests within the community. "It is so in all; the small and the great,—the poor and the rich,—irrespective of pursuits, productions, or degrees of civilization. . . ." As a result of such diversity, governmental actions, however equitable "on their face," necessarily have unequal effects. This inequality is a universal phenomenon; it is only the degree of inequality and oppressiveness that varies. A necessary consequence of the ordinary operations of government is that the community as a whole is divided into taxpayers and tax consumers. In effect, these "portions," "classes," "interests," "divisions," or "orders" are at war. Under the best of circumstances, the one's gain is the other's loss. What, then, can be expected from the ordinary unchecked actions of men as they are if not systematic aggrandizement by one group or party at the expense of the other? Publius's statelier prose exactly conveys Calhoun's own position: "If the impulse and the opportunity be suffered to coincide, we well know that neither moral nor religious motives can be relied on as an adequate control." [26]

The traditional distinctions between government of the one, the few, and the many are irrelevant here: in the absence of a constitution (in Calhoun's sense), all rulers oppress their subjects. Restated in purely American terms, Calhoun's critique was an extensive commentary upon, and correction of, *The Federalist*'s remedy for the "diseases most incident to republican government." It is a characteristic of popular government that natural groupings are allowed to assume political importance; there is no veneer of artificial classes or orders to conceal the natural variety of interests "resulting from diversity of pursuits, condition, situation and character of different portions of the people,—and from the action of the government itself." Publius seized upon this fact and developed safeguards that work, if anything, too well. He diagnosed the critical disease to be majority faction and prescribed a specific for it. But

[26] *Ibid.*, No. 10, p. 58.

in seeking to eliminate one form of the tyrannical virus—the unmitigated rule of the natural majority—he disarmed the community in the face of another form—the unmitigated rule of the
artificial majority centering about the control of government itself.
No provision had been made for the disease of party.[27]

Calhoun's reputation as a political theorist largely rests on his
analysis of the problem posed by party and his proposed solution
of it. His consideration of political parties led him, on the one
hand, to develop his views within the larger context of the problem
of identifying the common good and, on the other, to pay especial
attention to the particular question of class conflict. While the
Disquisition offers alternative suggestions of the ways in which
parties arise, in each case the concept of party remains the same.
For Calhoun, the political party was simply an instrument by
which men sought to capture the control of the government and its
patronage. His first explanation traces the genesis of party to that
natural diversity of interests and consequent conflict which Calhoun
saw as the critical and universal fact of social life. Where the
control of government is determined solely by the right of suffrage,
the struggle of interests takes the form of alliances to create or
maintain a majority. Party conflict is thus the inevitable consequence of government by numerical majority.

A more radical formulation is then suggested. Even if one were
to posit an entirely homogeneous community, without any diversity
of interests or inequality of condition, the mere fact of numerical
majority rule would suffice to bring parties into existence. "The
advantages of possessing the control of the powers of the government, and, thereby, of its honors and emoluments, are, of themselves, exclusive of all other considerations, ample to divide even
such a community into two great hostile parties." Governmental
action or, what was its equivalent for Calhoun, the advantage of
possessing governmental power leads to conflict and finally to the
formation of parties. The principle of concurrent majority rule
rests on this unavoidable diversity of interests, from which even
our hypothetical homogeneous community is not immune. There
are *always* at least two portions or interests in the community:
the ins and the outs.

[27] Crallé, *Works*, I, 13–15, 19–25, 37, 43, 61, 80.

Calhoun also traced the origin of parties to the need, "in the present condition of the world," for protection against external dangers.[28] The threat of such dangers gives rise to large defense establishments and even bigger government. The result is "sufficient to excite profoundly the ambition of the aspiring and the cupidity of the avaricious." It is not surprising that Calhoun saw unremitting and violent party conflict as the ultimate result, considering that he regarded these "most powerful passions of the human heart" as being beyond the reach of time, reflection, reason, discussion, entreaty, or remonstrance. Nor is there cause to wonder that he regarded the handiwork of the Founding Fathers as being deficient in the decisive respect. Calhoun's message seems to be that even if the poor should not always be with us, the same cannot be said of patronage and the pork barrel. Until the problem of "party-usage" is met and solved, none of the auxiliary protections and parchment barriers will prove of any avail. The task remains to form a constitutional government.[29]

It may be granted that the mere possession of governmental power creates an interest and party in opposition to those who have none. And yet the question remains: would such a government party interest suffice to keep the ins in? Would not an appeal have to be made, beyond an even numerous group of jobholders, to a still larger constituency? To embrace a majority of the whole electorate, would not the ruling party have to adopt a policy of systematic favoritism to a coalition of interests with something in common (say, a desire to promote home manufactures), with the consequent chance to exploit a minority with an opposite interest? Calhoun's notion of a governmental policy that benefits a majority at the expense of a minority seems to presuppose two elements of society so differently circumstanced that such a policy, in matching one set of interests, necessarily crosses the other. Underlying Calhoun's majorities and minorities are some grand

---

[28] Even here Calhoun successfully resisted using the word "nation."

[29] Crallé, *Works*, I, 16–18, 28, 33 f., 47; II, 245 f. (1833); VI, 202 (1832). Calhoun believed that the Americans are "greatly distinguished by the love of acquisition—I will not call it avarice—and the love of honorable distinction." The causes of these propensities are traced in an interesting speech in favor of increased compensation for members of Congress. *Ibid.*, II, 182 (1817).

divisions of society; party organizations do not simply supersede these natural divisions. If this is the case, Calhoun's critique of *The Federalist* may be restated. Publius assumed that a large republic splinters interests, so that none can rule solely in its own behalf. He erred in this, for the splinters—amounting to a majority —will discover a common interest that was really there all the while, but temporarily obscured by lesser differences. This majority will quickly discover a common interest that *government can promote* at the expense of the rest of society.

The case against party conflicts and numerical majority rule that is presented in the *Disquisition* appears to be quite independent of the bitter sectional disputes of the 1840's and 1850's. At least we must concede that the arguments cut deeper than the dominance of the North in the American political system. The right of a minority to transform itself into a majority and turn the rascals out was, Calhoun argued, only the right to be aggrandized and to aggrandize in turn. The contingency that marks one party's monopoly of power, far from moderating its tendency to be abusive, only heightens it.[30] In an effort to retain its advantages as long as possible, a party will "concentrate the control over its movements in fewer and fewer hands." Government by party leads inexorably to government by party leaders. Partisan fidelity and zeal are secured by party organization, caucuses, and discipline, but above all by patronage, "on which, in turn, depends that powerful, active and mercenary corps of expectants, created by the morbid moneyed action of the Government." In time, political parties must degenerate into factions, competing with one another in "gross appeals to the appetites of the lowest and most worthless portions of the community." Social sympathies are destroyed, and the good of the party places the good of the community in total eclipse. Finally, party strife is nothing less than *the* corrupter of communal life, poisoning the very wells of public and private morality. Not even what Calhoun admitted to be "a new and important political element"—a free press devoted to both edifying and reflecting public opinion—could counteract the baneful effects of party.[31]

[30] *Ibid.*, I, 23 f. This important proposition is asserted, but not defended or elaborated.
[31] *Ibid.*, I, 40–42, 47-50, 73–76; VI, 200 (1832).

Calhoun spoke often and clearly—and at length—about "the different interests, portions, or classes of the community," and occasionally, but obscurely, about "the common interests of the whole." Parties are condemned, not because they promote the interests of the part over the whole, or because they cater to man's selfish rather than social feelings, but because they do so excessively, unreasonably, perhaps even unnaturally. A party does ill when the mere machinery of getting and holding power dictates its objects and procedures, or when it may with impunity prescribe a governmental policy that unjustly overrides the claims of other parties, or when it embitters conflicts to the point that men no longer recognize any minimal common grounds. One cannot help being puzzled by Calhoun's notion of the common good. While it is the criterion by which he justified his proposed solution of the problem of party—the system of concurrent consent—it is by no means certain what he understood by the good or interest of the community or, for that matter, by the community itself. "Where the organism is perfect, every interest will be truly and fully represented, and *of course* the whole community must be so." [32] The community's interest is the sum of all its particular interests: the whole appears to be defined in terms of its parts. We wonder how the parts themselves are defined; we wonder what constitutes an "interest."

Calhoun rejected an infinite regress by which the sense of every portion would be determined by the concurrent majority of *its* parts. Within each portion the numerical majority would rule.[33] This is not to assume internally homogeneous portions, but rather the presence of an interest that overrides many lesser interests. Whatever diversity of interests there may be within a given minority portion, all the people of that portion have the same interest "against that of all others, and, of course, the government itself." Just as control of the government in order to determine a line of policy dictates a combination of kindred interests into a single ruling majority, so does effective opposition dictate a combination of

[32] *Ibid.*, I, 26, 69. (Italics supplied.)

[33] However, in his *Discourse on the Constitution and Government of the United States*, Calhoun did suggest a way of taking the concurrent consent of "the more strongly marked interests" of each of the several states. *Ibid.*, I, 397.

kindred elements left out of the government (and adversely affected by it) into one or a few counterforces. Political power is to be won or lost. With those alternatives before them, the lesser interests are forced to distinguish between minor wishes and essentials. The presumed hostility of every other portion serves to delimit the area within which a set of interest groups and individuals might trust the rule of a numerical majority "with confidence" that their several interests will not be abused. For Calhoun there was no whole transcending its parts. He went even further. Speaking of the larger community, he suggested that the requirements of constitutionalism (as he understood it) would largely be met if the concurrent consent were limited to "a few great and prominent interests only." Here again there is assumed a kind of combined partial interest that overrides many lesser interests.[34]

It is surely remarkable that Calhoun studiously avoided carrying this line of reasoning to what others chose to call "the nation." The only exception is when the larger community's very existence must be defended; then, and only then, must "every other consideration" yield.[35] The sole suggestion of an overarching common interest concerns the preservation of a system that allows particular interests to express themselves. It appears that men are to be prepared to lay down their lives, not for a nation, but for a process of government.

The principle by which constitutional governments are said to be preserved is compromise. In this they are distinguished sharply from all forms of absolute government, whose conservative principle, according to Calhoun, is force. It is clear that in constitutional governments each interest or portion has a negative by which it can protect itself against the predatory designs and interests of others. What is not clear is the source of the various groups' desire to compromise. The answer Calhoun offered is simple, if not altogether satisfying. The effect of the various groups' possession of a veto power is to cause them

to desist from attempting to adopt any measure calculated to promote the prosperity of one, or more, by sacrificing that of others; and thus

[34] The principal safeguard of these lesser interests appears to be their pettiness, because of which they can never be desirable objects of plunder.
[35] Crallé, *Works*, I, 10, 26–28, 36 f., 60.

to force them to unite in such measures only as would promote the prosperity of all, as the only means to prevent the suspension of the action of the government;—and, thereby, to avoid anarchy, the greatest of all evils. . . .

It would, perhaps, be more strictly correct to trace the conservative principle of constitutional governments to the necessity which compels the different interests, or portions, or orders, to compromise,—as the only way to promote their respective prosperity, and to avoid anarchy,—rather than to the compromise itself. No necessity can be more urgent and imperious, than that of avoiding anarchy. It is the same as that which makes government indispensable to preserve society; and is not less imperative than that which compels obedience to superior force. Traced to this source, the voice of a people,—uttered under the necessity of avoiding the greatest of calamities, through the organs of a government so constructed as to suppress the expression of all partial and selfish interests, and to give a full and faithful utterance to the sense of the whole community, in reference to its common welfare,—may, without impiety, be called *the voice of God*. To call any other so, would be impious.[36]

We may wonder at the aplomb with which compromise, so understood, is contrasted with force. Does not this compromise too rest on a kind of force? A dread of impending anarchy compels the groups to compromise and forces them to unite. (This is not to deny that there is a difference—and an important one—between an absolute government's force, which acts solely *from* the separate interest of one side *on* the interest of the other, and the necessity that forces to a compromise, making *each* party sacrifice part of its purpose for an object that *both* recognize as valuable to themselves.) We may be totally incredulous on learning now that constitutional government suppresses the expression of partial interests while giving voice to the sense of the whole community. Has Calhoun not taught us that the sense of the whole community is nothing but the sum of all partial and selfish interests? Calhoun's system rests upon the expression, not the suppression, of these interests; he was very far from "making the vain attempt" to bend human nature to his measures. If he expected government by the concurrent majority to produce harmony rather than discord, it was because under that system a great deal of controversial busi-

[36] *Ibid.*, I, 37–39.

ness would be removed from central control. In an effort to check encroachments on local concerns, lesser interests within a minority will find a common ground of resistance: the preservation and enlargement of the sphere of individual rights and liberties. The effect is to restrict the government to "its primary end,—the protection of the community," the business of internal and external security. The latter, of course, is precisely the kind of activity concerning which we might expect to find a compelling common interest and a reasonable prospect of compromise.[37]

The old science of politics, while not unaware of the important and even profound differences that divided men, never ceased emphasizing those interests that all men in the community shared and the common good that they esteemed. This traditional teaching is identified in the *Disquisition* as the erroneous premise of numerical majority rule and the remote cause of the eclipse of the common good. By mistakenly regarding all men as sharing the same interests and then offering the control of the government as the grand prize, the system of numerical majority rule *insures* that men's desire for honors and emoluments will turn them into bitter rivals "waging, under the forms of law, incessant hostilities against each other." The new science of politics starts from the opposite premise. By regarding all men as being interested, above everything else, in preserving what is peculiarly their own, the system of concurrent majority rule places men in a position where they can afford to conciliate one another. On second thought, they cannot afford *not* to conciliate. "Each [interest or portion] sees and feels that it can best promote its own prosperity by conciliating the goodwill, and promoting the prosperity of the others." Out of the mass of particular and conflicting interests, there emerges a true community of interests; "there would be patriotism, nationality,[38] harmony, and a struggle only for supremacy in promoting the common good of the whole." Love emerges as a by-product of a "process." Love emerges for that which makes it possible for each interest to preserve itself comfortably—namely, a process of government. It is

---

[37] *Ibid.*, I, 36 f., 59–61; II, 648 (1837).

[38] "Nationality" is mentioned twice again in the *Disquisition,* when praising the Roman and British constitutions. *Ibid.*, I, 104 f.

that process which turns out to be the common interest, the common good.

Calhoun went to some pains to show that the process of concurrent majority rule was not impracticable. More narrowly, the question is whether one does well to rely upon a disposition to harmonize that is said to lead to unanimity. Calhoun's answer is that "when something *must* be done,—and when it can be done only by the united consent of all,—the necessity of the case will force to a compromise." The principal example is that of a petit jury: the jurors are under the necessity of reaching some common opinion after giving a fair and impartial hearing to both sides. Guided by this necessity and a love of truth and justice, a jury usually reaches a verdict.[39] "Far more urgent," much more "imperious" and "overpowering," is the necessity that impels men to compromise in constitutional governments. And, we may add, far more difficult to reach is such a compromise, since the interests that are involved are our own.[40]

Yet Calhoun was convinced—if not convincing—that the impulse to compromise would be well-nigh irresistible. A fear of anarchy that would attend the suspension of governmental action, bolstered by "an ardent love of country" or "an exalted patriotism," would induce each portion to take an enlarged and public-spirited view of whatever sacrifice it might have to make.

But to form a juster estimate of the full force of this impulse to compromise, there must be added that, in governments of the concurrent majority, each portion, in order to advance its own peculiar interests, would have to conciliate all others, by showing a disposition

[39] It hardly requires noting that opposing counsel try to enhance the likelihood of a fair hearing by rejecting potential jurors who have an *interest* in the trial's outcome, to say nothing of the fact that a jury's failure to find a verdict rarely entails dire consequences for the jurymen. Calhoun also referred to the Polish *liberum veto* to show that even in its most extreme form the principle of concurrent majority rule was both practicable and compatible with "great power and splendor." *Ibid.*, I, 71 f. Has any other political thinker held that constitution to be a model of good government?

[40] *Ibid.*, I, 47–49, 64–68. This necessity was precisely what stamped the work of the Constitutional Convention of 1787 with "so much fairness, equity, and justice." *Ibid.*, I, 195 f.

to advance theirs; and, for this purpose, each would select those to represent it, whose wisdom, patriotism, and weight of character, would command the confidence of the others. Under its influence,—and with representatives so well qualified to accomplish the object for which they were selected,—the prevailing desire would be, to promote the common interests of the whole; and, hence, the competition would be, not which should yield the least to promote the common good, but which should yield the most. It is thus, that concession would cease to be considered a sacrifice,—would become a free-will offering on the altar of the country, and lose the name of compromise.[41]

In these lines we catch a glimpse of a common good that is truly common to all concerned, and not a mere composite of *n* interests. We can only surmise—for Calhoun did not declare himself unambiguously—that *this* common good is more or less identical with the effects of the Roman and British constitutions, with whose celebration the *Disquisition* concludes:

to unite and harmonize conflicting interests;—to strengthen attachments to the whole community, and to moderate that to the respective orders or classes; to rally all, in the hour of danger, around the standard of their country; to elevate the feeling of nationality, and to develop power, moral and physical, to an extraordinary extent.[42]

A calculating concern for others' interests becomes, somehow, a genuine concern for the common interests of the whole. Calhoun did not explain with sufficient clarity how this might be expected to come about. He had, however, all but maintained that a predominance of social feelings, or even an equality between social and individual feelings, is an impossibility. In the light of his psychological premises, we are justified in doubting whether these confidence-inspiring men are in a position to sacrifice their peculiar interests. Rather, are these not confidence men, making a *show* of concern for others? I suggest this interpretation: Calhoun believed that love of country comprehends, "within itself, a large portion both of our individual and social feelings." He believed that "few motives exert a greater sway." Satisfying some of *those* motives enables men to act as patriots. The selfishness that takes the form

41 *Ibid.*, I, 68–70.
42 *Ibid.*, I, 104.

of warring interests is not eradicated, but it is tamed and possibly even civilized.[43] By giving selfish interest its due as a fact of life— one might almost say, as a law of nature—it is possible to transcend it. Calhoun's system appears to elicit—perhaps even to require— men's thinking about the common good, or at least a kind of self- interest, so guided by very indirect considerations, that barely can be distinguished from genuine public-spiritedness.[44]

If Calhoun's discussion of the common good sheds light on a wide range of issues related to the problem of partisanship, it is not a very strong light. His treatment of class conflict has a narrower focus and in some respects is more illuminating. The inevitability of class divisions and the tendency of labor and capital to conflict are persistent themes in Calhoun's speeches and writings, from the *South Carolina Exposition* to the *Disquisition on Government*. He saw in the system of protective tariffs a mighty instrument for erect- ing an oligarchy. This system's tendency is, as the experience of Europe bears witness,

to make the poor poorer, and the rich richer. Heretofore, in our country, this tendency has displayed itself principally in its effects, as regards the different sections,—but the time will come when it will produce the same results between the several classes in the manufac- turing States. After we [the staple states] are exhausted, the contest will be between the capitalists and operatives; for into these two classes it must, ultimately, divide society.[45]

Calhoun was not prone to belittle the unique splendors of the United States. But in this respect, the American government—"per- fectly distinct from all others which have preceded it—a govern- ment founded on the rights of man; resting, not on authority, not

---

[43] "For the very nature of the group process (which our government shows in a fairly well-developed form) is this, that groups are freely com- bining, dissolving, and recombining in accordance with their interest lines. And the lion when he has satisfied his physical need will lie down quite lamb-like, however much louder his roars were than his appetite justified." Arthur F. Bentley, *The Process of Government* (Chicago, 1908), p. 359.

[44] Crallé, *Works*, I, 5, 68. The manner in which the President is elected makes him "look more to *the interest of the whole* [and] soften sectional feelings and asperity." Even aspirants to that office find it easier "to be more of a patriot than the partisan of any particular interest." *Ibid.*, IV, 87 f. (1842).

[45] *Ibid.*, VI, 25 f. (1828).

on prejudice, not on superstition, but reason"—could claim no
providential dispensation. While the Americans had "wisely exploded" the artificial distinctions of social classes, they had not
thereby secured an exemption from the threat of oligarchy. Calhoun
denied that "there now exists, or ever has existed, a wealthy and
civilized community in which one portion did not live on the labor
of another." In a small republic, this inequality would manifest itself in the conflict between capital and labor, with the ultimate establishment of an oligarchy. In an extensive republic, the inevitable
inequality "would tend more in a geographical direction" and result
even more swiftly—thanks to governmental favoritism—in a "moneyed oligarchy." It is not necessary to repeat here the argument that
sees in slavery a "positive good" and a more humane resolution of
the conflict between capital and labor than that prevailing in most
countries. It suffices to say that in the slave plantation and in the
states where the plantation was the predominant mode of economic
organization, Calhoun saw a harmony, union, and stability that
other portions, "less fortunately constituted," could not hope to
attain. More significantly, Calhoun saw in the slaveholding states
—"the conservative portion of the country"—a valuable, indeed
indispensable, guarantor of a political and economic equilibrium.
They provided what the North lacked: a "central point of union"
immune to "the agitation and conflicts growing out of the divisions
of wealth and poverty." Such is the reasoning that Calhoun addressed to the "sober and considerate portions" of Northern citizens, "who have a deep stake in the existing institutions of the
country." [46]

Some interpreters have had no difficulty in seeing in all this a
more or less open appeal for the planters and capitalist manufacturers to collaborate against the lower classes.[47] From the recorded
actions and opinions of Calhoun and of those who knew him, one
can no more easily *prove* that he worked for such a collaboration
than that he did not intend any such alliance. The question remains
moot. On another occasion, when speaking of the South's being on

[46] *Ibid.*, II, 152 (1816), 631 f. (1837); III, 180 (1838), 643 f. (1841);
IV, 360 f. (1847), 533 (1849); V, 207 f. (1836); VI, 64 (1831); *Correspondence*, p. 305 (1831).
[47] Consider *Correspondence*, pp. 655 f. (1845).

the conservative side in the conflict between Northern labor and capital, he went on to add: "against the aggression of one or the other side." He censured Webster for attaching his affections, not to local interests, but to local *class* interests. He condemned the Hamiltonian policy of systematically favoring "the great and powerful classes of society, with the view of binding them through their interest, to the support of the Government" as "uncongenial and dangerous" to the American system of government. He denied any hostility on his own part to the interests of manufacturers or laborers. He denied that slavery threatened the profits of Northern capitalists or the wages of Northern operatives. Most important of all, he denied that the social cleavage of rich and poor had any significance in the South. "With us the two great divisions of society are not the rich and poor, but white and black; and all the former, the poor as well as the rich, belong to the upper class. . . ."[48] Without appreciating the force of this assertion, one cannot fully understand the *Disquisition*'s teaching about class divisions and partisan conflicts.

Calhoun maintained that concurrent majority rule has a "more popular character" than numerical majority rule because it allows for the extension of the right of suffrage—"with safety"—to almost every adult male, "with few ordinary exceptions." Such an extension in a system of simple majoritarianism would entail the predominance of "the more ignorant and dependent portions of the community."

For, as the community becomes populous, wealthy, refined, and highly civilized, the difference between the rich and the poor will become more strongly marked; and the number of the ignorant and dependent greater in proportion to the rest of the community. With the increase of this difference, the tendency to conflict between them will become stronger; and, as the poor and dependent become more numerous in proportion, there will be, in governments of the numerical majority, no want of leaders among the wealthy and ambitious, to excite and direct them in their efforts to obtain the control.

The case is different in governments of the concurrent majority. There, mere numbers have not the absolute control; and the wealthy

[48] Crallé, *Works*, III, 180 (1838), 287 (1838), 392 f. (1839); IV, 183 f. (1842), 196 (1842), 385 f. (1847), 505 (1848).

220   RALPH LERNER

and intelligent being identified in interest with the poor and ignorant
of their respective portions or interests of the community, become
their leaders and protectors. And hence, as the latter would have
neither hope nor inducement to rally the former in order to obtain the
control, the right of suffrage, under such a government, may be safely
enlarged to the extent stated, without incurring the hazard to which
such enlargement would expose governments of the numerical majority.[49]

Hitherto we have understood Calhoun to say that the principal
division to which his political science must address itself is that of
tax consumers and taxpayers, or that of the ins and the outs. Here,
however, there is a suggestion that the problem posed by the natural
majority, the poor, still is the fundamental problem. This may be
taken as a tacit questioning of the efficacy of Publius's remedy for
the evil effects of majority factionalism. Of the greatest significance
for understanding Calhoun's thought is the quiet, almost casual,
assertion of an identity of interest of the wealthy and intelligent
with the poor and ignorant, in the concurrent majority system. How
is this deepest social cleavage bridged? What interest or interests
can so overwhelm the fear and envy of class conflict?

That there are such preponderant interests common to a particular portion or group is the very cornerstone of Calhoun's system.
Otherwise he would not have been able to assume that numerical
majorities will not be oppressive or tyrannical *within* any given
portion or group. But what would prevent any local numerical
majority from going through the same kind of changing alliances
as Calhoun observed with despair in the national government? We
well may wonder at the ease with which Calhoun believed a group
could define itself and identify its particular interest, considering his
own difficulties in defining the whole of which those groups are a
part and in identifying the community's general interest. I can think
of no present interest so overwhelming as to unify—without some
injustice—a majority of the politically relevant individuals of one
portion *vis-à-vis* all the other portions of the country. I can think
of only one interest that could harmonize individual interests
within a portion to the extent that Calhoun foresaw. And that interest is slavery.

[49] *Ibid.*, I, 45 f.

If this is so, how did Calhoun expect *national* harmony to be secured by the concurrent majority system in a community that included nonslave portions and economic class divisions? His answer, I believe, is suggested by the conservative role he saw for the South. The slaveholding portion would use its veto power to prevent the rich *or* the poor (perhaps especially the latter) from imposing their class interest upon the country. When labor seeks to level wealth, the South would oppose it; when capital seeks fiscal and commercial policies oppressive to labor and agrarians, the South would oppose it. For Calhoun, not the least of slavery's salutary effects was its making the South the balance of the American political system.

III

In the last analysis, the general applicability of Calhoun's system is open to serious question, thereby exposing him to the charge of "closet ingenuity." The least that can be said is that his difficulties are not peculiarly his own. If these difficulties leave his political theory in an unsatisfactory condition, they may, nonetheless, indicate the measure of Calhoun's current significance as a political scientist. Calhoun was one of the first to construct a science of politics on partially articulated principles that we fairly can identify as belonging to today's behavioral political science. Having built his theoretical teaching upon these principles or premises, he rigorously adhered to them well beyond the point at which his practical knowledge of political life cried "halt."

Yet halt he did, and the silent and unmarked substitution of other principles or premises in his argument makes the understanding, as well as the assessment, of Calhoun's teaching a slippery road indeed. His discussion of interest, for example, lacks nothing of modern sophistication. Constitution, institutional arrangements, the forms of legislation, the appearance of equitable generality that marks governmental actions—all were stripped away by Calhoun to reveal the harsher stuff of politics. With a deft hand he traced the course of the many and varicolored threads of interest as they arise out of geography, size, civilization, production, wealth, and office, and go on to color and give texture to political life as a

whole. But he did not stop at this; he went on to maintain in effect
that self-interest forms the warp and woof of every significant political act. It is only late in his argument—too late—that Senator
Calhoun reminded himself of what he had known since young manhood: that "our Union cannot safely stand on the cold calculations
of interest alone." [50] The threads of interest are too thin to bear the
heaviest burdens, too short to reach the highest goals of political
life. Interest was not a sufficient bond of political life because, for
Calhoun, those burdens and goals were not imaginary "spooks."

Again, Calhoun's discussion of groups or portions is a remarkable anticipation of the contemporary teaching. Both in his theoretical writing and in his speeches in the Senate, Calhoun showed a
keen understanding of the physics or mechanics of group politics.
This perhaps is not noteworthy in a man of long political experience. What is surprising is the extent to which Calhoun's discussion
of the portions proceeds in virtual disregard of that of which they
are parts. If he shunned the word "nation," it was not solely by
virtue of his nullifier's creed. The groups or portions have a kind of
tangible relevance, easily detectable in their marchings and coun-
termarchings across the political landscape. If there was a whole
or entity, what could it be if not the sum of all these discrete groupings? It is almost as though the larger community, which others
called the nation or the country, had become a piece of painted
scenery for Calhoun, lacking depth and significance, and gradually
to be forgotten as the spectators are absorbed in the action down-
stage. It is almost as though some hostile intruder must burst upon
the stage, tearing down the backdrop or putting a torch to it, for it
to be recalled in mind. And yet, there is something in Calhoun's
view that refuses to be satisfied with such a conception of the larger
political community. An admiration of foreign grandeur, a pride
of native achievements and promise—feelings that he would not or
could not repress—peep through the elaborate argument, disturbing its logical symmetry before it reaches its last necessary deduction.

Or consider, finally, Calhoun's lengthy discussion of concurrent
majority rule, in which a process of government becomes in itself
the common good. Given a whole that is the arithmetical sum of

[50] *Ibid.*, II, 42 (1812).

its parts, given parts that are engrossed in the single-minded pursuit of their self-interest, narrowly conceived, it is hardly cause
for amazement that the highest common denominator—the *only*
common denominator—is an agreement to persist with the game.
Hardly anyone thinks it needful or worth his while to justify the
game, and if someone does try to do so, he retreats willy-nilly to a
kind of argument and language that the serious players find quaint
at best. Calhoun's theory carries him far in this direction, though
it is the position that he least satisfactorily explained, defended, or
qualified. On the one hand, Calhoun's system moves from irreduci-
ble self-interest to enlarged patriotism by way of a dread of stalemate and anarchy. On the other hand, Calhoun considered that
man's nature (both its low and high elements, its need for both
preservation and perfection) made concurrent majority rule necessary and possible.

The *Disquisition on Government* might be considered as a pre-
scriptive set of "rules of the game," but Calhoun's defense of those
rules makes use of standards that fall outside the terms of the game.
At the same time, his conception of the common good or public
interest as a governmental process earns for him the reward due one
who anticipated by several generations this development in political
science. Calhoun was some kind of precursor or pioneer of a behavioral science of politics. Greater precision eludes us as long
as the line separating his reluctance from his confusion is so indis-
tinct.

This much, however, may safely be said: the modern understanding of parties and group politics shares much more with Calhoun
than with the man whom it customarily claims as its intellectual
forebear. Not the Madison of *The Federalist,* No. 10, but Calhoun,
saw parties as machines or instruments for capturing and monop-
olizing governmental power and privilege. Not Madison, but Calhoun, had the clearer and fuller understanding of the multifarious
and shifting alliances that constitute the political behavior of groups.
Similarly, it is Calhoun, more than Madison, who would talk about
group interests while stumbling over, or ignoring, the identification
of the common good.

Yet if one looks at Calhoun's system as a whole and contrasts
it with Publius's, it does not look altogether mean. Like Publius, he

built upon selfishness and made the pursuit of self-interest the
mainspring of civil society. But in criticizing Publius's solution,
Calhoun proceeded to develop a system that he believed would
induce the generality of men to think about the common good
(however vaguely perceived), albeit for selfish reasons. Publius
thought he knew what "the permanent and aggregate interests of
the community" were, but believed that the system he had devised
could dispense safely with much deep or widespread thinking about
them. Calhoun was less willing to rely on either the ancient devices
or the modern political discoveries to which Publius resorted. He
was not satisfied that the habits of a commercial people in a land
of great extent and diversity would suffice of themselves to secure
and preserve the common good. Something more—the kind of
character he expected the concurrent majority system to elicit—
was required to lead men to embrace broader goals than their immediate self-interest. Calhoun believed that there would always be
a need for thoughtful patriots. He still could envy the "pride and
elevation of sentiment" with which the ancients proclaimed: "*I am
a Roman citizen.*" [51]

I conclude: Calhoun's new science of politics tries to wed to the
narrow premises of a behavioral social science that barely looks
beyond the fact of self-interest, the ends held in esteem by a man
"of enlarged philosophical views, and of ardent patriotism." [52]

---

[51] *Ibid.,* I, 105.
[52] Charles Francis Adams, ed., *Memoirs of John Quincy Adams*
(Philadelphia, 1874–1877), V, 361 (October 15, 1821).

Bibliographical Essay

The study of Calhoun's political ideas and ideals should begin with the *Disquisition on Government* and the *Discourse on the Constitution and Government of the United States*. These two treatises, written during Calhoun's later years, were first published in 1851, the year after his death, as Volume I in Richard K. Crallé's six-volume *The Works of John C. Calhoun* (Charleston, S.C., New York, 1851–1856). Selections from Calhoun's major speeches as well as the Crallé text of the *Disquisition* are collected in *Calhoun: Basic Documents* (State College, Pa., 1952) edited by John M. Anderson. Calhoun's letters have been edited by J. F. Jameson, *Correspondence of John C. Calhoun, Annual Report of the American Historical Association for the Year 1899* (Washington, 1900), Vol. II, but the definitive collection of Calhoun's papers is currently being compiled. At present *The Papers of John C. Calhoun* (Columbia, S.C., 1959–) consists of the first volume edited by Robert L. Meriwether which covers the years 1801–1817.

Calhoun has been variously served by biographers. By far the best study is Charles M. Wiltse's three-volume *John C. Calhoun* (Indianapolis, 1944, 1949, 1951), subtitled *Nationalist, 1782–1828; Nullifier, 1829–1839;* and *Sectionalist, 1840–1850*. Despite a tendency to heighten Calhoun's stature by diminishing his rivals, Wiltse presents the fullest and most searching account of Calhoun's career. The best one-volume biography is Margaret L. Coit, *John C. Calhoun: American Portrait* (Boston, 1950), but students are also advised to consult the more critical if less readable account by Gerald M. Capers, *John C. Calhoun, Opportunist: A Reappraisal* (Gainesville, Fla., 1960). Arthur Styron, *The Cast-Iron Man: John C. Calhoun and American*

Democracy (New York, 1935), a combined eulogy of the South Carolinian and jeremiad on "modernism," is provocative but perverse. Earlier biographies also vary in quality. Still useful is John S. Jenkins, *John C. Calhoun* (Auburn and Buffalo, N. Y., 1857); but Hermann E. von Holst, *John C. Calhoun* (Boston, 1882), based in part on the *Diary* of John Quincy Adams, suffers from the same animus that characterizes the original observations. Both Gaillard Hunt, *John C. Calhoun* (Philadelphia, 1908) and William M. Meigs, *The Life of John C. Calhoun*, 2 vols. (New York, 1917) are factual and low-keyed narratives.

The most complete descriptive treatment of Calhoun's thought is August O. Spain, *The Political Theory of John C. Calhoun* (New York, 1951), but Richard N. Current's briefer *John C. Calhoun* (New York, 1963) is superior both in organization and analysis. Current's essay is a convincing refutation of the neo-Calhounite interpretation and a sensible revisionist commentary on Calhoun's original theories. In "John C. Calhoun: Marx of the Master Class," a chapter in *The American Political Tradition and the Men Who Made It* (New York, 1948) Richard Hofstadter develops themes of class and class conflict in Calhoun's thought similar to those suggested by Current. Two older essays are still particularly useful. Charles E. Merriam, "The Political Philosophy of John C. Calhoun" in *Studies in Southern History and Politics, Inscribed to William Archibald Dunning. . . .* (New York, 1914) is a succinct discussion of the basic political ideas. William E. Dodd's essay on Calhoun in his *Statesmen of the Old South, or from Radicalism to Conservative Revolt* (New York, 1911) depicts Calhoun as the transitional figure in the general Southern retreat from Jeffersonian liberalism to the conservative particularism of Jefferson Davis. Arthur Bestor, "State Sovereignty and Slavery: A Reinterpretation of Proslavery Constitutional Doctrine," *Journal of the Illinois State Historical Society,* LIV (Summer 1961), 1–64, is a fascinating account of the constitutional implications of the shift in the Southern defense of slavery from states' rights to the concept of state sovereignty. Finally, William W. Freehling, *Prelude to Conflict: The Nullification Crisis in South Carolina, 1816–1836* (New York, 1965) reassesses that crisis and throws new light on Calhoun's role in it.

Contributors

GERALD M. CAPERS, born in 1909, Professor of History at Newcombe College, Tulane University, is the author of *John C. Calhoun, Opportunist: A Reappraisal* (1960) and *Stephen A. Douglas: Defender of the Union* (1959).

MARGARET L. COIT, Associate Professor of Social Sciences at Fairleigh Dickinson University, won the Pulitzer Prize in 1950 for *John C. Calhoun: An American Portrait*. Her other books include *Mr. Baruch* (1957), *The Fight for the Union* (1961), and *The Sweep Westward* (1963).

RICHARD N. CURRENT, born in 1912, Professor of American History at the University of North Carolina at Greensboro, has written extensively on the National Period. Among his books are *The Last Full Measure* (1955), which won the Bancroft Prize, *Daniel Webster and the Rise of National Conservatism* (1955), *The Lincoln Nobody Knows* (1958), and *Lincoln and the First Shot* (1963).

JEFFERSON DAVIS (1808–1889), President of the Confederate States of America, brought a distinguished military and political record as well as a strong belief in Calhoun's doctrines to the Lost Cause. His major work was the two-volume *The Rise and Fall of the Confederate Government* (1881).

PETER F. DRUCKER, born in 1909, educator and management consultant, has written widely on problems of technology and industrial management. Among his books are *Concept of the Corporation*

(1946), *The New Society* (1950), *Landmarks of Tomorrow* (1959), and *Managing for Results* (1964).

WILLIAM W. FREEHLING, born in 1935, Associate Professor of American History at the University of Michigan, is the author of *Prelude to Civil War: The Nullification Controversy in South Carolina, 1816–1836*, which won both the Allan Nevins Prize and the Bancroft Prize.

RALPH H. GABRIEL, born in 1890, Professor Emeritus at Yale University, is the author of *The Course of American Democratic Thought* (1940) and *Traditional Values in American Life* (1959).

LOUIS HARTZ, born in 1919, Professor of Political Science at Harvard University and in 1955 recipient of the Woodrow Wilson Prize awarded by the American Political Science Association, has also written *Economic Policy and Democratic Thought* (1963) and *The Founding of New Societies* (1964).

ROBERT M. T. HUNTER (1809–1887), Virginia statesman and follower of Calhoun, is credited by some historians with the authorship of the 1843 campaign biography. Hunter served in Congress from 1837 to 1861, first in the House and after 1847 in the Senate. When Virginia seceded, he resigned his seat and became Confederate Secretary of State and subsequently a member of the Confederate Senate.

RALPH LERNER, Associate Professor of the Social Sciences at the University of Chicago, is co-editor of *Medieval Political Philosophy* (1963).

WILLIAM PETERFIELD TRENT (1862–1939), distinguished teacher and literary scholar, taught at the University of the South and for many years at Columbia University. The author of numerous biographical and literary studies, he founded the *Sewanee Review* and was also the co-editor of *The Cambridge History of American Literature*.

CHARLES M. WILTSE, born in 1907, Professor of History at Dartmouth College and Editor-in-Chief of the Daniel Webster Papers, is the author of the definitive three-volume biography of Calhoun, *The Jeffersonian Tradition in American Democracy* (1935), and *The New Nation* (1961).

JOHN L. THOMAS was born in Maine in 1926, attended Bowdoin College, and received a doctorate in American Civilization from Brown University. He has taught at Barnard and Harvard, and is now Associate Professor of American History at Brown. His book *The Liberator: William Lloyd Garrison* (1963) won the Allan Nevins Prize and the Bancroft Prize, and he has been a Guggenheim fellow. His other publications include *Slavery Attacked* (1965) and a recent edition of Edward Bellamy's *Looking Backward*.

❂

AÏDA DIPACE DONALD, General Editor of the American Profiles series, holds degrees from Barnard and Columbia, where she taught American history, and a doctorate from the University of Rochester. Mrs. Donald has been awarded A.A.U.W. and Fulbright fellowships and has edited *John F. Kennedy and the New Frontier*. She is also co-editor of the *Charles Francis Adams Diary*.

DATE DUE

NOV 13 '68			
DEC 2 '68			
OCT 20 '69			
NOV 5 '69			
NOV 17 '69			
DEC 10 '69			
JAN 12 '70			
OCT 5 '70			
OCT 20 '70			
OCT 11 '71			
DEC 8 '71			
NOV 14 '72			
FEB 13 '73			
FEB 27 '73			
NOV 15 '73			
OC 5 '82			
GAYLORD			PRINTED IN U.S.A.